Building Microservices

Sam Newman

Beijing · Boston · Farnham · Sebastopol · Tokyo

Building Microservices

by Sam Newman

Copyright © 2015 Sam Newman. All rights reserved.

Printed in the United States of America.

Published by O'Reilly Media, Inc., 1005 Gravenstein Highway North, Sebastopol, CA 95472.

O'Reilly books may be purchased for educational, business, or sales promotional use. Online editions are also available for most titles (*http://safaribooksonline.com*). For more information, contact our corporate/institutional sales department: 800-998-9938 or *corporate@oreilly.com*.

Editors: Mike Loukides and Brian MacDonald
Production Editor: Kristen Brown
Copyeditor: Rachel Monaghan
Proofreader: Jasmine Kwityn

Indexer: Judith McConville
Interior Designer: David Futato
Cover Designer: Ellie Volckhausen
Illustrator: Rebecca Demarest

February 2015:   First Edition

Revision History for the First Edition
2015-01-30:   First Release
2015-02-27:   Second Release
2015-08-28:   Third Release
2016-01-29:   Fourth Release

See *http://oreilly.com/catalog/errata.csp?isbn=9781491950357* for release details.

978-1-491-95035-7

[LSI]

Table of Contents

Preface

Microservices are an approach to distributed systems that promote the use of finely grained services with their own lifecycles, which collaborate together. Because microservices are primarily modeled around business domains, they avoid the problems of traditional tiered architectures. Microservices also integrate new technologies and techniques that have emerged over the last decade, which helps them avoid the pitfalls of many service-oriented architecture implementations.

This book is full of concrete examples of microservice use around the world, including in organizations like Netflix, Amazon, Gilt, and the REA group, who have all found that the increased autonomy this architecture gives their teams is a huge advantage.

Who Should Read This Book

The scope of this book is broad, as the implications of fine-grained microservice architectures are also broad. As such, it should appeal to people interested in aspects of design, development, deployment, testing, and maintenance of systems. Those of you who have already embarked on the journey toward finer-grained architectures, whether for a greenfield application or as part of decomposing an existing, more monolithic system, will find plenty of practical advice to help you. It will also help those of you who want to know what all the fuss is about, so that you can determine whether microservices are right for you.

Why I Wrote This Book

I started thinking about the topic of application architectures many years ago, when working to help people deliver their software faster. I realized that while infrastructure automation, testing, and continuous delivery techniques could help, if the fundamental design of the system doesn't make it easy to make changes, then there are limits to what can be accomplished.

At the same time, many organizations were experimenting with finer-grained architectures to accomplish similar goals, but also to achieve things like improved scaling, increasing autonomy of teams, or to more easily embrace new technologies. My own experiences, as well as those of my colleagues at ThoughtWorks and elsewhere, reinforced the fact that using larger numbers of services with their own independent lifecycles resulted in more headaches that had to be dealt with. In many ways, this book was imagined as a one-stop shop that would help encompass the wide variety of topics that are necessary for understanding microservices—something that would have helped me greatly in the past!

A Word on Microservices Today

Microservices is a fast-moving topic. Although the idea is not new (even if the term itself is), experiences from people all over the world, along with the emergence of new technologies, are having a profound effect on how they are used. Due to the fast pace of change, I have tried to focus this book on ideas more than specific technologies, knowing that implementation details always change faster than the thoughts behind them. Nonetheless, I fully expect that in a few years from now we'll have learned even more about where microservices fit, and how to use them well.

So while I have done my best to distill out the essence of the topic in this book, if this topic interests you, be prepared for many years of continuous learning to keep on top of the state of the art!

Navigating This Book

This book is primarily organized in a topic-based format. As such, you may want to jump into the specific topics that interest you the most. While I have done my best to reference terms and ideas in the earlier chapters, I'd like to think that even people who consider themselves fairly experienced will find something of interest in all chapters here. I would certainly suggest that you take a look at Chapter 2, which touches on the breadth of the topic as well as providing some framing for how I go about things in case if you want to dive deeper into some of the later topics.

For people new to the subject, I've structured the chapters in a way that I hope will make sense to read from beginning to end.

Here is an overview of what we cover:

Chapter 1, Microservices
> We'll begin with an introduction to microservices, including the key benefits as well as some of the downsides.

Chapter 2, The Evolutionary Architect

This chapter discusses the difficulties we face in terms of making trade-offs as architects, and covers specifically just how many things we need to think about with microservices.

Chapter 3, How to Model Services

Here we'll start to define the boundary of microservices, using techniques from domain-driven design to help focus our thinking.

Chapter 4, Integration

This is where we start getting a bit deeper into specific technology implications, as we discuss what sorts of service collaboration techniques will help us most. We'll also delve into the topic of user interfaces and integrating with legacy and commercial off-the-shelf (COTS) products.

Chapter 5, Splitting the Monolith

Many people get interested in microservices as an antidote to large, hard-to-change monolithic systems, and this is exactly what we'll cover in detail in this chapter.

Chapter 6, Deployment

Although this book is primarily theoretical, few topics in the book have been as impacted by recent changes in technology as deployment, which we'll explore here.

Chapter 7, Testing

This chapter goes deep into the topic of testing, an area of particular concern when handling the deployment of multiple discrete services. Of particular note will be the role that consumer-driven contracts can play in helping us ensure the quality of our software.

Chapter 8, Monitoring

Testing our software before production doesn't help if problems occur once we go live, and this chapter explores how we can monitor our fine-grained systems and deal with some of the emergent complexity of distributed systems.

Chapter 9, Security

Here we'll examine the security aspects of microservices and consider how to handle user-to-service and service-to-service authentication and authorization. Security is a very important topic in computing, one that is all too readily ignored. Although I am in no way a security expert, I hope that this chapter will at least help you consider some of the aspects you need to be aware of when building systems, and microservice systems in particular.

Chapter 10, Conway's Law and System Design

This chapter focuses on the interplay of organizational structure and architecture. Many organizations have realized that trouble will occur if you don't keep the two in harmony. We'll attempt to get to the bottom of this dilemma, and consider some different ways to align system design with the structure of your teams.

Chapter 11, Microservices at Scale

This is where we start looking at doing all of this at scale, so that we can handle the increased chance of failure that can happen with large numbers of services, as well as large volumes of traffic.

Chapter 12, Bringing It All Together

The final chapter attempts to distill down the core essence of what makes microservices different. It includes a list of seven microservices principles, as well as a wrap-up of the key points of the book.

Conventions Used in This Book

The following typographical conventions are used in this book:

Italic

Indicates new terms, URLs, email addresses, filenames, and file extensions.

`Constant width`

Used for program listings, as well as within paragraphs to refer to program elements such as variable or function names, databases, data types, environment variables, statements, and keywords.

`Constant width bold`

Shows commands or other text that should be typed literally by the user.

`Constant width italic`

Shows text that should be replaced with user-supplied values or by values determined by context.

Safari® Books Online

 *Safari Books Online* is an on-demand digital library that delivers expert content in both book and video form from the world's leading authors in technology and business.

Technology professionals, software developers, web designers, and business and creative professionals use Safari Books Online as their primary resource for research, problem solving, learning, and certification training.

Safari Books Online offers a range of plans and pricing for enterprise, government, education, and individuals.

Members have access to thousands of books, training videos, and prepublication manuscripts in one fully searchable database from publishers like O'Reilly Media, Prentice Hall Professional, Addison-Wesley Professional, Microsoft Press, Sams, Que, Peachpit Press, Focal Press, Cisco Press, John Wiley & Sons, Syngress, Morgan Kaufmann, IBM Redbooks, Packt, Adobe Press, FT Press, Apress, Manning, New Riders, McGraw-Hill, Jones & Bartlett, Course Technology, and hundreds more. For more information about Safari Books Online, please visit us online.

How to Contact Us

Please address comments and questions concerning this book to the publisher:

O'Reilly Media, Inc.
1005 Gravenstein Highway North
Sebastopol, CA 95472
800-998-9938 (in the United States or Canada)
707-829-0515 (international or local)
707-829-0104 (fax)

We have a web page for this book, where we list errata, examples, and any additional information. You can access this page at *http://bit.ly/building-microservices*.

To comment or ask technical questions about this book, send email to *bookquestions@oreilly.com*.

For more information about our books, courses, conferences, and news, see our website at *http://www.oreilly.com*.

Find us on Facebook: *http://facebook.com/oreilly*

Follow us on Twitter: *http://twitter.com/oreillymedia*

Watch us on YouTube: *http://www.youtube.com/oreillymedia*

Acknowledgments

This book is dedicated to Lindy Stephens, without whom it wouldn't exist. She encouraged me to start on this journey, supported me throughout the often stressful process of writing, and is the best partner I could have ever asked for. I would also like to dedicate this to my dad, Howard Newman, who has always been there for me. This is for both of you.

I would like to single out Ben Christensen, Venkat Subramaniam, and Martin Fowler for providing detailed feedback throughout the writing process, helping shape what this book became. I'd also like to thank James Lewis, with whom I have consumed many beers discussing the ideas presented in this book. This book would be a shadow of itself without their help and guidance.

In addition, many others provided help and feedback on early versions of the book. Specifically, I would like to thank (in no particular order) Kane Venables, Anand Krishnaswamy, Kent McNeil, Charles Haynes, Chris Ford, Aidy Lewis, Will Thames, Jon Eaves, Rolf Russell, Badrinath Janakiraman, Daniel Bryant, Ian Robinson, Jim Webber, Stewart Gleadow, Evan Bottcher, Eric Sword, Olivia Leonard, and all my other colleagues at ThoughtWorks and across the industry who have helped me get this far.

Finally, I would like to thank all the people at O'Reilly, including Mike Loukides for getting me on board, my editor Brian MacDonald, Rachel Monaghan, Kristen Brown, Betsy Waliszewski, and all the other people who have helped in ways I may never know about.

CHAPTER 1

Microservices

For many years now, we have been finding better ways to build systems. We have been learning from what has come before, adopting new technologies, and observing how a new wave of technology companies operate in different ways to create IT systems that help make both their customers and their own developers happier.

Eric Evans's book *Domain-Driven Design* (Addison-Wesley) helped us understand the importance of representing the real world in our code, and showed us better ways to model our systems. The concept of continuous delivery showed how we can more effectively and efficiently get our software into production, instilling in us the idea that we should treat every check-in as a release candidate. Our understanding of how the Web works has led us to develop better ways of having machines talk to other machines. Alistair Cockburn's concept of hexagonal architecture (*http://bit.ly/ 1GZuFW9*) guided us away from layered architectures where business logic could hide. Virtualization platforms allowed us to provision and resize our machines at will, with infrastructure automation giving us a way to handle these machines at scale. Some large, successful organizations like Amazon and Google espoused the view of small teams owning the full lifecycle of their services. And, more recently, Netflix has shared with us ways of building antifragile systems at a scale that would have been hard to comprehend just 10 years ago.

Domain-driven design. Continuous delivery. On-demand virtualization. Infrastructure automation. Small autonomous teams. Systems at scale. Microservices have emerged from this world. They weren't invented or described before the fact; they emerged as a trend, or a pattern, from real-world use. But they exist only because of all that has gone before. Throughout this book, I will pull strands out of this prior work to help paint a picture of how to build, manage, and evolve microservices.

Many organizations have found that by embracing fine-grained, microservice architectures, they can deliver software faster and embrace newer technologies. Microservices give us significantly more freedom to react and make different decisions, allowing us to respond faster to the inevitable change that impacts all of us.

What Are Microservices?

Microservices are small, autonomous services that work together. Let's break that definition down a bit and consider the characteristics that make microservices different.

Small, and Focused on Doing One Thing Well

Codebases grow as we write code to add new features. Over time, it can be difficult to know where a change needs to be made because the codebase is so large. Despite a drive for clear, modular monolithic codebases, all too often these arbitrary in-process boundaries break down. Code related to similar functions starts to become spread all over, making fixing bugs or implementations more difficult.

Within a monolithic system, we fight against these forces by trying to ensure our code is more cohesive, often by creating abstractions or modules. Cohesion—the drive to have related code grouped together—is an important concept when we think about microservices. This is reinforced by Robert C. Martin's definition of the *Single Responsibility Principle* (*http://bit.ly/1zOFMxl*), which states "Gather together those things that change for the same reason, and separate those things that change for different reasons."

Microservices take this same approach to independent services. We focus our service boundaries on business boundaries, making it obvious where code lives for a given piece of functionality. And by keeping this service focused on an explicit boundary, we avoid the temptation for it to grow too large, with all the associated difficulties that this can introduce.

The question I am often asked is *how small is small?* Giving a number for lines of code is problematic, as some languages are more expressive than others and can therefore do more in fewer lines of code. We must also consider the fact that we could be pulling in multiple dependencies, which themselves contain many lines of code. In addition, some part of your domain may be legitimately complex, requiring more code. Jon Eaves at RealEstate.com.au in Australia characterizes a microservice as something that could be rewritten in two weeks, a rule of thumb that makes sense for his particular context.

Another somewhat trite answer I can give is *small enough and no smaller*. When speaking at conferences, I nearly always ask the question *who has a system that is too big and that you'd like to break down*? Nearly everyone raises their hands. We seem to have a very good sense of what is too big, and so it could be argued that once a piece of code no longer *feels* too big, it's probably small enough.

A strong factor in helping us answer *how small?* is how well the service aligns to team structures. If the codebase is too big to be managed by a small team, looking to break it down is very sensible. We'll talk more about organizational alignment later on.

When it comes to how small is small enough, I like to think in these terms: the smaller the service, the more you maximize the benefits and downsides of microservice architecture. As you get smaller, the benefits around interdependence increase. But so too does some of the complexity that emerges from having more and more moving parts, something that we will explore throughout this book. As you get better at handling this complexity, you can strive for smaller and smaller services.

Autonomous

Our microservice is a separate entity. It might be deployed as an isolated service on a platform as a service (PAAS), or it might be its own operating system process. We try to avoid packing multiple services onto the same machine, although the definition of *machine* in today's world is pretty hazy! As we'll discuss later, although this isolation can add some overhead, the resulting simplicity makes our distributed system much easier to reason about, and newer technologies are able to mitigate many of the challenges associated with this form of deployment.

All communication between the services themselves are via network calls, to enforce separation between the services and avoid the perils of tight coupling.

These services need to be able to change independently of each other, and be deployed by themselves without requiring consumers to change. We need to think about what our services should expose, and what they should allow to be hidden. If there is too much sharing, our consuming services become coupled to our internal representations. This decreases our autonomy, as it requires additional coordination with consumers when making changes.

Our service exposes an application programming interface (API), and collaborating services communicate with us via those APIs. We also need to think about what technology is appropriate to ensure that this itself doesn't couple consumers. This may mean picking technology-agnostic APIs to ensure that we don't constrain technology choices. We'll come back time and again to the importance of good, decoupled APIs throughout this book.

Without decoupling, everything breaks down for us. The golden rule: can you make a change to a service and deploy it by itself without changing anything else? If the answer is no, then many of the advantages we discuss throughout this book will be hard for you to achieve.

To do decoupling well, you'll need to model your services right and get the APIs right. I'll be talking about that a lot.

Key Benefits

The benefits of microservices are many and varied. Many of these benefits can be laid at the door of any distributed system. Microservices, however, tend to achieve these benefits to a greater degree primarily due to how far they take the concepts behind distributed systems and service-oriented architecture.

Technology Heterogeneity

With a system composed of multiple, collaborating services, we can decide to use different technologies inside each one. This allows us to pick the right tool for each job, rather than having to select a more standardized, one-size-fits-all approach that often ends up being the lowest common denominator.

If one part of our system needs to improve its performance, we might decide to use a different technology stack that is better able to achieve the performance levels required. We may also decide that how we store our data needs to change for different parts of our system. For example, for a social network, we might store our users' interactions in a graph-oriented database to reflect the highly interconnected nature of a social graph, but perhaps the posts the users make could be stored in a document-oriented data store, giving rise to a heterogeneous architecture like the one shown in Figure 1-1.

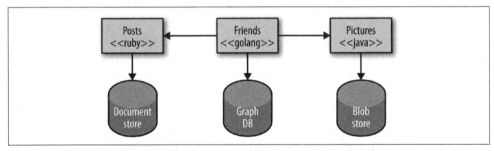

Figure 1-1. Microservices can allow you to more easily embrace different technologies

With microservices, we are also able to adopt technology more quickly, and understand how new advancements may help us. One of the biggest barriers to trying out and adopting new technology is the risks associated with it. With a monolithic application, if I want to try a new programming language, database, or framework, any change will impact a large amount of my system. With a system consisting of multiple services, I have multiple new places in which to try out a new piece of technology. I can pick a service that is perhaps lowest risk and use the technology there, knowing that I can limit any potential negative impact. Many organizations find this ability to more quickly absorb new technologies to be a real advantage for them.

Embracing multiple technologies doesn't come without an overhead, of course. Some organizations choose to place some constraints on language choices. Netflix and Twitter, for example, mostly use the Java Virtual Machine (JVM) as a platform, as they have a very good understanding of the reliability and performance of that system. They also develop libraries and tooling for the JVM that make operating at scale much easier, but make it more difficult for non-Java-based services or clients. But neither Twitter nor Netflix use only one technology stack for all jobs, either. Another counterpoint to concerns about mixing in different technologies is the size. If I really can rewrite my microservice in two weeks, you may well mitigate the risks of embracing new technology.

As you'll find throughout this book, just like many things concerning microservices, it's all about finding the right balance. We'll discuss how to make technology choices in Chapter 2, which focuses on evolutionary architecture; and in Chapter 4, which deals with integration, you'll learn how to ensure that your services can evolve their technology independently of each other without undue coupling.

Resilience

A key concept in resilience engineering is the bulkhead. If one component of a system fails, but that failure doesn't cascade, you can isolate the problem and the rest of the system can carry on working. Service boundaries become your obvious bulkheads. In a monolithic service, if the service fails, everything stops working. With a monolithic system, we can run on multiple machines to reduce our chance of failure, but with microservices, we can build systems that handle the total failure of services and degrade functionality accordingly.

We do need to be careful, however. To ensure our microservice systems can properly embrace this improved resilience, we need to understand the new sources of failure that distributed systems have to deal with. Networks can and will fail, as will machines. We need to know how to handle this, and what impact (if any) it should have on the end user of our software.

We'll talk more about better handling resilience, and how to handle failure modes, in Chapter 11.

Scaling

With a large, monolithic service, we have to scale everything together. One small part of our overall system is constrained in performance, but if that behavior is locked up in a giant monolithic application, we have to handle scaling everything as a piece. With smaller services, we can just scale those services that need scaling, allowing us to run other parts of the system on smaller, less powerful hardware, like in Figure 1-2.

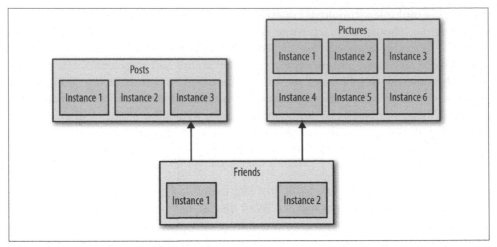

Figure 1-2. You can target scaling at just those microservices that need it

Gilt, an online fashion retailer, adopted microservices for this exact reason. Starting in 2007 with a monolithic Rails application, by 2009 Gilt's system was unable to cope with the load being placed on it. By splitting out core parts of its system, Gilt was better able to deal with its traffic spikes, and today has over 450 microservices, each one running on multiple separate machines.

When embracing on-demand provisioning systems like those provided by Amazon Web Services, we can even apply this scaling on demand for those pieces that need it. This allows us to control our costs more effectively. It's not often that an architectural approach can be so closely correlated to an almost immediate cost savings.

Ease of Deployment

A one-line change to a million-line-long monolithic application requires the whole application to be deployed in order to release the change. That could be a large-impact, high-risk deployment. In practice, large-impact, high-risk deployments end up happening infrequently due to understandable fear. Unfortunately, this means that our changes build up and build up between releases, until the new version of our application hitting production has masses of changes. And the bigger the delta between releases, the higher the risk that we'll get something wrong!

With microservices, we can make a change to a single service and deploy it independently of the rest of the system. This allows us to get our code deployed faster. If a problem does occur, it can be isolated quickly to an individual service, making fast rollback easy to achieve. It also means we can get our new functionality out to customers faster. This is one of the main reasons why organizations like Amazon and Netflix use these architectures—to ensure they remove as many impediments as possible to getting software out the door.

The technology in this space has changed greatly in the last couple of years, and we'll be looking more deeply into the topic of deployment in a microservice world in Chapter 6.

Organizational Alignment

Many of us have experienced the problems associated with large teams and large codebases. These problems can be exacerbated when the team is distributed. We also know that smaller teams working on smaller codebases tend to be more productive.

Microservices allow us to better align our architecture to our organization, helping us minimize the number of people working on any one codebase to hit the sweet spot of team size and productivity. We can also shift ownership of services between teams to try to keep people working on one service colocated. We will go into much more detail on this topic when we discuss Conway's law in Chapter 10.

Composability

One of the key promises of distributed systems and service-oriented architectures is that we open up opportunities for reuse of functionality. With microservices, we allow for our functionality to be consumed in different ways for different purposes. This can be especially important when we think about how our consumers use our software. Gone is the time when we could think narrowly about either our desktop website or mobile application. Now we need to think of the myriad ways that we might want to weave together capabilities for the Web, native application, mobile web, tablet app, or wearable device. As organizations move away from thinking in terms of narrow channels to more holistic concepts of customer engagement, we need architectures that can keep up.

With microservices, think of us opening up seams in our system that are addressable by outside parties. As circumstances change, we can build things in different ways. With a monolithic application, I often have one coarse-grained seam that can be used from the outside. If I want to break that up to get something more useful, I'll need a hammer! In Chapter 5, I'll discuss ways for you to break apart existing monolithic systems, and hopefully change them into some reusable, re-composable microservices.

Optimizing for Replaceability

If you work at a medium-size or bigger organization, chances are you are aware of some big, nasty legacy system sitting in the corner. The one no one wants to touch. The one that is vital to how your company runs, but that happens to be written in some odd Fortran variant and runs only on hardware that reached end of life 25 years ago. Why hasn't it been replaced? You know why: it's too big and risky a job.

With our individual services being small in size, the cost to replace them with a better implementation, or even delete them altogether, is much easier to manage. How often have you deleted more than a hundred lines of code in a single day and not worried too much about it? With microservices often being of similar size, the barriers to rewriting or removing services entirely are very low.

Teams using microservice approaches are comfortable with completely rewriting services when required, and just killing a service when it is no longer needed. When a codebase is just a few hundred lines long, it is difficult for people to become emotionally attached to it, and the cost of replacing it is pretty small.

What About Service-Oriented Architecture?

Service-oriented architecture (SOA) is a design approach where multiple services collaborate to provide some end set of capabilities. A service here typically means a completely separate operating system process. Communication between these services occurs via calls across a network rather than method calls within a process boundary.

SOA emerged as an approach to combat the challenges of the large monolithic applications. It is an approach that aims to promote the reusability of software; two or more end-user applications, for example, could both use the same services. It aims to make it easier to maintain or rewrite software, as theoretically we can replace one service with another without anyone knowing, as long as the semantics of the service don't change too much.

SOA at its heart is a very sensible idea. However, despite many efforts, there is a lack of good consensus on how to do SOA *well*. In my opinion, much of the industry has failed to look holistically enough at the problem and present a compelling alternative to the narrative set out by various vendors in this space.

Many of the problems laid at the door of SOA are actually problems with things like communication protocols (e.g., SOAP), vendor middleware, a lack of guidance about service granularity, or the wrong guidance on picking places to split your system. We'll tackle each of these in turn throughout the rest of the book. A cynic might suggest that vendors co-opted (and in some cases drove) the SOA movement as a way to sell more products, and those selfsame products in the end undermined the goal of SOA.

Much of the conventional wisdom around SOA doesn't help you understand how to split something big into something small. It doesn't talk about how big is too big. It doesn't talk enough about real-world, practical ways to ensure that services do not become overly coupled. The number of things that go unsaid is where many of the pitfalls associated with SOA originate.

The microservice approach has emerged from real-world use, taking our better understanding of systems and architecture to do SOA well. So you should instead think of microservices as a specific approach for SOA in the same way that XP or Scrum are specific approaches for Agile software development.

Other Decompositional Techniques

When you get down to it, many of the advantages of a microservice-based architecture come from its granular nature and the fact that it gives you many more choices as to how to solve problems. But could similar decompositional techniques achieve the same benefits?

Shared Libraries

A very standard decompositional technique that is built into virtually any language is breaking down a codebase into multiple libraries. These libraries may be provided by third parties, or created in your own organization.

Libraries give you a way to share functionality between teams and services. I might create a set of useful collection utilities, for example, or perhaps a statistics library that can be reused.

Teams can organize themselves around these libraries, and the libraries themselves can be reused. But there are some drawbacks.

First, you lose true technology heterogeneity. The library typically has to be in the same language, or at the very least run on the same platform. Second, the ease with which you can scale parts of your system independently from each other is curtailed. Next, unless you're using dynamically linked libraries, you cannot deploy a new library without redeploying the entire process, so your ability to deploy changes in isolation is reduced. And perhaps the kicker is that you lack the obvious seams around which to erect architectural safety measures to ensure system resiliency.

Shared libraries do have their place. You'll find yourself creating code for common tasks that aren't specific to your business domain that you want to reuse across the organization, which is an obvious candidate for becoming a reusable library. You do need to be careful, though. Shared code used to communicate between services can become a point of coupling, something we'll discuss in Chapter 4.

Services can and should make heavy use of third-party libraries to reuse common code. But they don't get us all the way there.

Modules

Some languages provide their own modular decomposition techniques that go beyond simple libraries. They allow some lifecycle management of the modules, such that they can be deployed into a running process, allowing you to make changes without taking the whole process down.

The Open Source Gateway Initiative (OSGI) is worth calling out as one technology-specific approach to modular decomposition. Java itself doesn't have a true concept of modules, and we'll have to wait at least until Java 9 to see this added to the language. OSGI, which emerged as a framework to allow plug-ins to be installed in the Eclipse Java IDE, is now used as a way to retrofit a module concept in Java via a library.

The problem with OSGI is that it is trying to enforce things like module lifecycle management without enough support in the language itself. This results in more work having to be done by module authors to deliver on proper module isolation. Within a process boundary, it is also much easier to fall into the trap of making modules overly coupled to each other, causing all sorts of problems. My own experience with OSGI, which is matched by that of colleagues in the industry, is that even with good teams it is easy for OSGI to become a much bigger source of complexity than its benefits warrant.

Erlang follows a different approach, in which modules are baked into the language runtime. Thus, Erlang is a very mature approach to modular decomposition. Erlang modules can be stopped, restarted, and upgraded without issue. Erlang even supports running more than one version of the module at a given time, allowing for more graceful module upgrading.

The capabilities of Erlang's modules are impressive indeed, but even if we are lucky enough to use a platform with these capabilities, we still have the same shortcomings as we do with normal shared libraries. We are strictly limited in our ability to use new technologies, limited in how we can scale independently, can drift toward integration techniques that are overly coupling, and lack seams for architectural safety measures.

There is one final observation worth sharing. Technically, it should be possible to create well-factored, independent modules within a single monolithic process. And yet we rarely see this happen. The modules themselves soon become tightly coupled with the rest of the code, surrendering one of their key benefits. Having a process boundary separation does enforce clean hygiene in this respect (or at least makes it harder to do the wrong thing!). I wouldn't suggest that this should be the main driver for process separation, of course, but it is interesting that the promises of modular separation within process boundaries rarely deliver in the real world.

So while modular decomposition within a process boundary may be something you want to do as well as decomposing your system into services, by itself it won't help solve everything. If you are a pure Erlang shop, the quality of Erlang's module implementation may get you a very long way, but I suspect many of you are not in that situation. For the rest of us, we should see modules as offering the same sorts of benefits as shared libraries.

No Silver Bullet

Before we finish, I should call out that microservices are no free lunch or silver bullet, and make for a bad choice as a golden hammer. They have all the associated complexities of distributed systems, and while we have learned a lot about how to manage distributed systems well (which we'll discuss throughout the book) it is still hard. If you're coming from a monolithic system point of view, you'll have to get much better at handling deployment, testing, and monitoring to unlock the benefits we've covered so far. You'll also need to think differently about how you scale your systems and ensure that they are resilient. Don't also be surprised if things like distributed transactions or CAP theorem start giving you headaches, either!

Every company, organization, and system is different. A number of factors will play into whether or not microservices are right for you, and how aggressive you can be in adopting them. Throughout each chapter in this book I'll attempt to give you guidance highlighting the potential pitfalls, which should help you chart a steady path.

Summary

Hopefully by now you know what a microservice is, what makes it different from other compositional techniques, and what some of the key advantages are. In each of the following chapters we will go into more detail on how to achieve these benefits and how to avoid some of the common pitfalls.

There are a number of topics to cover, but we need to start somewhere. One of the main challenges that microservices introduce is a shift in the role of those who often guide the evolution of our systems: the architects. We'll look next at some different approaches to this role that can ensure we get the most out of this new architecture.

CHAPTER 2

The Evolutionary Architect

As we have seen so far, microservices give us a lot of choice, and accordingly a lot of decisions to make. For example, how many different technologies should we use, should we let different teams use different programming idioms, and should we split or merge a service? How do we go about making these decisions? With the faster pace of change, and the more fluid environment that these architectures allow, the role of the architect also has to change. In this chapter, I'll take a fairly opinionated view of what the role of an architect is, and hopefully launch one final assault on the ivory tower.

Inaccurate Comparisons

> *You keep using that word. I do not think it means what you think it means.*
> —Inigo Montoya, from
> *The Princess Bride*

Architects have an important job. They are in charge of making sure we have a joined-up technical vision, one that should help us deliver the system our customers need. In some places, they may only have to work with one team, in which case the role of the architect and technical lead is often the same. In others, they may be defining the vision for an entire program of work, coordinating with multiple teams across the world, or perhaps even an entire organization. At whatever level they operate, the role is a tricky one to pin down, and despite it often being the obvious career progression for developers in enterprise organizations, it is also a role that gets more criticism than virtually any other. More than any other role, architects can have a direct impact on the quality of the systems built, on the working conditions of their colleagues, and on their organization's ability to respond to change, and yet we so frequently seem to get this role wrong. Why is that?

Our industry is a young one. This is something we seem to forget, and yet we have only been creating programs that run on what we recognize as computers for around 70 years. Therefore, we are constantly looking to other professions in an attempt to explain what we do. We aren't medical doctors or engineers, but nor are we plumbers or electricians. Instead, we fall into some middle ground, which makes it hard for society to understand us, or for us to understand where we fit.

So we borrow from other professions. We call ourselves software "engineers," or "architects." But we aren't, are we? Architects and engineers have a rigor and discipline we could only dream of, and their importance in society is well understood. I remember talking to a friend of mine, the day before he became a qualified architect. "Tomorrow," he said, "if I give you advice down at the pub about how to build something and it's wrong, I get held to account. I could get sued, as in the eyes of the law I am now a qualified architect and I should be held responsible if I get it wrong." The importance of these jobs to society means that there are required qualifications people have to meet. In the UK, for example, a minimum of seven years study is required before you can be called an architect. But these jobs are also based on a body of knowledge going back thousands of years. And us? Not quite. Which is also why I view most forms of IT certification as worthless, as we know so little about what *good* looks like.

Part of us wants recognition, so we borrow names from other professions that already have the recognition we as an industry crave. But this can be doubly harmful. First, it implies we know what we are doing, when we plainly don't. I wouldn't say that buildings and bridges never fall down, but they fall down much less than the number of times our programs will crash, making comparisons with engineers quite unfair. Second, the analogies break down very quickly when given even a cursory glance. To turn things around, if bridge building were like programming, halfway through we'd find out that the far bank was now 50 meters farther out, that it was actually mud rather than granite, and that rather than building a footbridge we were instead building a road bridge. Our software isn't constrained by the same physical rules that real architects or engineers have to deal with, and what we create is designed to flex and adapt and evolve with user requirements.

Perhaps the term *architect* has done the most harm. The idea of someone who draws up detailed plans for others to interpret, and expects this to be carried out. The balance of part artist, part engineer, overseeing the creation of what is normally a singular vision, with all other viewpoints being subservient, except for the occasional objection from the structural engineer regarding the laws of physics. In our industry, this view of the architect leads to some terrible practices. Diagram after diagram, page after page of documentation, created with a view to inform the construction of the perfect system, without taking into account the fundamentally unknowable future. Utterly devoid of any understanding as to how hard it will be to implement, or whether or not it will actually work, let alone having any ability to change as we learn more.

When we compare ourselves to engineers or architects, we are in danger of doing everyone a disservice. Unfortunately, we are stuck with the word *architect* for now. So the best we can do is to redefine what it means in our context.

An Evolutionary Vision for the Architect

Our requirements shift more rapidly than they do for people who design and build buildings—as do the tools and techniques at our disposal. The things we create are not fixed points in time. Once launched into production, our software will continue to evolve as the way it is used changes. For most things we create, we have to accept that once the software gets into the hands of our customers we will have to react and adapt, rather than it being a never-changing artifact. Thus, our architects need to shift their thinking away from creating the perfect end product, and instead focus on helping create a framework in which the right systems can emerge, and continue to grow as we learn more.

Although I have spent much of the chapter so far warning you off comparing ourselves too much to other professions, there is one analogy that I like when it comes to the role of the IT architect and that I think better encapsulates what we want this role to be. Erik Doernenburg first shared with me the idea that we should think of our role more as town planners than architects for the built environment. The role of the town planner should be familiar to any of you who have played SimCity before. A town planner's role is to look at a multitude of sources of information, and then attempt to optimize the layout of a city to best suit the needs of the citizens today, taking into account future use. The way he influences how the city evolves, though, is interesting. He does not say, "build this specific building there"; instead, he *zones a city*. So as in SimCity, you might designate part of your city as an industrial zone, and another part as a residential zone. It is then up to other people to decide what exact buildings get created, but there are restrictions: if you want to build a factory, it will need to be in an industrial zone. Rather than worrying too much about what happens in one zone, the town planner will instead spend far more time working out how people and utilities move from one zone to another.

More than one person has likened a city to a living creature. The city changes over time. It shifts and evolves as its occupants use it in different ways, or as external forces shape it. The town planner does his best to anticipate these changes, but accepts that trying to exert direct control over all aspects of what happens is futile.

The comparison with software should be obvious. As our users use our software, we need to react and change. We cannot foresee everything that will happen, and so rather than plan for any eventuality, we should plan to allow for change by avoiding the urge to overspecify every last thing. Our city—the system—needs to be a good, happy place for everyone who uses it. One thing that people often forget is that our system doesn't just accommodate users; it also accommodates developers and operations people who also have to work there, and who have the job of making sure it can change as required. To borrow a term from Frank Buschmann, architects have a duty to ensure that the system is *habitable* for developers too.

A town planner, just like an architect, also needs to know when his plan isn't being followed. As he is less prescriptive, the number of times he needs to get involved to correct direction should be minimal, but if someone decides to build a sewage plant in a residential area, he needs to be able to shut it down.

So our architects as town planners need to set direction in broad strokes, and only get involved in being highly specific about implementation detail in limited cases. They need to ensure that the system is fit for purpose now, but also a platform for the future. And they need to ensure that it is a system that makes users and developers equally happy. This sounds like a pretty tall order. Where do we start?

Zoning

So, to continue the metaphor of the architect as town planner for a moment, what are our zones? These are our service boundaries, or perhaps coarse-grained groups of services. As architects, we need to worry much less about what happens *inside* the zone than what happens *between* the zones. That means we need to spend time thinking about how our services talk to each other, or ensuring that we can properly monitor the overall health of our system. How involved we get inside the zone will vary somewhat. Many organizations have adopted microservices in order to maximize for autonomy of teams, something we'll expand on in Chapter 10. If you are in such an organization, you will rely more on the team to make the right local decision.

But between the zones, or the boxes on our traditional architecture diagram, we need to be careful; getting things wrong here leads to all sorts of problems and can be very hard to correct.

Within each service, you may be OK with the team who owns that zone picking a different technology stack or data store. Other concerns may kick in here, of course. Your inclination to let teams pick the right tool for the job may be tempered by the fact that it becomes harder to hire people or move them between teams if you have 10 different technology stacks to support. Similarly, if each team picks a completely different data store, you may find yourself lacking enough experience to run any of them at scale. Netflix, for example, has mostly standardized on Cassandra as a data-store technology. Although it may not be the best fit for all of its cases, Netflix feels that the value gained by building tooling and expertise around Cassandra is more important than having to support and operate at scale multiple other platforms that may be a better fit for certain tasks. Netflix is an extreme example, where scale is likely the strongest overriding factor, but you get the idea.

Between services is where things can get messy, however. If one service decides to expose REST over HTTP, another makes use of protocol buffers, and a third uses Java RMI, then integration can become a nightmare as consuming services have to understand and support multiple styles of interchange. This is why I try to stick to the guideline that we should "be worried about what happens between the boxes, and be liberal in what happens inside."

The Coding Architect

If we are to ensure that the systems we create are habitable for our developers, then our architects need to understand the impact of their decisions. At the very least, this means spending time with the team, and ideally it should mean that these developers actually spend time coding with the team too. For those of you who practice pair programming, it becomes a simple matter for an architect to join a team for a short period as one member of the pair. Ideally, you should work on normal stories, to really understand what *normal* work is like. I cannot emphasize how important it is for the architect to actually sit with the team! This is significantly more effective than having a call or just looking at her code.

As for how often you should do this, that depends greatly on the size of the team(s) you are working with. But the key is that it should be a routine activity. If you are working with four teams, for example, spending half a day with each team every four weeks ensures you build an awareness and improved communications with the teams you are working with.

A Principled Approach

Rules are for the obedience of fools and the guidance of wise men.
—Generally attributed to Douglas Bader

Making decisions in system design is all about trade-offs, and microservice architectures give us lots of trade-offs to make! When picking a datastore, do we pick a platform that we have less experience with, but that gives us better scaling? Is it OK for us to have two different technology stacks in our system? What about three? Some decisions can be made completely on the spot with information available to us, and these are the easiest to make. But what about those decisions that might have to be made on incomplete information?

Framing here can help, and a great way to help frame our decision making is to define a set of principles and practices that guide it, based on goals that we are trying to achieve. Let's look at each in turn.

Strategic Goals

The role of the architect is already daunting enough, so luckily we usually don't have to also define strategic goals! Strategic goals should speak to where your company is going, and how it sees itself as best making its customers happy. These will be high-level goals, and may not include technology at all. They could be defined at a company level or a division level. They might be things like "Expand into Southeast Asia to unlock new markets," or "Let the customer achieve as much as possible using self-service." The key is that this is where your organization is headed, so you need to make sure the technology is aligned to it.

If you're the person defining the company's technical vision, this may mean you'll need to spend more time with the nontechnical parts of your organization (or *the business*, as they are often called). What is the driving vision for the business? And how does it change?

Principles

Principles are rules you have made in order to align what you are doing to some larger goal, and will sometimes change. For example, if one of your strategic goals as an organization is to decrease the time to market for new features, you may define a principle that says that delivery teams have full control over the lifecycle of their software to ship whenever they are ready, independently of any other team. If another goal is that your organization is moving to aggressively grow its offering in other countries, you may decide to implement a principle that the entire system must be portable to allow for it to be deployed locally in order to respect sovereignty of data.

You probably don't want loads of these. Fewer than 10 is a good number—small enough that people can remember them, or to fit on small posters. The more principles you have, the greater the chance that they overlap or contradict each other.

Heroku's 12 Factors (*http://www.12factor.net/*) are a set of design principles structured around the goal of helping you create applications that work well on the Heroku platform. They also may well make sense in other contexts. Some of the principles are actually constraints based on behaviors your application needs to exhibit in order to work on Heroku. A constraint is really something that is very hard (or virtually impossible) to change, whereas principles are things we decide to choose. You may decide to explicitly call out those things that are principles versus those that are constraints, to help indicate those things you really can't change. Personally, I think there can be some value in keeping them in the same list to encourage challenging constraints every now and then and see if they really are immovable!

Practices

Our practices are how we ensure our principles are being carried out. They are a set of detailed, practical guidance for performing tasks. They will often be technology-specific, and should be low level enough that any developer can understand them. Practices could include coding guidelines, the fact that all log data needs to be captured centrally, or that HTTP/REST is the standard integration style. Due to their technical nature, practices will often change more often than principles.

As with principles, sometimes practices reflect constraints in your organization. For example, if you support only CentOS, this will need to be reflected in your practices.

Practices should underpin our principles. A principle stating that delivery teams control the full lifecycle of their systems may mean you have a practice stating that all services are deployed into isolated AWS accounts, providing self-service management of the resources and isolation from other teams.

Combining Principles and Practices

One person's principles are another's practices. You might decide to call the use of HTTP/REST a principle rather than a practice, for example. And that would be fine. The key point is that there is value in having overarching ideas that guide how the system evolves, and in having enough detail so that people know how to implement those ideas. For a small enough group, perhaps a single team, combining principles and practices might be OK. However, for larger organizations, where the technology and working practices may differ, you may want a different set of practices in different places, as long as they both map to a common set of principles. A .NET team, for example, might have one set of practices, and a Java team another, with a set of practices common to both. The principles, though, could be the same for both.

A Real-World Example

My colleague Evan Bottcher developed the diagram shown in Figure 2-1 in the course of working with one of our clients. The figure shows the interplay of goals, principles, and practices in a very clear format. Over the course of a couple years, the practices on the far right will change fairly regularly, whereas the principles remain fairly static. A diagram such as this can be printed nicely on a single sheet of paper and shared, and each idea is simple enough for the average developer to remember. There is, of course, more detail behind each point here, but being able to articulate this in summary form is very useful.

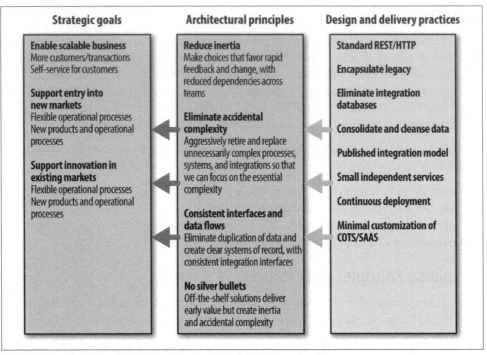

Figure 2-1. A real-world example of principles and practices

It makes sense to have documentation supporting some of these items. In the main, though, I like the idea of having example code that you can look at, inspect, and run, which embodies these ideas. Even better, we can create tooling that does the right thing out of the box. We'll discuss that in more depth momentarily.

The Required Standard

When you're working through your practices and thinking about the trade-offs you need to make, one of the core balances to find is how much variability to allow in your system. One of the key ways to identify what should be constant from service to service is to define what a well-behaved, good service looks like. What is a "good citizen" service in your system? What capabilities does it need to have to ensure that your system is manageable and that one bad service doesn't bring down the whole system? And, as with people, what a good citizen is in one context does not reflect what it looks like somewhere else. Nonetheless, there are some common characteristics of well-behaved services that I think are fairly important to observe. These are the few key areas where allowing too much divergence can result in a pretty torrid time. As Ben Christensen from Netflix puts it, when we think about the bigger picture, "it needs to be a cohesive system made of many small parts with autonomous lifecycles but all coming together." So we need to find the balance between optimizing for autonomy of the individual microservice without losing sight of the bigger picture. Defining clear attributes that each service should have is one way of being clear as to where that balance sits.

Monitoring

It is essential that we are able to draw up coherent, cross-service views of our system health. This has to be a system-wide view, not a service-specific view. As we'll discuss in Chapter 8, knowing the health of an individual service is useful, but often only when you're trying to diagnose a wider problem or understand a larger trend. To make this as easy as possible, I would suggest ensuring that all services emit health and general monitoring-related metrics in the same way.

You might choose to adopt a push mechanism, where each service needs to push this data into a central location. For your metrics this might be Graphite, and for your health it might be Nagios. Or you might decide to use polling systems that scrape data from the nodes themselves. But whatever you pick, try to keep it standardized. Make the technology inside the box opaque, and don't require that your monitoring systems change in order to support it. Logging falls into the same category here: we need it in one place.

Interfaces

Picking a small number of defined interface technologies helps integrate new consumers. Having one standard is a good number. Two isn't too bad, either. Having 20 different styles of integration is bad. This isn't just about picking the technology and the protocol. If you pick HTTP/REST, for example, will you use verbs or nouns? How will you handle pagination of resources? How will you handle versioning of end points?

Architectural Safety

We cannot afford for one badly behaved service to ruin the party for everyone. We have to ensure that our services shield themselves accordingly from unhealthy, downstream calls. The more services we have that do not properly handle the potential failure of downstream calls, the more fragile our systems will be. This means you will probably want to mandate as a minimum that each downstream service gets its own connection pool, and you may even go as far as to say that each also uses a circuit breaker. This will get covered in more depth when we discuss microservices at scale in Chapter 11.

Playing by the rules is important when it comes to response codes, too. If your circuit breakers rely on HTTP codes, and one service decides to send back 2XX codes for errors, or confuses 4XX codes with 5XX codes, then these safety measures can fall apart. Similar concerns would apply even if you're not using HTTP; knowing the difference between a request that was OK and processed correctly, a request that was bad and thus prevented the service from doing anything with it, and a request that might be OK but we can't tell because the server was down is key to ensuring we can fail fast and track down issues. If our services play fast and loose with these rules, we end up with a more vulnerable system.

Governance Through Code

Getting together and agreeing on how things can be done is a good idea. But spending time making sure people are following these guidelines is less fun, as is placing a burden on developers to implement all these standard things you expect each service to do. I am a great believer in making it easy to do the right thing. Two techniques I have seen work well here are using exemplars and providing service templates.

Exemplars

Written documentation is good, and useful. I clearly see the value; after all, I've written this book. But developers also like code, and code they can run and explore. If you have a set of standards or best practices you would like to encourage, then having exemplars that you can point people to is useful. The idea is that people can't go far wrong just by imitating some of the better parts of your system.

Ideally, these should be real-world services you have that get things right, rather than isolated services that are just implemented to be *perfect examples*. By ensuring your exemplars are actually being used, you ensure that all the principles you have actually make sense.

Tailored Service Template

Wouldn't it be great if you could make it really easy for all developers to follow most of the guidelines you have with very little work? What if, out of the box, the developers had most of the code in place to implement the core attributes that each service needs?

Dropwizard (*http://dropwizard.io/*) and Karyon (*http://bit.ly/1JtA6KX*) are two open source, JVM-based microcontainers. They work in similar ways, pulling together a set of libraries to provide features like health checking, serving HTTP, or exposing metrics. So, out of the box, you have a service complete with an embedded servlet container that can be launched from the command line. This is a great way to get going, but why stop there? While you're at it, why not take something like a Dropwizard or Karyon, and add more features so that it becomes compliant for your context?

For example, you might want to mandate the use of circuit breakers. In that case, you might integrate a circuit breaker library like Hystrix (*http://bit.ly/1wxQtwW*). Or you might have a practice that all your metrics need to be sent to a central Graphite server, so perhaps pull in an open source library like Dropwizard's Metrics (*http://bit.ly/1yVt4LN*) and configure it so that, out of the box, response times and error rates are pushed automatically to a known location.

By tailoring such a service template for your own set of development practices, you ensure that teams can get going faster, and also that developers have to go out of their way to make their services badly behaved.

Of course, if you embraced multiple disparate technology stacks, you'd need a matching service template for each. This may be a way you subtly constrain language choices in your teams, though. If the in-house service template supports only Java, then people may be discouraged from picking alternative stacks if they have to do lots more work themselves. Netflix, for example, is especially concerned with aspects like fault tolerance, to ensure that the outage of one part of its system cannot take everything down. To handle this, a large amount of work has been done to ensure that there are client libraries on the JVM to provide teams with the tools they need to keep their services well behaved. Anyone introducing a new technology stack would mean having to reproduce all this effort. The main concern for Netflix is less about the duplicated effort, and more about the fact that it is so easy to get this wrong. The risk of a service getting newly implemented fault tolerance wrong is high if it could impact more of the system. Netflix mitigates this by using *sidecar services*, which communicate locally with a JVM that is using the appropriate libraries.

You do have to be careful that creating the service template doesn't become the job of a central tools or architecture team who dictates how things should be done, albeit via code. Defining the practices you use should be a collective activity, so ideally your team(s) should take joint responsibility for updating this template (an internal open source approach works well here).

I have also seen many a team's morale and productivity destroyed by having a mandated framework thrust upon them. In a drive to improve code reuse, more and more work is placed into a centralized framework until it becomes an overwhelming monstrosity. If you decide to use a tailored service template, think very carefully about what its job is. Ideally, its use should be purely optional, but if you are going to be more forceful in its adoption you need to understand that ease of use for the developers has to be a prime guiding force.

Also be aware of the perils of shared code. In our desire to create reusable code, we can introduce sources of coupling between services. At least one organization I spoke to is so worried about this that it actually copies its service template code manually into each service. This means that an upgrade to the core service template takes longer to be applied across its system, but this is less concerning to it than the danger of coupling. Other teams I have spoken to have simply treated the service template as a shared binary dependency, although they have to be very diligent in not letting the tendency for DRY (don't repeat yourself) result in an overly coupled system! This is a nuanced topic, so we'll explore it in more detail in Chapter 4.

Technical Debt

We are often put in situations where we cannot follow through to the letter on our technical vision. Often, we need to make a choice to cut a few corners to get some urgent features out. This is just one more trade-off that we'll find ourselves having to make. Our technical vision exists for a reason. If we deviate from this reason, it might have a short-term benefit but a long-term cost. A concept that helps us understand this trade-off is technical debt. When we accrue technical debt, just like debt in the real world it has an ongoing cost, and is something we want to pay down.

Sometimes technical debt isn't just something we cause by taking shortcuts. What happens if our vision for the system changes, but not all of our system matches? In this situation, too, we have created new sources of technical debt.

The architect's job is to look at the bigger picture, and understand this balance. Having some view as to the level of debt, and where to get involved, is important. Depending on your organization, you might be able to provide gentle guidance, but have the teams themselves decide how to track and pay down the debt. For other organizations, you may need to be more structured, perhaps maintaining a debt log that is reviewed regularly.

Exception Handling

So our principles and practices guide how our systems should be built. But what happens when our system deviates from this? Sometimes we make a decision that is just an exception to the rule. In these cases, it might be worth capturing such a decision in a log somewhere for future reference. If enough *exceptions* are found, it may eventually make sense to change the principle or practice to reflect a new understanding of the world. For example, we might have a practice that states that we will always use MySQL for data storage. But then we see compelling reasons to use Cassandra for highly scalable storage, at which point we change our practice to say, "Use MySQL for most storage requirements, unless you expect large growth in volumes, in which case use Cassandra."

It's probably worth reiterating, though, that every organization is different. I've worked with some companies where the development teams have a high degree of trust and autonomy, and there the principles are lightweight (and the need for overt exception handling is greatly reduced if not eliminated). In more structured organizations in which developers have less freedom, tracking exceptions may be vital to ensure that the rules put in place properly reflect the challenges people are facing. With all that said, I am a fan of microservices as a way of optimizing for autonomy of teams, giving them as much freedom as possible to solve the problem at hand. If you are working in an organization that places lots of restrictions on how developers can do their work, then microservices may not be for you.

Governance and Leading from the Center

Part of what architects need to handle is governance. What do I mean by *governance*? It turns out the Control Objectives for Information and Related Technology (COBIT) has a pretty good definition:

> Governance ensures that enterprise objectives are achieved by evaluating stakeholder needs, conditions and options; setting direction through prioritisation and decision making; and monitoring performance, compliance and progress against agreed-on direction and objectives.
>
> —COBIT 5

Governance can apply to multiple things in the forum of IT. We want to focus on the aspect of technical governance, something I feel is the job of the architect. If one of the architect's jobs is ensuring there is a technical vision, then governance is about ensuring what we are building matches this vision, and evolving the vision if needed.

Architects are responsible for a lot of things. They need to ensure there is a set of principles that can guide development, and that these principles match the organization's strategy. They need to make sure as well that these principles don't require working practices that make developers miserable. They need to keep up to date with new technology, and know when to make the right trade-offs. This is an awful lot of responsibility. All that, and they also need to carry people with them—that is, to ensure that the colleagues they are working with understand the decisions being made and are brought in to carry them out. Oh, and as we've already mentioned: they need to spend some time with the teams to understand the impact of their decisions, and perhaps even code too.

A tall order? Absolutely. But I am firmly of the opinion that they shouldn't do this alone. A properly functioning governance group can work together to share the work and shape the vision.

Normally, governance is a group activity. It could be an informal chat with a small enough team, or a more structured regular meeting with formal group membership for a larger scope. This is where I think the principles we covered earlier should be discussed and changed as required. This group needs to be led by a technologist, and to consist predominantly of people who are executing the work being governed. This group should also be responsible for tracking and managing technical risks.

A model I greatly favor is having the architect chair the group, but having the bulk of the group drawn from the technologists of each delivery team—the leads of each team at a minimum. The architect is responsible for making sure the group works, but the group as a whole is responsible for governance. This shares the load, and ensures that there is a higher level of buy-in. It also ensures that information flows freely from the teams into the group, and as a result, the decision making is much more sensible and informed.

Sometimes, the group may make decisions with which the architect disagrees. At this point, what is the architect to do? Having been in this position before, I can tell you this is one of the most challenging situations to face. Often, I take the approach that I should go with the group decision. I take the view that I've done my best to convince people, but ultimately I wasn't convincing enough. The group is often much wiser than the individual, and I've been proven wrong more than once! And imagine how disempowering it can be for a group to have been given space to come up with a decision, and then ultimately be ignored. But sometimes I have overruled the group. But why, and when? How do you pick the lines?

Think about teaching children to ride a bike. You can't ride it for them. You watch them wobble, but if you stepped in every time it looked like they might fall off, then they'd never learn, and in any case they fall off far less than you think they will! But if you see them about to veer into traffic, or into a nearby duck pond, then you have to step in. Likewise, as an architect, you need to have a firm grasp of when, figuratively, your team is steering into a duck pond. You also need to be aware that even if you know you are right and overrule the team, this can undermine your position and also make the team feel that they don't have a say. Sometimes the right thing is to go along with a decision you don't agree with. Knowing when to do this and when not to is tough, but is sometimes vital.

Building a Team

Being the main point person responsible for the technical vision of your system and ensuring that you're executing on this vision isn't just about making technology decisions. It's the people you work with who will be doing the work. Much of the role of the technical leader is about helping grow them—to help them understand the vision themselves—and also ensuring that they can be active participants in shaping and implementing the vision too.

Helping the people around you on their own career growth can take many forms, most of which are outside the scope of this book. There is one aspect, though, where a microservice architecture is especially relevant. With larger, monolithic systems, there are fewer opportunities for people to step up and *own* something. With microservices, on the other hand, we have multiple autonomous codebases that will have their own independent lifecycles. Helping people step up by having them take ownership of individual services before accepting more responsibility can be a great way to help them achieve their own career goals, and at the same time lightens the load on whoever is in charge!

I am a strong believer that great software comes from great people. If you worry only about the technology side of the equation, you're missing way more than half of the picture.

Summary

To summarize this chapter, here are what I see as the core responsibilities of the evolutionary architect:

Vision
Ensure there is a clearly communicated technical vision for the system that will help your system meet the requirements of your customers and organization

Empathy
Understand the impact of your decisions on your customers and colleagues

Collaboration
Engage with as many of your peers and colleagues as possible to help define, refine, and execute the vision

Adaptability
Make sure that the technical vision changes as your customers or organization requires it

Autonomy
Find the right balance between standardizing and enabling autonomy for your teams

Governance
Ensure that the system being implemented fits the technical vision

The evolutionary architect is one who understands that pulling off this feat is a constant balancing act. Forces are always pushing you one way or another, and understanding where to push back or where to go with the flow is often something that comes only with experience. But the worst reaction to all these forces that push us toward change is to become more rigid or fixed in our thinking.

While much of the advice in this chapter can apply to any systems architect, microservices give us many more decisions to make. Therefore, being better able to balance all of these trade-offs is essential.

In the next chapter, we'll take some of our newfound awareness of the architect's role with us as we start thinking about how to find the right boundaries for our microservices.

CHAPTER 3

How to Model Services

My opponent's reasoning reminds me of the heathen, who, being asked on what the world stood, replied, "On a tortoise." But on what does the tortoise stand? "On another tortoise."

—Joseph Barker (1854)

So you know what microservices are, and hopefully have a sense of their key benefits. You're probably eager now to go and start making them, right? But where to start? In this chapter, we'll look at how to think about the boundaries of your microservices that will hopefully maximize the upsides and avoid some of the potential downsides. But first, we need something to work with.

Introducing MusicCorp

Books about ideas work better with examples. Where possible, I'll be sharing stories from real-world situations, but I've found it's also useful to have a fictional domain with which to work. Throughout the book, we'll be returning to this domain, seeing how the concept of microservices works within this world.

So let's turn our attention to the cutting-edge online retailer MusicCorp. MusicCorp was recently a brick-and-mortar retailer, but after the bottom dropped out of the gramophone record business it focused more and more of its efforts online. The company has a website, but feels that now is the time to double-down on the online world. After all, those iPods are just a passing fad (Zunes are way better, obviously) and music fans are quite happy to wait for CDs to arrive at their doorsteps. Quality over convenience, right? And while we're at it, what's this Spotify thing people keep talking about—some sort of skin treatment for teenagers?

Despite being a little behind the curve, MusicCorp has grand ambitions. Luckily, it has decided that its best chance of taking over the world is by making sure it can make changes as easily as possible. Microservices for the win!

What Makes a Good Service?

Before the team from MusicCorp tears off into the distance, creating service after service in an attempt to deliver eight-track tapes to all and sundry, let's put the brakes on and talk a bit about the most important underlying idea we need to keep in mind. What makes a good service? If you've survived a failed SOA implementation, you may have some idea where I'm going next. But just in case you aren't that (un)fortunate, I want you to focus on two key concepts: *loose coupling* and *high cohesion*. We'll talk in detail throughout the book about other ideas and practices, but they are all for naught if we get these two thing wrong.

Despite the fact that these two terms are used a lot, especially in the context of object-oriented systems, it is worth discussing what they mean in terms of microservices.

Loose Coupling

When services are loosely coupled, a change to one service should not require a change to another. The whole point of a microservice is being able to make a change to one service and deploy it, without needing to change any other part of the system. This is really quite important.

What sort of things cause tight coupling? A classic mistake is to pick an integration style that tightly binds one service to another, causing changes inside the service to require a change to consumers. We'll discuss how to avoid this in more depth in Chapter 4.

A loosely coupled service knows as little as it needs to about the services with which it collaborates. This also means we probably want to limit the number of different types of calls from one service to another, because beyond the potential performance problem, chatty communication can lead to tight coupling.

High Cohesion

We want related behavior to sit together, and unrelated behavior to sit elsewhere. Why? Well, if we want to change behavior, we want to be able to change it in one place, and release that change as soon as possible. If we have to change that behavior in lots of different places, we'll have to release lots of different services (perhaps at the same time) to deliver that change. Making changes in lots of different places is slower, and deploying lots of services at once is risky—both of which we want to avoid.

So we want to find boundaries within our problem domain that help ensure that related behavior is in one place, and that communicate with other boundaries as loosely as possible.

The Bounded Context

Eric Evans's book *Domain-Driven Design* (Addison-Wesley) focuses on how to create systems that model real-world domains. The book is full of great ideas like using ubiquitous language, repository abstractions, and the like, but there is one very important concept Evans introduces that completely passed me by at first: *bounded context*. The idea is that any given domain consists of multiple bounded contexts, and residing within each are things (Eric uses the word *model* a lot, which is probably better than *things*) that do not need to be communicated outside as well as things that are shared externally with other bounded contexts. Each bounded context has an explicit interface, where it decides what models to share with other contexts.

Another definition of bounded contexts I like is "a specific responsibility enforced by explicit boundaries."[1] If you want information from a bounded context, or want to make requests of functionality within a bounded context, you communicate with its explicit boundary using models. In his book, Evans uses the analogy of cells, where "[c]ells can exist because their membranes define what is in and out and determine what can pass."

Let's return for a moment to the MusicCorp business. Our domain is the whole business in which we are operating. It covers everything from the warehouse to the reception desk, from finance to ordering. We may or may not model all of that in our software, but that is nonetheless the domain in which we are operating. Let's think about parts of that domain that look like the bounded contexts that Evans refers to. At MusicCorp, our warehouse is a hive of activity—managing orders being shipped out (and the odd return), taking delivery of new stock, having forklift truck races, and so on. Elsewhere, the finance department is perhaps less fun-loving, but still has a very important function inside our organization. These employees manage payroll, keep the company accounts, and produce important reports. Lots of reports. They probably also have interesting desk toys.

Shared and Hidden Models

For MusicCorp, we can then consider the finance department and the warehouse to be two separate bounded contexts. They both have an explicit interface to the outside world (in terms of inventory reports, pay slips, etc.), and they have details that only they need to know about (forklift trucks, calculators).

Now the finance department doesn't need to know about the detailed inner workings of the warehouse. It does need to know some things, though—for example it needs to know about stock levels to keep the accounts up to date. Figure 3-1 shows an example

---

1 *http://bit.ly/bounded-context-explained*

context diagram. We see concepts that are internal to the warehouse, like Picker (people who pick orders), shelves that represent stock locations, and so on. Likewise, the company's general ledger is integral to finance but is not shared externally here.

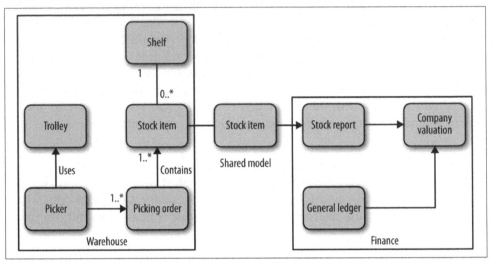

Figure 3-1. A shared model between the finance department and the warehouse

To be able to work out the valuation of the company, though, the finance employees need information about the stock we hold. The stock item then becomes a shared model between the two contexts. However, note that we don't need to blindly expose everything about the stock item from the warehouse context. For example, although internally we keep a record on a stock item as to where it should live within the warehouse, that doesn't need to be exposed in the shared model. So there is the internal-only representation, and the external representation we expose. In many ways, this foreshadows the discussion around REST in Chapter 4.

Sometimes we may encounter models with the same name that have very different meanings in different contexts too. For example, we might have the concept of a return, which represents a customer sending something back. Within the context of the customer, a return is all about printing a shipping label, dispatching a package, and waiting for a refund. For the warehouse, this could represent a package that is about to arrive, and a stock item that needs to be restocked. It follows that within the warehouse we store additional information associated with the return that relates to the tasks to be carried out; for example, we may generate a restock request. The shared model of the return becomes associated with different processes and supporting entities within each bounded context, but that is very much an internal concern within the context itself.

Modules and Services

By thinking clearly about what models should be shared, and not sharing our internal representations, we avoid one of the potential pitfalls that can result in tight coupling (the opposite of what we want). We have also identified a boundary within our domain where all like-minded business capabilities should live, giving us the high cohesion we want. These bounded contexts, then, lend themselves extremely well to being compositional boundaries.

As we discussed in Chapter 1, we have the option of using modules within a process boundary to keep related code together and attempt to reduce the coupling to other modules in the system. When you're starting out on a new codebase, this is probably a good place to begin. So once you have found your bounded contexts in your domain, make sure they are modeled within your codebase as modules, with shared and hidden models.

These modular boundaries then become excellent candidates for microservices. In general, microservices should cleanly align to bounded contexts. Once you become very proficient, you may decide to skip the step of keeping the bounded context modeled as a module within a more monolithic system, and jump straight for a separate service. When starting out, however, keep a new system on the more monolithic side; getting service boundaries wrong can be costly, so waiting for things to stabilize as you get to grips with a new domain is sensible. We'll discuss this more in Chapter 5, along with techniques to help break apart existing systems into microservices.

So, if our service boundaries align to the bounded contexts in our domain, and our microservices represent those bounded contexts, we are off to an excellent start in ensuring that our microservices are loosely coupled and strongly cohesive.

Premature Decomposition

At ThoughtWorks, we ourselves experienced the challenges of splitting out microservices too quickly. Aside from consulting, we also create a few products. One of them is SnapCI, a hosted continuous integration and continuous delivery tool (we'll discuss those concepts later in Chapter 6). The team had previously worked on another similar tool, Go-CD, a now open source continuous delivery tool that can be deployed locally rather than being hosted in the cloud.

Although there was some code reuse very early on between the SnapCI and Go-CD projects, in the end SnapCI turned out to be a completely new codebase. Nonetheless, the previous experience of the team in the domain of CD tooling emboldened them to move more quickly in identifying boundaries, and building their system as a set of microservices.

After a few months, though, it became clear that the use cases of SnapCI were subtly different enough that the initial take on the service boundaries wasn't quite right. This led to lots of changes being made across services, and an associated high cost of change. Eventually the team merged the services back into one monolithic system, giving them time to better understand where the boundaries should exist. A year later, the team was then able to split the monolithic system apart into microservices, whose boundaries proved to be much more stable. This is far from the only example of this situation I have seen. Prematurely decomposing a system into microservices can be costly, especially if you are new to the domain. In many ways, having an existing codebase you want to decompose into microservices is much easier than trying to go to microservices from the beginning.

Business Capabilities

When you start to think about the bounded contexts that exist in your organization, you should be thinking not in terms of data that is shared, but about the capabilities those contexts provide the rest of the domain. The warehouse may provide the capability to get a current stock list, for example, or the finance context may well expose the end-of-month accounts or let you set up payroll for a new recruit. These capabilities may require the interchange of information—shared models—but I have seen too often that thinking about *data* leads to anemic, CRUD-based (create, read, update, delete) services. So ask first "What does this context do?", and then "So what data does it need to do that?"

When modeled as services, these capabilities become the key operations that will be exposed over the wire to other collaborators.

Turtles All the Way Down

At the start, you will probably identify a number of coarse-grained bounded contexts. But these bounded contexts can in turn contain further bounded contexts. For example, you could decompose the warehouse into capabilities associated with order fulfillment, inventory management, or goods receiving. When considering the boundaries of your microservices, first think in terms of the larger, coarser-grained contexts, and then subdivide along these nested contexts when you're looking for the benefits of splitting out these seams.

I have seen these nested contexts remaining hidden to other, collaborating microservices to great effect. To the outside world, they are still making use of business capabilities in the warehouse, but they are unaware that their requests are actually being mapped transparently to two or more separate services, as you can see in Figure 3-2. Sometimes, you will decide it makes more sense for the higher-level bounded context to not be explicitly modeled as a service boundary, as in Figure 3-3, so rather than a single warehouse boundary, you might instead split out inventory, order fulfillment, and goods receiving.

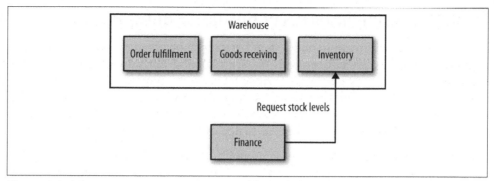

Figure 3-2. Microservices representing nested bounded contexts hidden inside the warehouse

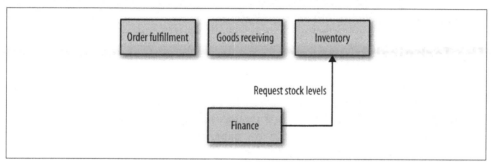

Figure 3-3. The bounded contexts inside the warehouse being popped up into their own top-level contexts

In general, there isn't a hard-and-fast rule as to what approach makes the most sense. However, whether you choose the nested approach over the full separation approach should be based on your organizational structure. If order fulfillment, inventory management, and goods receiving are managed by different teams, they probably deserve their status as *top-level* microservices. If, on the other hand, all of them are managed by one team, then the nested model makes more sense. This is because of the interplay of organizational structures and software architecture, which we will discuss toward the end of the book in Chapter 10.

Another reason to prefer the nested approach could be to chunk up your architecture to simplify testing. For example, when testing services that consume the warehouse, I don't have to stub each service inside the warehouse context, just the more coarse-grained API. This can also give you a unit of isolation when considering larger-scoped tests. I may, for example, decide to have end-to-end tests where I launch all services inside the warehouse context, but for all other collaborators I might stub them out. We'll explore more about testing and isolation in Chapter 7.

Communication in Terms of Business Concepts

The changes we implement to our system are often about changes the business wants to make to how the system behaves. We are changing functionality—capabilities—that are exposed to our customers. If our systems are decomposed along the bounded contexts that represent our domain, the changes we want to make are more likely to be isolated to one, single microservice boundary. This reduces the number of places we need to make a change, and allows us to deploy that change quickly.

It's also important to think of the communication between these microservices in terms of the same business concepts. The modeling of your software after your business domain shouldn't stop at the idea of bounded contexts. The same terms and ideas that are shared between parts of your organization should be reflected in your interfaces. It can be useful to think of forms being sent between these microservices, much as forms are sent around an organization.

The Technical Boundary

It can be useful to look at what can go wrong when services are modeled incorrectly. A while back, a few colleagues and I were working with a client in California, helping the company adopt some cleaner code practices and move more toward automated testing. We'd started with some of the low-hanging fruit, such as service decomposition, when we noticed something much more worrying. I can't go into too much detail as to what the application did, but it was a public-facing application with a large, global customer base.

The team, and system, had grown. Originally one person's vision, the system had taken on more and more features, and more and more users. Eventually, the organization decided to increase the capacity of the team by having a new group of developers based in Brazil take on some of the work. The system got split up, with the front half of the application being essentially stateless, implementing the public-facing website, as shown in Figure 3-4. The back half of the system was simply a remote procedure call (RPC) interface over a data store. Essentially, imagine you'd taken a repository layer in your codebase and made this a separate service.

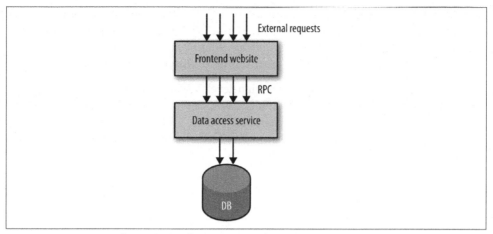

Figure 3-4. A service boundary split across a technical seam

Changes frequently had to be made to both services. Both services spoke in terms of low-level, RPC-style method calls, which were overly brittle (we'll discuss this further in Chapter 4). The service interface was also very chatty too, resulting in performance issues. This resulted in the need for elaborate RPC-batching mechanisms. I called this *onion architecture*, as it had lots of layers and made me cry when we had to cut through it.

Now on the face of it, the idea of splitting the previously monolithic system along geographical/organizational lines makes perfect sense, as we'll expand on in Chapter 10. Here, however, rather than taking a vertical, business-focused slice through the stack, the team picked what was previously an in-process API and made a horizontal slice.

Making decisions to model service boundaries along technical seams isn't always wrong. I have certainly seen this make lots of sense when an organization is looking to achieve certain performance objectives, for example. However, it should be your secondary driver for finding these seams, not your primary one.

Summary

In this chapter, you've learned a bit about what makes a good service, and how to find seams in our problem space that give us the dual benefits of both loose coupling and high cohesion. Bounded contexts are a vital tool in helping us find these seams, and by aligning our microservices to these boundaries we ensure that the resulting system has every chance of keeping those virtues intact. We've also got a hint about how we can subdivide our microservices further, something we'll explore in more depth later. And we also introduced MusicCorp, the example domain that we will use throughout this book.

The ideas presented in Eric Evans's *Domain-Driven Design* are very useful to us in finding sensible boundaries for our services, and I've just scratched the surface here. I recommend Vaughn Vernon's book *Implementing Domain-Driven Design* (Addison-Wesley) to help you understand the practicalities of this approach.

Although this chapter has been mostly high-level, we need to get much more technical in the next. There are many pitfalls associated with implementing interfaces between services that can lead to all sorts of trouble, and we will have to take a deep dive into this topic if we are to keep our systems from becoming a giant, tangled mess.

CHAPTER 4

Integration

Getting integration right is the single most important aspect of the technology associated with microservices in my opinion. Do it well, and your microservices retain their autonomy, allowing you to change and release them independent of the whole. Get it wrong, and disaster awaits. Hopefully once you've read this chapter you'll learn how to avoid some of the biggest pitfalls that have plagued other attempts at SOA and could yet await you in your journey to microservices.

Looking for the Ideal Integration Technology

There is a bewildering array of options out there for how one microservice can talk to another. But which is the right one: SOAP? XML-RPC? REST? Protocol buffers? We'll dive into those in a moment, but before we do, let's think about what we want out of whatever technology we pick.

Avoid Breaking Changes

Every now and then, we may make a change that requires our consumers to also change. We'll discuss how to handle this later, but we want to pick technology that ensures this happens as rarely as possible. For example, if a microservice adds new fields to a piece of data it sends out, existing consumers shouldn't be impacted.

Keep Your APIs Technology-Agnostic

If you have been in the IT industry for more than 15 minutes, you don't need me to tell you that we work in a space that is changing rapidly. The one certainty *is* change. New tools, frameworks, and languages are coming out all the time, implementing new ideas that can help us work faster and more effectively. Right now, you might be a .NET shop. But what about in a year from now, or five years from now? What if you want to experiment with an alternative technology stack that might make you more productive?

I am a big fan of keeping my options open, which is why I am such a fan of microservices. It is also why I think it is very important to ensure that you keep the APIs used for communication between microservices technology-agnostic. This means avoiding integration technology that dictates what technology stacks we can use to implement our microservices.

Make Your Service Simple for Consumers

We want to make it easy for consumers to use our service. Having a beautifully factored microservice doesn't count for much if the cost of using it as a consumer is sky high! So let's think about what makes it easy for consumers to use our wonderful new service. Ideally, we'd like to allow our clients full freedom in their technology choice, but on the other hand, providing a client library can ease adoption. Often, however, such libraries are incompatible with other things we want to achieve. For example, we might use client libraries to make it easy for consumers, but this can come at the cost of increased coupling.

Hide Internal Implementation Detail

We don't want our consumers to be bound to our internal implementation. This leads to increased coupling. This means that if we want to change something inside our microservice, we can break our consumers by requiring them to also change. That increases the cost of change—the exact result we are trying to avoid. It also means we are less likely to want to make a change for fear of having to upgrade our consumers, which can lead to increased technical debt within the service. So any technology that pushes us to expose internal representation detail should be avoided.

Interfacing with Customers

Now that we've got a few guidelines that can help us select a good technology to use for integration between services, let's look at some of the most common options out there and try to work out which one works best for us. To help us think this through, let's pick a real-world example from MusicCorp.

Customer creation at first glance could be considered a simple set of CRUD operations, but for most systems it is more complex than that. Enrolling a new customer may need to kick off additional processes, like setting up financial payments or sending out welcome emails. And when we change or delete a customer, other business processes might get triggered as well.

So with that in mind, we should look at some different ways in which we might want to work with customers in our MusicCorp system.

The Shared Database

By far the most common form of integration that I or any of my colleagues see in the industry is database (DB) integration. In this world, if other services want information from a service, they reach into the database. And if they want to change it, they reach into the database! This is really simple when you first think about it, and is probably the fastest form of integration to start with—which probably explains its popularity.

Figure 4-1 shows our registration UI, which creates customers by performing SQL operations directly on the database. It also shows our call center application that views and edits customer data by running SQL on the database. And the warehouse updates information about customer orders by querying the database. This is a common enough pattern, but it's one fraught with difficulties.

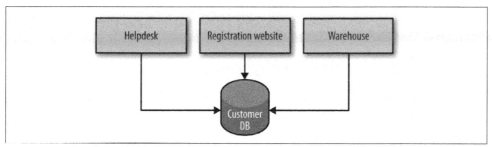

Figure 4-1. Using DB integration to access and change customer information

First, we are allowing external parties to view and bind to internal implementation details. The data structures I store in the DB are fair game to all; they are shared in their entirety with all other parties with access to the database. If I decide to change my schema to better represent my data, or make my system easier to maintain, I can break my consumers. The DB is effectively a very large, shared API that is also quite brittle. If I want to change the logic associated with, say, how the helpdesk manages customers and this requires a change to the database, I have to be extremely careful that I don't break parts of the schema used by other services. This situation normally results in requiring a large amount of regression testing.

Second, my consumers are tied to a specific technology choice. Perhaps right now it makes sense to store customers in a relational database, so my consumers use an appropriate (potentially DB-specific) driver to talk to it. What if over time we realize we would be better off storing data in a nonrelational database? Can it make that decision? So consumers are intimately tied to the implementation of the customer service. As we discussed earlier, we really want to ensure that implementation detail is hidden from consumers to allow our service a level of autonomy in terms of how it changes its internals over time. Goodbye, loose coupling.

Finally, let's think about behavior for a moment. There is going to be logic associated with how a customer is changed. Where is that logic? If consumers are directly manipulating the DB, then they have to own the associated logic. The logic to perform the same sorts of manipulation to a customer may now be spread among multiple consumers. If the warehouse, registration UI, and call center UI all need to edit customer information, I need to fix a bug or change the behavior in three different places, and deploy those changes too. Goodbye, cohesion.

Remember when we talked about the core principles behind good microservices? Strong cohesion and loose coupling—with database integration, we lose both things. Database integration makes it easy for services to share data, but does nothing about *sharing behavior*. Our internal representation is exposed over the wire to our consumers, and it can be very difficult to avoid making breaking changes, which inevitably leads to a fear of any change at all. Avoid at (nearly) all costs.

For the rest of the chapter, we'll explore different styles of integration that involve collaborating services, which themselves hide their own internal representations.

Synchronous Versus Asynchronous

Before we start diving into the specifics of different technology choices, we should discuss one of the most important decisions we can make in terms of how services collaborate. Should communication be synchronous or asynchronous? This fundamental choice inevitably guides us toward certain implementation detail.

With synchronous communication, a call is made to a remote server, which blocks until the operation completes. With asynchronous communication, the caller doesn't wait for the operation to complete before returning, and may not even care whether or not the operation completes at all.

Synchronous communication can be easier to reason about. We know when things have completed successfully or not. Asynchronous communication can be very useful for long-running jobs, where keeping a connection open for a long period of time between the client and server is impractical. It also works very well when you need low latency, where blocking a call while waiting for the result can slow things down. Due to the nature of mobile networks and devices, firing off requests and assuming things have worked (unless told otherwise) can ensure that the UI remains responsive even if the network is highly laggy. On the flipside, the technology to handle asynchronous communication can be a bit more involved, as we'll discuss shortly.

These two different modes of communication can enable two different idiomatic styles of collaboration: *request/response* or *event-based*. With request/response, a client initiates a request and waits for the response. This model clearly aligns well to synchronous communication, but can work for asynchronous communication too. I might kick off an operation and register a callback, asking the server to let me know when my operation has completed.

With an event-based collaboration, we invert things. Instead of a client initiating requests asking for things to be done, it instead says *this thing happened* and expects other parties to know what to do. We never tell anyone else what to do. Event-based systems by their nature are asynchronous. The smarts are more evenly distributed— that is, the business logic is not centralized into core brains, but instead pushed out more evenly to the various collaborators. Event-based collaboration is also highly decoupled. The client that emits an event doesn't have any way of knowing who or what will react to it, which also means that you can add new subscribers to these events without the client ever needing to know.

So are there any other drivers that might push us to pick one style over another? One important factor to consider is how well these styles are suited for solving an often-complex problem: how do we handle processes that span service boundaries and may be long running?

Orchestration Versus Choreography

As we start to model more and more complex logic, we have to deal with the problem of managing business processes that stretch across the boundary of individual services. And with microservices, we'll hit this limit sooner than usual. Let's take an example from MusicCorp, and look at what happens when we create a customer:

1. A new record is created in the loyalty points bank for the customer.
2. Our postal system sends out a welcome pack.
3. We send a welcome email to the customer.

This is very easy to model conceptually as a flowchart, as we do in Figure 4-2.

When it comes to actually implementing this flow, there are two styles of architecture we could follow. With orchestration, we rely on a central brain to guide and drive the process, much like the conductor in an orchestra. With choreography, we inform each part of the system of its job, and let it work out the details, like dancers all finding their way and reacting to others around them in a ballet.

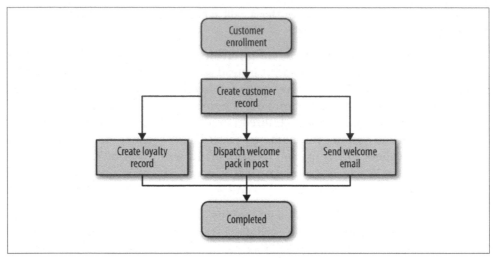

Figure 4-2. The process for creating a new customer

Let's think about what an orchestration solution would look like for this flow. Here, probably the simplest thing to do would be to have our customer service act as the central brain. On creation, it talks to the loyalty points bank, email service, and postal service as we see in Figure 4-3, through a series of request/response calls. The customer service itself can then track where a customer is in this process. It can check to see if the customer's account has been set up, or the email sent, or the post delivered. We get to take the flowchart in Figure 4-2 and model it directly into code. We could even use tooling that implements this for us, perhaps using an appropriate rules engine. Commercial tools exist for this very purpose in the form of business process modeling software. Assuming we use synchronous request/response, we could even know if each stage has worked.

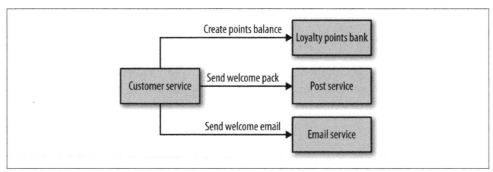

Figure 4-3. Handling customer creation via orchestration

The downside to this orchestration approach is that the customer service can become too much of a central governing authority. It can become the hub in the middle of a web, and a central point where logic starts to live. I have seen this approach result in a small number of smart "god" services telling anemic CRUD-based services what to do.

With a choreographed approach, we could instead just have the customer service emit an event in an asynchronous manner, saying *Customer created*. The email service, postal service, and loyalty points bank then just subscribe to these events and react accordingly, as in Figure 4-4. This approach is significantly more decoupled. If some other service needed to reach to the creation of a customer, it just needs to subscribe to the events and do its job when needed. The downside is that the explicit view of the business process we see in Figure 4-2 is now only implicitly reflected in our system.

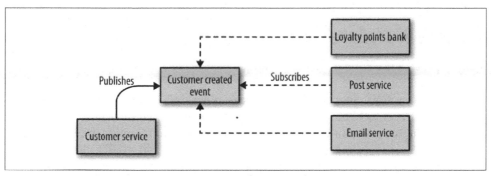

Figure 4-4. Handling customer creation via choreography

This means additional work is needed to ensure that you can monitor and track that the right things have happened. For example, would you know if the loyalty points bank had a bug and for some reason didn't set up the correct account? One approach I like for dealing with this is to build a monitoring system that explicitly matches the view of the business process in Figure 4-2, but then tracks what each of the services does as independent entities, letting you see odd exceptions mapped onto the more explicit process flow. The flowchart we saw earlier isn't the driving force, but just one lens through which we can see how the system is behaving.

In general, I have found that systems that tend more toward the choreographed approach are more loosely coupled, and are more flexible and amenable to change. You do need to do extra work to monitor and track the processes across system boundaries, however. I have found most heavily orchestrated implementations to be extremely brittle, with a higher cost of change. With that in mind, I strongly prefer aiming for a choreographed system, where each service is smart enough to understand its role in the whole dance.

There are quite a few factors to unpack here. Synchronous calls are simpler, and we get to know if things worked straightaway. If we like the semantics of request/

response but are dealing with longer-lived processes, we could just initiate asynchronous requests and wait for callbacks. On the other hand, asynchronous event collaboration helps us adopt a choreographed approach, which can yield significantly more decoupled services—something we want to strive for to ensure our services are independently releasable.

We are, of course, free to mix and match. Some technologies will fit more naturally into one style or another. We do, however, need to appreciate some of the different technical implementation details that will further help us make the right call.

To start with, let's look at two technologies that fit well when we are considering request/response: remote procedure call (RPC) and REpresentational State Transfer (REST).

Remote Procedure Calls

Remote procedure call refers to the technique of making a local call and having it execute on a remote service somewhere. There are a number of different types of RPC technology out there. Some of this technology relies on having an interface definition (SOAP, Thrift, protocol buffers). The use of a separate interface definition can make it easier to generate client and server stubs for different technology stacks, so, for example, I could have a Java server exposing a SOAP interface, and a .NET client generated from the Web Service Definition Language (WSDL) definition of the interface. Other technology, like Java RMI, calls for a tighter coupling between the client and server, requiring that both use the same underlying technology but avoid the need for a shared interface definition. All these technologies, however, have the same, core characteristic in that they make a remote call look like a local call.

Many of these technologies are binary in nature, like Java RMI, Thrift, or protocol buffers, while SOAP uses XML for its message formats. Some implementations are tied to a specific networking protocol (like SOAP, which makes nominal use of HTTP), whereas others might allow you to use different types of networking protocols, which themselves can provide additional features. For example, TCP offers guarantees about delivery, whereas UDP doesn't but has a much lower overhead. This can allow you to use different networking technology for different use cases.

Those RPC implementations that allow you to generate client and server stubs help you get started very, very fast. I can be sending content over a network boundary in no time at all. This is often one of the main selling points of RPC: its ease of use. The fact that I can just make a normal method call and theoretically ignore the rest is a huge boon.

Some RPC implementations, though, do come with some downsides that can cause issues. These issues aren't always apparent initially, but nonetheless they can be severe enough to outweigh the benefits of being so easy to get up and running quickly.

Technology Coupling

Some RPC mechanisms, like Java RMI, are heavily tied to a specific platform, which can limit which technology can be used in the client and server. Thrift and protocol buffers have an impressive amount of support for alternative languages, which can reduce this downside somewhat, but be aware that sometimes RPC technology comes with restrictions on interoperability.

In a way, this technology coupling can be a form of exposing internal technical implementation details. For example, the use of RMI ties not only the client to the JVM, but the server too.

Local Calls Are Not Like Remote Calls

The core idea of RPC is to hide the complexity of a remote call. Many implementations of RPC, though, hide too much. The drive in some forms of RPC to make remote method calls look like local method calls hides the fact that these two things are very different. I can make large numbers of local, in-process calls without worrying overly about the performance. With RPC, though, the cost of marshalling and unmarshalling payloads can be significant, not to mention the time taken to send things over the network. This means you need to think differently about API design for remote interfaces versus local interfaces. Just taking a local API and trying to make it a service boundary without any more thought is likely to get you in trouble. In some of the worst examples, developers may be using remote calls without knowing it, if the abstraction is overly opaque.

You need to think about the network itself. Famously, the first of the fallacies of distributed computing is "The network is reliable" (*http://bit.ly/1LbdCzY*). Networks aren't reliable. They can and will fail, even if your client and the server you are speaking to are fine. They can fail fast, they can fail slow, and they can even malform your packets. You should assume that your networks are plagued with malevolent entities ready to unleash their ire on a whim. Therefore, the failure modes you can expect are different. A failure could be caused by the remote server returning an error, or by you making a bad call. Can you tell the difference, and if so, can you do anything about it? And what do you do when the remote server just starts responding slowly? We'll cover this topic when we talk about resiliency in Chapter 11.

Brittleness

Some of the most popular implementations of RPC can lead to some nasty forms of brittleness, Java's RMI being a very good example. Let's consider a very simple Java interface that we have decided to make a remote API for our customer service. Example 4-1 declares the methods we are going to expose remotely. Java RMI then generates the client and server stubs for our method.

Example 4-1. Defining a service endpoint using Java RMI

```
import java.rmi.Remote;
import java.rmi.RemoteException;

public interface CustomerRemote extends Remote {
  public Customer findCustomer(String id) throws RemoteException;

  public Customer createCustomer(String firstname, String surname, String emailAddress)
      throws RemoteException;
}
```

In this interface, `createCustomer` takes the first name, surname, and email address. What happens if we decide to allow the `Customer` object to also be created with just an email address? We could add a new method at this point pretty easily, like so:

```
...
public Customer createCustomer(String emailAddress) throws RemoteException;
...
```

The problem is that now we need to regenerate the client stubs too. Clients that want to consume the new method need the new stubs, and depending on the nature of the changes to the specification, consumers that don't need the new method may also need to have their stubs upgraded too. This is manageable, of course, but to a point. The reality is that changes like this are fairly common. RPC endpoints often end up having a large number of methods for different ways of creating or interacting with objects. This is due in part to the fact that we are still thinking of these remote calls as local ones.

There is another sort of brittleness, though. Let's take a look at what our `Customer` object looks like:

```
public class Customer implements Serializable {
  private String firstName;
  private String surname;
  private String emailAddress;
  private String age;
}
```

Now, what if it turns out that although we expose the `age` field in our `Customer` objects, none of our consumers ever use it? We decide we want to remove this field. But if the server implementation removes `age` from its definition of this type, and we don't do the same to all the consumers, then even though they never used the field, the code associated with deserializing the `Customer` object on the consumer side will break. To roll out this change, I would have to deploy both a new server and clients at the same time. This is a key challenge with any RPC mechanism that promotes the use of binary stub generation: you don't get to separate client and server deployments. If you use this technology, lock-step releases may be in your future.

Similar problems occur if I want to restructure the Customer object even if I didn't remove fields—for example, if I wanted to encapsulate firstName and surname into a new naming type to make it easier to manage. I could, of course, fix this by passing around dictionary types as the parameters of my calls, but at that point, I lose many of the benefits of the generated stubs because I'll still have to manually match and extract the fields I want.

In practice, objects used as part of binary serialization across the wire can be thought of as *expand-only* types. This brittleness results in the types being exposed over the wire and becoming a mass of fields, some of which are no longer used but can't be safely removed.

Is RPC Terrible?

Despite its shortcomings, I wouldn't go so far as to call RPC terrible. Some of the common implementations that I have encountered can lead to the sorts of problems I have outlined here. Due to the challenges of using RMI, I would certainly give that technology a wide berth. Many operations fall quite nicely into the RPC-based model, and more modern mechanisms like protocol buffers or Thrift mitigate some of the sins of the past by avoiding the need for lock-step releases of client and server code.

Just be aware of some of the potential pitfalls associated with RPC if you're going to pick this model. Don't abstract your remote calls to the point where the network is completely hidden, and ensure that you can evolve the server interface without having to insist on lock-step upgrades for clients. Finding the right balance for your client code is important, for example. Make sure your clients aren't oblivious to the fact that a network call is going to be made. Client libraries are often used in the context of RPC, and if not structured right they can be problematic. We'll talk more about them shortly.

Compared to database integration, RPC is certainly an improvement when we think about options for request/response collaboration. But there's another option to consider.

REST

REpresentational State Transfer (REST) is an architectural style inspired by the Web. There are many principles and constraints behind the REST style, but we are going to focus on those that really help us when we face integration challenges in a microservices world, and when we're looking for an alternative style to RPC for our service interfaces.

Most important is the concept of resources. You can think of a resource as a thing that the service itself knows about, like a Customer. The server creates different representations of this Customer on request. How a resource is shown externally is completely decoupled from how it is stored internally. A client might ask for a JSON representation of a Customer, for example, even if it is stored in a completely different format. Once a client has a representation of this Customer, it can then make requests to change it, and the server may or may not comply with them.

There are many different styles of REST, and I touch only briefly on them here. I strongly recommend you take a look at the Richardson Maturity Model (*http://bit.ly/ 1fh2AGt*), where the different styles of REST are compared.

REST itself doesn't really talk about underlying protocols, although it is most commonly used over HTTP. I have seen implementations of REST using very different protocols before, such as serial or USB, although this can require a lot of work. Some of the features that HTTP gives us as part of the specification, such as verbs, make implementing REST over HTTP easier, whereas with other protocols you'll have to handle these features yourself.

REST and HTTP

HTTP itself defines some useful capabilities that play very well with the REST style. For example, the HTTP verbs (e.g., GET, POST, and PUT) already have well-understood meanings in the HTTP specification as to how they should work with resources. The REST architectural style actually tells us that methods should behave the same way on all resources, and the HTTP specification happens to define a bunch of methods we can use. GET retrieves a resource in an idempotent way, and POST creates a new resource. This means we can avoid lots of different createCustomer or editCustomer methods. Instead, we can simply POST a customer representation to request that the server create a new resource, and initiate a GET request to retrieve a representation of a resource. Conceptually, there is one *endpoint* in the form of a Customer resource in these cases, and the operations we can carry out upon it are baked into the HTTP protocol.

HTTP also brings a large ecosystem of supporting tools and technology. We get to use HTTP caching proxies like Varnish and load balancers like mod_proxy, and many monitoring tools already have lots of support for HTTP out of the box. These building blocks allow us to handle large volumes of HTTP traffic and route them smartly, in a fairly transparent way. We also get to use all the available security controls with HTTP to secure our communications. From basic auth to client certs, the HTTP ecosystem gives us lots of tools to make the security process easier, and we'll explore that topic more in Chapter 9. That said, to get these benefits, you have to use HTTP well. Use it badly, and it can be as insecure and hard to scale as any other technology out there. Use it right, though, and you get a lot of help.

Note that HTTP can be used to implement RPC too. SOAP, for example, gets routed over HTTP, but unfortunately uses very little of the specification. Verbs are ignored, as are simple things like HTTP error codes. All too often, it seems, the existing, well-understood standards and technology are ignored in favor of new standards that can only be implemented using brand-new technology—conveniently provided by the same companies that help design the new standards in the first place!

Hypermedia As the Engine of Application State

Another principle introduced in REST that can help us avoid the coupling between client and server is the concept of *hypermedia as the engine of application state* (often abbreviated as HATEOAS, and boy, did it need an abbreviation). This is fairly dense wording and a fairly interesting concept, so let's break it down a bit.

Hypermedia is a concept whereby a piece of content contains links to various other pieces of content in a variety of formats (e.g., text, images, sounds). This should be pretty familiar to you, as it's what the average web page does: you follow links, which are a form of hypermedia controls, to see related content. The idea behind HATEOAS is that clients should perform interactions (potentially leading to state transitions) with the server via these links to other resources. It doesn't need to know where exactly customers live on the server by knowing which URI to hit; instead, the client looks for and navigates links to find what it needs.

This is a bit of an odd concept, so let's first step back and consider how people interact with a web page, which we've already established is rich with hypermedia controls.

Think of the Amazon.com shopping site. The location of the shopping cart has changed over time. The graphic has changed. The link has changed. But as humans we are smart enough to still see a shopping cart, know what it is, and interact with it. We have an understanding of what a shopping cart means, even if the exact form and underlying control used to represent it has changed. We know that if we want to view the cart, this is the control we want to interact with. This is why web pages can change incrementally over time. As long as these implicit contracts between the customer and the website are still met, changes don't need to be breaking changes.

With hypermedia controls, we are trying to achieve the same level of *smarts* for our electronic consumers. Let's look at a hypermedia control that we might have for MusicCorp. We've accessed a resource representing a catalog entry for a given album in Example 4-2. Along with information about the album, we see a number of hypermedia controls.

Example 4-2. Hypermedia controls used on an album listing

```
<album>
  <name>Give Blood</name>
  <link rel="/artist" href="/artist/theBrakes" /> ❶
  <description>
    Awesome, short, brutish, funny and loud. Must buy!
  </description>
```

```
<link rel="/instantpurchase" href="/instantPurchase/1234" /> ❷
</album>
```

❶ This hypermedia control shows us where to find information about the artist.

❷ And if we want to purchase the album, we now know where to go.

In this document, we have two hypermedia controls. The client reading such a document needs to know that a control with a relation of `artist` is where it needs to navigate to get information about the artist, and that `instantpurchase` is part of the protocol used to purchase the album. The client has to understand the semantics of the API in much the same way as a human being needs to understand that on a shopping website the cart is where the items to be purchased will be.

As a client, I don't need to know which URI scheme to access to *buy* the album, I just need to access the resource, find the buy control, and navigate to that. The buy control could change location, the URI could change, or the site could even send me to another service altogether, and as a client I wouldn't care. This gives us a huge amount of decoupling between the client and server.

We are greatly abstracted from the underlying detail here. We could completely change the implementation of how the control is presented as long as the client can still find a control that matches its understanding of the protocol, in the same way that a shopping cart control might go from being a simple link to a more complex JavaScript control. We are also free to add new controls to the document, perhaps representing new state transitions that we can perform on the resource in question. We would end up breaking our consumers only if we fundamentally changed the semantics of one of the controls so it behaved very differently, or if we removed a control altogether.

Using these controls to decouple the client and server yields significant benefits over time that greatly offset the small increase in the time it takes to get these protocols up and running. By following the links, the client gets to progressively discover the API, which can be a really handy capability when we are implementing new clients.

One of the downsides is that this navigation of controls can be quite chatty, as the client needs to follow links to find the operation it wants to perform. Ultimately, this is a trade-off. I would suggest you start with having your clients navigate these controls first, then optimize later if necessary. Remember that we have a large amount of help out of the box by using HTTP, which we discussed earlier. The evils of premature optimization have been well documented before, so I don't need to expand upon them here. Also note that a lot of these approaches were developed to create distributed hypertext systems, and not all of them fit! Sometimes you'll find yourself just wanting good old-fashioned RPC.

Personally, I am a fan of using links to allow consumers to navigate API endpoints. The benefits of progressive discovery of the API and reduced coupling can be significant. However, it is clear that not everyone is sold, as I don't see it being used anywhere near as much as I would like. I think a large part of this is that there is some initial upfront work required, but the rewards often come later.

JSON, XML, or Something Else?

The use of standard textual formats gives clients a lot of flexibility as to how they consume resources, and REST over HTTP lets us use a variety of formats. The examples I have given so far used XML, but at this stage, JSON is a much more popular content type for services that work over HTTP.

The fact that JSON is a much simpler format means that consumption is also easier. Some proponents also cite its relative compactness when compared to XML as another winning factor, although this isn't often a real-world issue.

JSON does have some downsides, though. XML defines the `link` control we used earlier as a hypermedia control. The JSON standard doesn't define anything similar, so in-house styles are frequently used to shoe-horn this concept in. The Hypertext Application Language (HAL) (*http://bit.ly/hal-spec*) attempts to fix this by defining some common standards for hyperlinking for JSON (and XML too, although arguably XML needs less help). If you follow the HAL standard, you can use tools like the web-based HAL browser for exploring hypermedia controls, which can make the task of creating a client much easier.

We aren't limited to these two formats, of course. We can send pretty much anything over HTTP if we want, even binary. I am seeing more and more people just using HTML as a format instead of XML. For some interfaces, the HTML can do double duty as a UI and an API, although there are pitfalls to be avoided here, as the interactions of a human and a computer are quite different! But it is certainly an attractive idea. There are lots of HTML parsers out there, after all.

Personally, though, I am still a fan of XML. Some of the tool support is better. For example, if I want to extract only certain parts of the payload (a technique we'll discuss more in "Versioning" on page 62) I can use XPATH, which is a well-understood standard with lots of tool support, or even CSS selectors, which many find even easier. With JSON, I have JSONPATH, but this is not widely supported. I find it odd that people pick JSON because it is nice and lightweight, then try and push concepts into it like hypermedia controls that already exist in XML. I accept, though, that I am probably in the minority here and that JSON is the format of choice for most people!

Beware Too Much Convenience

As REST has become more popular, so too have the frameworks that help us create RESTFul web services. However, some of these tools trade off too much in terms of short-term gain for long-term pain; in trying to get you going fast, they can encourage some bad behaviors. For example, some frameworks actually make it very easy to simply take database representations of objects, deserialize them into in-process objects, and then directly expose these externally. I remember at a conference seeing this demonstrated using Spring Boot and cited as a major advantage. The inherent coupling that this setup promotes will in most cases cause far more pain than the effort required to properly decouple these concepts.

There is a more general problem at play here. How we decide to store our data, and how we expose it to our consumers, can easily dominate our thinking. One pattern I saw used effectively by one of our teams was to delay the implementation of proper persistence for the microservice, until the interface had stabilized enough. For an interim period, entities were just persisted in a file on local disk, which is obviously not a suitable long-term solution. This ensured that how the consumers wanted to use the service drove the design and implementation decisions. The rationale given, which was borne out in the results, was that it is too easy for the way we store domain entities in a backing store to overtly influence the models we send over the wire to collaborators. One of the downsides with this approach is that we are deferring the work required to wire up our data store. I think for new service boundaries, however, this is an acceptable trade-off.

Downsides to REST Over HTTP

In terms of ease of consumption, you cannot easily generate a client stub for your REST over HTTP application protocol like you can with RPC. Sure, the fact that HTTP is being used means that you get to take advantage of all the excellent HTTP client libraries out there, but if you want to implement and use hypermedia controls as a client you are pretty much on your own. Personally, I think client libraries could do much better at this than they do, and they are certainly better now than in the past, but I have seen this apparent increased complexity result in people backsliding into smuggling RPC over HTTP or building shared client libraries. Shared code between client and server can be very dangerous, as we'll discuss in "DRY and the Perils of Code Reuse in a Microservice World" on page 59.

A more minor point is that some web server frameworks don't actually support all the HTTP verbs well. That means that it might be easy for you to create a handler for GET or POST requests, but you may have to jump through hoops to get PUT or DELETE requests to work. Proper REST frameworks like Jersey don't have this problem, and you can normally work around this, but if you are locked into certain framework choices this might limit what style of REST you can use.

Performance may also be an issue. REST over HTTP payloads can actually be more compact than SOAP because it supports alternative formats like JSON or even binary, but it will still be nowhere near as lean a binary protocol as Thrift might be. The overhead of HTTP for each request may also be a concern for low-latency requirements.

HTTP, while it can be suited well to large volumes of traffic, isn't great for low-latency communications when compared to alternative protocols that are built on top of Transmission Control Protocol (TCP) or other networking technology. Despite the name, WebSockets, for example, has very little to do with the Web. After the initial HTTP handshake, it's just a TCP connection between client and server, but it can be a much more efficient way for you to stream data for a browser. If this is something you're interested in, note that you aren't really using much of HTTP, let alone anything to do with REST.

For server-to-server communications, if extremely low latency or small message size is important, HTTP communications in general may not be a good idea. You may need to pick different underlying protocols, like User Datagram Protocol (UDP), to achieve the performance you want, and many RPC frameworks will quite happily run on top of networking protocols other than TCP.

Consumption of the payloads themselves requires more work than is provided by some RPC implementations that support advanced serialization and deserialization mechanisms. These can become a coupling point in their own right between client and server, as implementing tolerant readers is a nontrivial activity (we'll discuss this shortly), but from the point of view of getting up and running, they can be very attractive.

Despite these disadvantages, REST over HTTP is a sensible default choice for service-to-service interactions. If you want to know more, I recommend *REST in Practice* (O'Reilly), which covers the topic of REST over HTTP in depth.

Implementing Asynchronous Event-Based Collaboration

We've talked for a bit about some technologies that can help us implement request/response patterns. What about event-based, asynchronous communication?

Technology Choices

There are two main parts we need to consider here: a way for our microservices to emit events, and a way for our consumers to find out those events have happened.

Traditionally, message brokers like RabbitMQ try to handle both problems. Producers use an API to publish an event to the broker. The broker handles subscriptions, allowing consumers to be informed when an event arrives. These brokers can even handle the state of consumers, for example by helping keep track of what messages they have seen before. These systems are normally designed to be scalable and resilient, but that doesn't come for free. It can add complexity to the development process, because it is another system you may need to run to develop and test your services. Additional machines and expertise may also be required to keep this infrastructure up and running. But once it does, it can be an incredibly effective way to implement loosely coupled, event-driven architectures. In general, I'm a fan.

Do be wary, though, about the world of middleware, of which the message broker is just a small part. Queues in and of themselves are perfectly sensible, useful things. However, vendors tend to want to package lots of software with them, which can lead to more and more smarts being pushed into the middleware, as evidenced by things like the Enterprise Service Bus. Make sure you know what you're getting: keep your middleware dumb, and keep the smarts in the endpoints.

Another approach is to try to use HTTP as a way of propagating events. ATOM is a REST-compliant specification that defines semantics (among other things) for publishing feeds of resources. Many client libraries exist that allow us to create and consume these feeds. So our customer service could just publish an event to such a feed when our customer service changes. Our consumers just poll the feed, looking for changes. On one hand, the fact that we can reuse the existing ATOM specification and any associated libraries is useful, and we know that HTTP handles scale very well. However, HTTP is not good at low latency (where some message brokers excel), and we still need to deal with the fact that the consumers need to keep track of what messages they have seen and manage their own polling schedule.

I have seen people spend an age implementing more and more of the behaviors that you get out of the box with an appropriate message broker to make ATOM work for some use cases. For example, the Competing Consumer pattern describes a method whereby you bring up multiple worker instances to compete for messages, which works well for scaling up the number of workers to handle a list of independent jobs. However, we want to avoid the case where two or more workers see the same message, as we'll end up doing the same task more than we need to. With a message broker, a standard queue will handle this. With ATOM, we now need to manage our own shared state among all the workers to try to reduce the chances of reproducing effort.

If you already have a good, resilient message broker available to you, consider using it to handle publishing and subscribing to events. But if you don't already have one, give ATOM a look, but be aware of the sunk-cost fallacy. If you find yourself wanting more and more of the support that a message broker gives you, at a certain point you might want to change your approach.

In terms of what we actually send over these asynchronous protocols, the same considerations apply as with synchronous communication. If you are currently happy with encoding requests and responses using JSON, stick with it.

Complexities of Asynchronous Architectures

Some of this asynchronous stuff seems fun, right? Event-driven architectures seem to lead to significantly more decoupled, scalable systems. And they can. But these programming styles do lead to an increase in complexity. This isn't just the complexity required to manage publishing and subscribing to messages as we just discussed, but also in the other problems we might face. For example, when considering long-running async request/response, we have to think about what to do when the response comes back. Does it come back to the same node that initiated the request? If so, what if that node is down? If not, do I need to store information somewhere so I can react accordingly? Short-lived async can be easier to manage if you've got the right APIs, but even so, it is a different way of thinking for programmers who are accustomed to intra-process synchronous message calls.

Time for a cautionary tale. Back in 2006, I was working on building a pricing system for a bank. We would look at market events, and work out which items in a portfolio needed to be repriced. Once we determined the list of things to work through, we put these all onto a message queue. We were making use of a grid to create a pool of pricing workers, allowing us to scale up and down the pricing farm on request. These workers used the competing consumer pattern, each one gobbling messages as fast as possible until there was nothing left to process.

The system was up and running, and we were feeling rather smug. One day, though, just after we pushed a release out, we hit a nasty problem. Our workers kept dying. And dying. And dying.

Eventually, we tracked down the problem. A bug had crept in whereby a certain type of pricing request would cause a worker to crash. We were using a transacted queue: as the worker died, its lock on the request timed out, and the pricing request was put back on the queue—only for another worker to pick it up and die. This was a classic example of what Martin Fowler calls a catastrophic failover (*http://bit.ly/1EmZMss*).

Aside from the bug itself, we'd failed to specify a maximum retry limit for the job on the queue. We fixed the bug itself, and also configured a maximum retry. But we also realized we needed a way to view, and potentially replay, these bad messages. We ended up having to implement a message hospital (or dead letter queue), where messages got sent if they failed. We also created a UI to view those messages and retry them if needed. These sorts of problems aren't immediately obvious if you are only familiar with synchronous point-to-point communication.

The associated complexity with event-driven architectures and asynchronous programming in general leads me to believe that you should be cautious in how eagerly you start adopting these ideas. Ensure you have good monitoring in place, and strongly consider the use of correlation IDs, which allow you to trace requests across process boundaries, as we'll cover in depth in Chapter 8.

I also strongly recommend *Enterprise Integration Patterns* (Addison-Wesley), which contains a lot more detail on the different programming patterns that you may need to consider in this space.

Services as State Machines

Whether you choose to become a REST ninja, or stick with an RPC-based mechanism like SOAP, the core concept of the service as a state machine is powerful. We've spoken before (probably ad nauseum by this point) about our services being fashioned around bounded contexts. Our customer microservice *owns* all logic associated with behavior in this context.

When a consumer wants to change a customer, it sends an appropriate request to the customer service. The customer service, based on its logic, gets to decide if it accepts that request or not. Our customer service controls all lifecycle events associated with the customer itself. We want to avoid dumb, anemic services that are little more than CRUD wrappers. If the decision about what changes are allowed to be made to a customer leak out of the customer service itself, we are losing cohesion.

Having the lifecycle of key domain concepts explicitly modeled like this is pretty powerful. Not only do we have one place to deal with collisions of state (e.g., someone trying to update a customer that has already been removed), but we also have a place to attach behavior based on those state changes.

I still think that REST over HTTP makes for a much more sensible integration technology than many others, but whatever you pick, keep this idea in mind.

Reactive Extensions

Reactive extensions, often shortened to Rx, are a mechanism to compose the results of multiple calls together and run operations on them. The calls themselves could be blocking or nonblocking calls. At its heart, Rx inverts traditional flows. Rather than asking for some data, then performing operations on it, you observe the outcome of an operation (or set of operations) and react when something changes. Some implementations of Rx allow you to perform functions on these observables, such as RxJava, which allows traditional functions like `map` or `filter` to be used.

The various Rx implementations have found a very happy home in distributed systems. They allow us to abstract out the details of how calls are made, and reason about things more easily. I observe the result of a call to a downstream service. I don't care if it was a blocking or nonblocking call, I just wait for the response and react. The beauty is that I can compose multiple calls together, making handling concurrent calls to downstream services much easier.

As you find yourself making more service calls, especially when making multiple calls to perform a single operation, take a look at the reactive extensions for your chosen technology stack. You may be surprised how much simpler your life can become.

DRY and the Perils of Code Reuse in a Microservice World

One of the acronyms we developers hear a lot is DRY: don't repeat yourself. Though its definition is sometimes simplified as trying to avoid duplicating code, DRY more accurately means that we want to avoid duplicating our system *behavior and knowledge*. This is very sensible advice in general. Having lots of lines of code that do the same thing makes your codebase larger than needed, and therefore harder to reason about. When you want to change behavior, and that behavior is duplicated in many parts of your system, it is easy to forget everywhere you need to make a change, which can lead to bugs. So using DRY as a mantra, in general, makes sense.

DRY is what leads us to create code that can be reused. We pull duplicated code into abstractions that we can then call from multiple places. Perhaps we go as far as making a shared library that we can use everywhere! This approach, however, can be deceptively dangerous in a microservice architecture.

One of the things we want to avoid at all costs is overly coupling a microservice and consumers such that any small change to the microservice itself can cause unnecessary changes to the consumer. Sometimes, however, the use of shared code can create this very coupling. For example, at one client we had a library of common domain objects that represented the core entities in use in our system. This library was used by all the services we had. But when a change was made to one of them, all services had to be updated. Our system communicated via message queues, which also had to be drained of their now *invalid* contents, and woe betide you if you forgot.

If your use of shared code ever leaks outside your service boundary, you have introduced a potential form of coupling. Using common code like logging libraries is fine, as they are internal concepts that are invisible to the outside world. RealEstate.com.au makes use of a tailored service template to help bootstrap new service creation. Rather than make this code shared, the company copies it for every new service to ensure that coupling doesn't leak in.

My general rule of thumb: don't violate DRY within a microservice, but be relaxed about violating DRY across all services. The evils of too much coupling between services are far worse than the problems caused by code duplication. There is one specific use case worth exploring further, though.

Client Libraries

I've spoken to more than one team who has insisted that creating client libraries for your services is an essential part of creating services in the first place. The argument is that this makes it easy to use your service, and avoids the duplication of code required to consume the service itself.

The problem, of course, is that if the same people create both the server API and the client API, there is the danger that logic that should exist on the server starts leaking into the client. I should know: I've done this myself. The more logic that creeps into the client library, the more cohesion starts to break down, and you find yourself having to change multiple clients to roll out fixes to your server. You also limit technology choices, especially if you mandate that the client library has to be used.

A model for client libraries I like is the one for Amazon Web Services (AWS). The underlying SOAP or REST web service calls can be made directly, but everyone ends up using just one of the various software development kits (SDKs) that exist, which provide abstractions over the underlying API. These SDKs, though, are written by the community or AWS people other than those who work on the API itself. This degree of separation seems to work, and avoids some of the pitfalls of client libraries. Part of the reason this works so well is that the client is in charge of when the upgrade happens. If you go down the path of client libraries yourself, make sure this is the case.

Netflix in particular places special emphasis on the client library, but I worry that people view that purely through the lens of avoiding code duplication. In fact, the client libraries used by Netflix are as much (if not more) about ensuring reliability and scalability of their systems. The Netflix client libraries handle service discovery, failure modes, logging, and other aspects that aren't actually about the nature of the service itself. Without these shared clients, it would be hard to ensure that each piece of client/server communications behaved well at the massive scale at which Netflix operates. Their use at Netflix has certainly made it easy to get up and running and increased productivity while also ensuring the system behaves well. However, according to at least one person at Netflix, over time this has led to a degree of coupling between client and server that has been problematic.

If the client library approach is something you're thinking about, it can be important to separate out client code to handle the underlying transport protocol, which can deal with things like service discovery and failure, from things related to the destination service itself. Decide whether or not you are going to insist on the client library being used, or if you'll allow people using different technology stacks to make calls to the underlying API. And finally, make sure that the clients are in charge of when to upgrade their client libraries: we need to ensure we maintain the ability to release our services independently of each other!

Access by Reference

One consideration I want to touch on is how we pass around information about our domain entities. We need to embrace the idea that a microservice will encompass the lifecycle of our core domain entities, like the Customer. We've already talked about the importance of the logic associated with changing this Customer being held in the customer service, and that if we want to change it we have to issue a request to the customer service. But it also follows that we should consider the customer service as being the source of truth for Customers.

When we retrieve a given Customer resource from the customer service, we get to see what that resource looked like when we made the request. It is possible that after we requested that Customer resource, something else has changed it. What we have in effect is a memory of what the Customer resource once looked like. The longer we hold on to this memory, the higher the chance that this memory will be false. Of course, if we avoid requesting data more than we need to, our systems can become much more efficient.

Sometimes this memory is good enough. Other times you need to know if it has changed. So whether you decide to pass around a memory of what an entity once looked like, make sure you also include a reference to the original resource so that the new state can be retrieved.

Let's consider the example where we ask the email service to send an email when an order has been shipped. Now we could send in the request to the email service with the customer's email address, name, and order details. However, if the email service is actually queuing up these requests, or pulling them from a queue, things could change in the meantime. It might make more sense to just send a URI for the Customer and Order resources, and let the email server go look them up when it is time to send the email.

A great counterpoint to this emerges when we consider event-based collaboration. With events, we're saying *this happened*, but we need to know *what* happened. If we're receiving updates due to a Customer resource changing, for example, it could be valuable to us to know what the Customer looked like when the event occurred. As long as we also get a reference to the entity itself so we can look up its current state, then we can get the best of both worlds.

There are other trade-offs to be made here, of course, when we're accessing by reference. If we always go to the customer service to look at the information associated with a given Customer, the load on the customer service can be too great. If we provide additional information when the resource is retrieved, letting us know at what time the resource was in the given state and perhaps how long we can consider this information to be *fresh*, then we can do a lot with caching to reduce load. HTTP gives us much of this support out of the box with a wide variety of cache controls, some of which we'll discuss in more detail in Chapter 11.

Another problem is that some of our services might not need to know about the whole Customer resource, and by insisting that they go look it up we are potentially increasing coupling. It could be argued, for example, that our email service should be more dumb, and that we should just send it the email address and name of the customer. There isn't a hard-and-fast rule here, but be very wary of passing around data in requests when you don't know its freshness.

Versioning

In every single talk I have ever done about microservices, I get asked *how do you do versioning?* People have the legitimate concern that eventually they will have to make a change to the interface of a service, and they want to understand how to manage that. Let's break down the problem a bit and look at the various steps we can take to handle it.

Defer It for as Long as Possible

The best way to reduce the impact of making breaking changes is to avoid making them in the first place. You can achieve much of this by picking the right integration technology, as we've discussed throughout this chapter. Database integration is a great example of technology that can make it very hard to avoid breaking changes. REST, on the other hand, helps because changes to internal implementation detail are less likely to result in a change to the service interface.

Another key to deferring a breaking change is to encourage good behavior in your clients, and avoid them binding too tightly to your services in the first place. Let's consider our email service, whose job it is to send out emails to our customers from time to time. It gets asked to send an order shipped email to customer with the ID 1234. It goes off and retrieves the customer with that ID, and gets back something like the response shown in Example 4-3.

Example 4-3. Sample response from the customer service

```
<customer>
  <firstname>Sam</firstname>
  <lastname>Newman</lastname>
  <email>sam@magpiebrain.com</email>
  <telephoneNumber>555-1234-5678</telephoneNumber>
</customer>
```

Now to send the email, we need only the firstname, lastname, and email fields. We don't need to know the telephoneNumber. We want to simply pull out those fields we care about, and ignore the rest. Some binding technology, especially that used by strongly typed languages, can attempt to bind *all* fields whether the consumer wants them or not. What happens if we realize that no one is using the telephoneNumber and we decide to remove it? This could cause consumers to break needlessly.

Likewise, what if we wanted to restructure our Customer object to support more details, perhaps adding some further structure as in Example 4-4? The data our email service wants is still there, and still with the same name, but if our code makes very explicit assumptions as to where the firstname and lastname fields will be stored, then it could break again. In this instance, we could instead use XPath to pull out the fields we care about, allowing us to be ambivalent about where the fields are, as long as we can find them. This pattern—of implementing a reader able to ignore changes we don't care about—is what Martin Fowler calls a Tolerant Reader (*http://bit.ly/1yISOdQ*).

Example 4-4. A restructured Customer resource: the data is all still there, but can our consumers find it?

```
<customer>
  <naming>
    <firstname>Sam</firstname>
    <lastname>Newman</lastname>
    <nickname>Magpiebrain</nickname>
    <fullname>Sam "Magpiebrain" Newman</fullname>
  </naming>
  <email>sam@magpiebrain.com</email>
</customer>
```

The example of a client trying to be as flexible as possible in consuming a service demonstrates Postel's Law (*http://bit.ly/1Cs7dfR*) (otherwise known as the *robustness principle*), which states: "Be conservative in what you do, be liberal in what you accept from others." The original context for this piece of wisdom was the interaction of devices over networks, where you should expect all sorts of odd things to happen. In the context of our request/response interaction, it can lead us to try our best to allow the service being consumed to change without requiring us to change.

Catch Breaking Changes Early

It's crucial to make sure we pick up changes that will break consumers as soon as possible, because even if we choose the best possible technology, breaks can still happen. I am strongly in favor of using consumer-driven contracts, which we'll cover in Chapter 7, to help spot these problems early on. If you're supporting multiple different client libraries, running tests using each library you support against the latest service is another technique that can help. Once you realize you are going to break a consumer, you have the choice to either try to avoid the break altogether or else embrace it and start having the right conversations with the people looking after the consuming services.

Use Semantic Versioning

Wouldn't it be great if as a client you could look just at the version number of a service and know if you can integrate with it? *Semantic versioning (http://semver.org/)* is a specification that allows just that. With semantic versioning, each version number is in the form `MAJOR.MINOR.PATCH`. When the `MAJOR` number increments, it means that backward incompatible changes have been made. When `MINOR` increments, new functionality has been added that should be backward compatible. Finally, a change to `PATCH` states that bug fixes have been made to existing functionality.

To see how useful semantic versioning can be, let's look at a simple use case. Our helpdesk application is built to work against version 1.2.0 of the customer service. If a new feature is added, causing the customer service to change to 1.3.0, our helpdesk application should see no change in behavior and shouldn't be expected to make any changes. We couldn't guarantee that we could work against version 1.1.0 of the customer service, though, as we may rely on functionality added in the 1.2.0 release. We could also expect to have to make changes to our application if a new 2.0.0 release of the customer service comes out.

You may decide to have a semantic version for the service, or even for an individual endpoint on a service if you are coexisting them as detailed in the next section.

This versioning scheme allows us to pack a lot of information and expectations into just three fields. The full specification outlines in very simple terms the expectations clients can have of changes to these numbers, and can simplify the process of communicating about whether changes should impact consumers. Unfortunately, I haven't seen this approach used enough in the context of distributed systems.

Coexist Different Endpoints

If we've done all we can to avoid introducing a breaking interface change, our next job is to limit the impact. The thing we want to avoid is forcing consumers to upgrade in lock-step with us, as we always want to maintain the ability to release microservices independently of each other. One approach I have used successfully to handle this is to coexist both the old and new interfaces in the same running service. So if we want to release a breaking change, we deploy a new version of the service that exposes both the old and new versions of the endpoint.

This allows us to get the new microservice out as soon as possible, along with the new interface, but give time for consumers to move over. Once all of the consumers are no longer using the old endpoint, you can remove it along with any associated code, as shown in Figure 4-5.

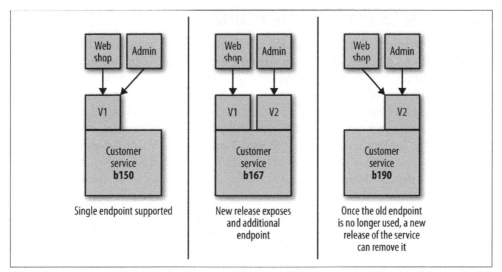

Figure 4-5. Coexisting different endpoint versions allows consumers to migrate gradually

When I last used this approach, we had gotten ourselves into a bit of a mess with the number of consumers we had and the number of breaking changes we had made. This meant that we were actually coexisting three different versions of the endpoint. This is not something I'd recommend! Keeping all the code around and the associated testing required to ensure they all worked was absolutely an additional burden. To make this more manageable, we internally transformed all requests to the V1 endpoint to a V2 request, and then V2 requests to the V3 endpoint. This meant we could clearly delineate what code was going to be retired when the old endpoint(s) died.

This is in effect an example of the expand and contract pattern, which allows us to phase breaking changes in. We *expand* the capabilities we offer, supporting both old and new ways of doing something. Once the old consumers do things in the new way, we *contract* our API, removing the old functionality.

If you are going to coexist endpoints, you need a way for callers to route their requests accordingly. For systems making use of HTTP, I have seen this done with both version numbers in request headers and also in the URI itself—for example, */v1/customer/* or */v2/customer/*. I'm torn as to which approach makes the most sense. On the one hand, I like URIs being opaque to discourage clients from hardcoding URI templates, but on the other hand, this approach does make things very obvious and can simplify request routing.

For RPC, things can be a little trickier. I have handled this with protocol buffers by putting my methods in different namespaces—for example, `v1.createCustomer` and `v2.createCustomer`—but when you are trying to support different versions of the same types being sent over the network, this can become really painful.

Use Multiple Concurrent Service Versions

Another versioning solution often cited is to have different versions of the service live at once, and for older consumers to route their traffic to the older version, with newer versions seeing the new one, as shown in Figure 4-6. This is the approach used sparingly by Netflix in situations where the cost of changing older consumers is too high, especially in rare cases where legacy devices are still tied to older versions of the API. Personally, I am not a fan of this idea, and understand why Netflix uses it rarely. First, if I need to fix an internal bug in my service, I now have to fix and deploy two different sets of services. This would probably mean I have to branch the codebase for my service, and this is always problematic. Second, it means I need smarts to handle directing consumers to the right microservice. This behavior inevitably ends up sitting in middleware somewhere or a bunch of nginx scripts, making it harder to reason about the behavior of the system. Finally, consider any persistent state our service might manage. Customers created by either version of the service need to be stored and made visible to all services, no matter which version was used to create the data in the first place. This can be an additional source of complexity.

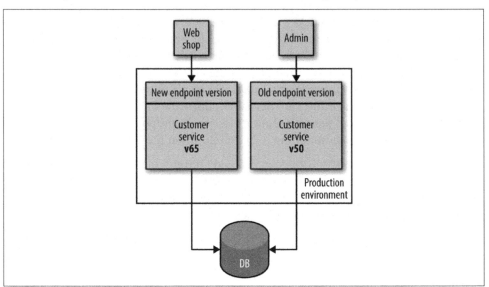

Figure 4-6. Running multiple versions of the same service to support old endpoints

Coexisting concurrent service versions for a short period of time can make perfect sense, especially when you're doing things like blue/green deployments or canary releases (we'll be discussing these patterns more in Chapter 7). In these situations, we may be coexisting versions only for a few minutes or perhaps hours, and normally will have only two different versions of the service present at the same time. The longer it takes for you to get consumers upgraded to the newer version and released, the more you should look to coexist different endpoints in the same microservice rather than coexist entirely different versions. I remain unconvinced that this work is worthwhile for the average project.

User Interfaces

So far, we haven't really touched on the world of the user interface. A few of you out there might just be providing a cold, hard, clinical API to your customers, but many of us find ourselves wanting to create beautiful, functional user interfaces that will delight our customers. But we really do need to think about them in the context of integration. The user interface, after all, is where we'll be pulling all these microservices together into something that makes sense to our customers.

In the past, when I first started computing, we were mostly talking about big, fat clients that ran on our desktops. I spent many hours with Motif and then Swing trying to make my software as nice to use as possible. Often these systems were just for the creation and manipulation of local files, but many of them had a server-side component. My first job at ThoughtWorks involved creating a Swing-based electronic point-of-sale system that was just part of a large number of moving parts, most of which were on the server.

Then came the Web. We started thinking of our UIs as being *thin* instead, with more logic on the server side. In the beginning, our server-side programs rendered the entire page and sent it to the client browser, which did very little. Any interactions were handled on the server side, via GETs and POSTs triggered by the user clicking on links or filling in forms. Over time, JavaScript became a more popular option to add dynamic behavior to the browser-based UI, and some applications could now be argued to be as *fat* as the old desktop clients.

Toward Digital

Over the last couple of years, organizations have started to move away from thinking that web or mobile should be treated differently; they are instead thinking about digital more holistically. What is the best way for our customers to use the services we offer? And what does that do to our system architecture? The understanding that we cannot predict exactly how a customer might end up interacting with our company has driven adoption of more granular APIs, like those delivered by microservices. By combining the capabilities our services expose in different ways, we can curate different experiences for our customers on their desktop application, mobile device, wearable device, or even in physical form if they visit our brick-and-mortar store.

So think of user interfaces as compositional layers—places where we weave together the various strands of the capabilities we offer. So with that in mind, how do we pull all these strands together?

Constraints

Constraints are the different forms in which our users interact with our system. On a desktop web application, for example, we consider constraints such as what browser visitors are using, or their resolution. But mobile has brought a whole host of new constraints. The way our mobile applications communicate with the server can have an impact. It isn't just about pure bandwidth concerns, where the limitations of mobile networks can play a part. Different sorts of interactions can drain battery life, leading to some cross customers.

The nature of interactions changes, too. I can't easily right-click on a tablet. On a mobile phone, I may want to design my interface to be used mostly one-handed, with most operations being controlled by a thumb. Elsewhere, I might allow people to interact with services via SMS in places where bandwidth is at a premium—the use of SMS as an interface is huge in the global south, for example.

So, although our core services—our core offering—might be the same, we need a way to adapt them for the different constraints that exist for each type of interface. When we look at different styles of user interface composition, we need to ensure that they address this challenge. Let's look at a few models of user interfaces to see how this might be achieved.

API Composition

Assuming that our services already speak XML or JSON to each other via HTTP, an obvious option available to us is to have our user interface interact directly with these APIs, as in Figure 4-7. A web-based UI could use JavaScript GET requests to retrieve data, or POST requests to change it. Even for native mobile applications, initiating HTTP communications is fairly straightforward. The UI would then need to create the various components that make up the interface, handling synchronization of state and the like with the server. If we were using a binary protocol for service-to-service communication, this would be more difficult for web-based clients, but could be fine for native mobile devices.

There are a couple of downsides with this approach. First, we have little ability to tailor the responses for different sorts of devices. For example, when I retrieve a customer record, do I need to pull back all the same data for a mobile shop as I do for a helpdesk application? One solution to this approach is to allow consumers to specify what fields to pull back when they make a request, but this assumes that each service supports this form of interaction.

Another key question: who creates the user interface? The people who look after the services are removed from how their services are surfaced to the users—for example, if another team is creating the UI, we could be drifting back into the bad old days of layered architecture where making even small changes requires change requests to multiple teams.

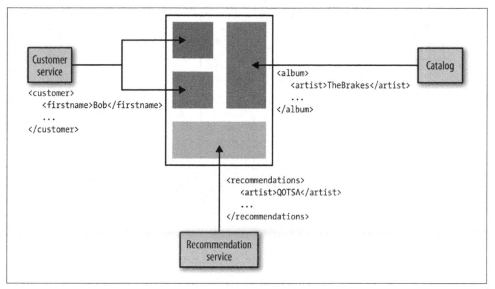

Figure 4-7. Using multiple APIs to present a user interface

This communication could also be fairly chatty. Opening lots of calls directly to services can be quite intensive for mobile devices, and could be a very inefficient use of a customer's mobile plan! Having an API gateway can help here, as you could expose calls that aggregate multiple underlying calls, although that itself can have some downsides that we'll explore shortly.

UI Fragment Composition

Rather than having our UI make API calls and map everything back to UI controls, we could have our services provide parts of the UI directly, and then just pull these fragments in to create a UI, as in Figure 4-8. Imagine, for example, that the recommendation service provides a recommendation widget that is combined with other controls or UI fragments to create an overall UI. It might get rendered as a box on a web page along with other content.

A variation of this approach that can work well is to assemble a series of coarser-grained parts of a UI. So rather than creating small widgets, you are assembling entire panes of a thick client application, or perhaps a set of pages for a website.

These coarser-grained fragments are served up from server-side apps that are in turn making the appropriate API calls. This model works best when the fragments align well to team ownership. For example, perhaps the team that looks after order management in the music shop serves up all the pages associated with order management.

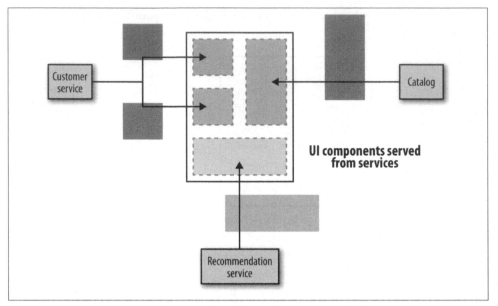

Figure 4-8. Services directly serving up UI components for assembly

You still need some sort of assembly layer to pull these parts together. This could be as simple as some server-side templating, or, where each set of pages comes from a different app, perhaps you'll need some smart URI routing.

One of the key advantages of this approach is that the same team that makes changes to the services can also be in charge of making changes to those parts of the UI. It allows us to get changes out faster. But there are some problems with this approach.

First, ensuring consistency of the user experience is something we need to address. Users want to have a seamless experience, not to feel that different parts of the interface work in different ways, or present a different design language. There are techniques to avoid this problem, though, such as living style guides, where assets like HTML components, CSS, and images can be shared to help give some level of consistency.

Another problem is harder to deal with. What happens with native applications or thick clients? We can't serve up UI components. We could use a hybrid approach and use native applications to serve up HTML components, but this approach has been shown time and again to have downsides. So if you need a native experience, we will have to fall back to an approach where the frontend application makes API calls and handles the UI itself. But even if we consider web-only UIs, we still may want very different treatments for different types of devices. Building responsive components can help, of course.

There is one key problem with this approach that I'm not sure can be solved. Sometimes the capabilities offered by a service do not fit neatly into a widget or a page. Sure, I might want to surface recommendations in a box on a page on our website, but what if I want to weave in dynamic recommendations elsewhere? When I search, I want the type ahead to automatically trigger fresh recommendations, for example. The more cross-cutting a form of interaction is, the less likely this model will fit and the more likely it is that we'll fall back to just making API calls.

Backends for Frontends

A common solution to the problem of chatty interfaces with backend services, or the need to vary content for different types of devices, is to have a server-side aggregation endpoint, or API gateway. This can marshal multiple backend calls, vary and aggregate content if needed for different devices, and serve it up, as we see in Figure 4-9. I've seen this approach lead to disaster when these server-side endpoints become thick layers with too much behavior. They end up getting managed by separate teams, and being another place where logic has to change whenever some functionality changes.

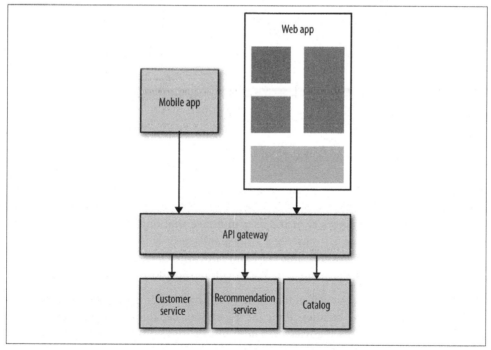

Figure 4-9. Using a single monolithic gateway to handle calls to/from UIs

The problem that can occur is that normally we'll have one giant layer for all our services. This leads to everything being thrown in together, and suddenly we start to lose isolation of our various user interfaces, limiting our ability to release them independently. A model I prefer and that I've seen work well is to restrict the use of these backends to one specific user interface or application, as we see in Figure 4-10.

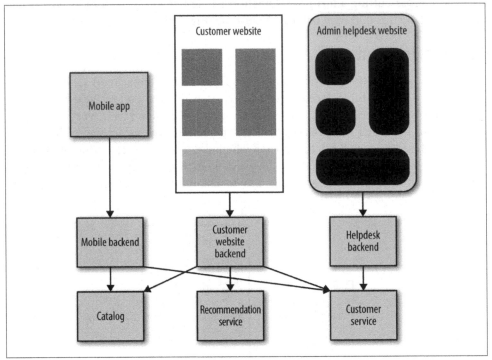

Figure 4-10. Using dedicated backends for frontends

This pattern is sometimes referred to as *backends for frontends (BFFs)*. It allows the team focusing on any given UI to also handle its own server-side components. You can see these backends as parts of the user interface that happen to be embedded in the server. Some types of UI may need a minimal server-side footprint, while others may need a lot more. If you need an API authentication and authorization layer, this can sit between our BFFs and our UIs. We'll explore this more in Chapter 9.

The danger with this approach is the same as with any aggregating layer; it can take on logic it shouldn't. The business logic for the various capabilities these backends use should stay in the services themselves. These BFFs should only contain behavior specific to delivering a particular user experience.

A Hybrid Approach

Many of the aforementioned options don't need to be one-size-fits-all. I could see an organization adopting the approach of fragment-based assembly to create a website, but using a backends-for-frontends approach when it comes to its mobile application. The key point is that we need to retain cohesion of the underlying capabilities that we offer our users. We need to ensure that logic associated with ordering music or changing customer details lives inside those services that handle those operations, and doesn't get smeared all over our system. Avoiding the trap of putting too much behavior into any intermediate layers is a tricky balancing act.

Integrating with Third-Party Software

We've looked at approaches to breaking apart existing systems that are under our control, but what about when we can't change the things we talk to? For many valid reasons, the organizations we work for buy commercial off-the-shelf software (COTS) or make use of software as a service (SaaS) offerings over which we have little control. So how do we integrate with them sensibly?

If you're reading this book, you probably work at an organization that writes code. You might write software for your own internal purposes or for an external client, or both. Nonetheless, even if you are an organization with the ability to create a significant amount of custom software, you'll still use software products provided by external parties, be they commercial or open source. Why is this?

First, your organization almost certainly has a greater demand for software than can be satisfied internally. Think of all the products you use, from office productivity tools like Excel to operating systems to payroll systems. Creating all of those for your own use would be a mammoth undertaking. Second, and most important, it wouldn't be cost effective! The cost for you to build your own email system, for example, is likely to dwarf the cost of using an existing combination of mail server and client, even if you go for commercial options.

My clients often struggle with the question "Should I build, or should I buy?" In general, the advice I and my colleagues give when having this conversation with the average enterprise organization boils down to "Build if it is unique to what you do, and can be considered a strategic asset; buy if your use of the tool isn't that special."

For example, the average organization would not consider its payroll system to be a strategic asset. People on the whole get paid the same the world over. Likewise, most organizations tend to buy content management systems (CMSes) off the shelf, as their use of such a tool isn't considered something that is key to their business. On the other hand, I was involved early on in rebuilding the *Guardian's* website, and there the decision was made to build a bespoke content management system, as it was core to the newspaper's business.

So the notion that we will occasionally encounter commercial, third-party software is sensible, and to be welcomed. However, many of us end up cursing some of these systems. Why is that?

Lack of Control

One challenge associated with integrating with and extending the capabilities of COTS products like CMS or SaaS tools is that typically many of the technical decisions have been made for you. How do you integrate with the tool? That's a vendor decision. Which programming language can you use to extend the tool? Up to the vendor. Can you store the configuration for the tool in version control, and rebuild from scratch, so as to enable continuous integration of customizations? It depends on choices the vendor makes.

If you are lucky, how easy—or hard—it is to work with the tool from a development point of view has been considered as part of the tool selection process. But even then, you are effectively ceding some level of control to an outside party. The trick is to bring the integration and customization work back on to your terms.

Customization

Many tools that enterprise organizations purchase sell themselves on their ability to be heavily customized *just for you*. Beware! Often, due to the nature of the tool chain you have access to, the cost of customization can be more expensive than building something bespoke from scratch! If you've decided to buy a product but the particular capabilities it provides aren't that special to you, it might make more sense to change how your organization works rather than embark on complex customization.

Content management systems are a great example of this danger. I have worked with multiple CMSes that by design do not support continuous integration, that have terrible APIs, and for which even a minor-point upgrade in the underlying tool can break any customizations you have made.

Salesforce is especially troublesome in this regard. For many years it has pushed its Force.com platform, which requires the use of a programming language, Apex, that exists only within the Force.com ecosystem!

Integration Spaghetti

Another challenge is how you integrate with the tool. As we discussed earlier, thinking carefully about how you integrate between services is important, and ideally you want to standardize on a small number of types of integration. But if one product decides to use a proprietary binary protocol, another some flavor of SOAP, and another XML-RPC, what are you left with? Even worse are the tools that allow you to reach right inside their underlying data stores, leading to all the same coupling issues we discussed earlier.

On Your Own Terms

COTS and SAAS products absolutely have their place, and it isn't feasible (or sensible) for most of us to build everything from scratch. So how do we resolve these challenges? The key is to move things back on to your own terms.

The core idea here is to do any customizations on a platform you control, and to limit the number of different consumers of the tool itself. To explore this idea in detail, let's look at a couple of examples.

Example: CMS as a service

In my experience, the CMS is one of the most commonly used product that needs to be customized or integrated with. The reason for this is that unless you want a basic static site, the average enterprise organization wants to enrich the functionality of its website with dynamic content like customer records or the latest product offerings. The source of this dynamic content is typically other services inside the organization, which you may have actually built yourself.

The temptation—and often the selling point of the CMS—is that you can customize the CMS to pull in all this special content and display it to the outside world. However, the development environment for the average CMS is *terrible*.

Let's look at what the average CMS specializes in, and what we probably bought it for: content creation and content management. Most CMSes are pretty bad even at doing page layout, typically providing drag-and-drop tools that don't cut the mustard. And even then, you end up needing to have someone who understands HTML and CSS to fine-tune the CMS templates. They tend to be terrible platforms on which to build custom code.

The answer? Front the CMS with your own service that provides the website to the outside world, as shown in Figure 4-11. Treat the CMS as a service whose role is to allow for the creation and retrieval of content. In your own service, you write the code and integrate with services how you want. You have control over scaling the website (many commercial CMSes provide their own proprietary add-ons to handle load), and you can pick the templating system that makes sense.

Most CMSes also provide APIs to allow for content creation, so you also have the ability to front that with your own service façade. For some situations, we've even used such a façade to abstract out the APIs for retrieving content.

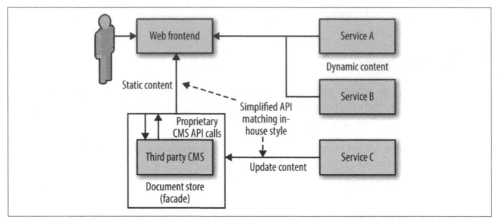

Figure 4-11. Hiding a CMS using your own service

We've used this pattern multiple times across ThoughtWorks in the last few years, and I've done this more than once myself. One notable example was a client that was looking to push out a new website for its products. Initially, it wanted to build the entire solution on the CMS, but it had yet to pick one. We instead suggested this approach, and started development of the fronting website. While waiting for the CMS tool to be selected, we *faked* it by having a web service that just surfaced static content. We ended up going live with the site well before the CMS was selected by using our fake content service in production to surface content to the live site. Later on, we were able to just drop in the eventually selected tool without any change to the fronting application.

Using this approach, we keep the scope of what the CMS does down to a minimum and move customizations onto our own technology stack.

Example: The multirole CRM system

The CRM—or Customer Relationship Management—tool is an often-encountered beast that can instill fear in the heart of even the hardiest architect. This sector, as typified by vendors like Salesforce or SAP, is rife with examples of tools that try to do everything for you. This can lead to the tool itself becoming a single point of failure, and a tangled knot of dependencies. Many implementations of CRM tools I have seen are among the best examples of *adhesive* (as opposed to cohesive) services.

The scope of such a tool typically starts small, but over time it becomes an increasingly important part of how your organization works. The problem is that the direction and choices made around this now-vital system are often made by the tool vendor itself, not by you.

I was involved recently in an exercise to try to wrest some control back. The organization I was working with realized that although it was using the CRM tool for a lot of things, it wasn't getting the value of the increasing costs associated with the platform. At the same time, multiple internal systems were using the less-than-ideal CRM APIs for integration. We wanted to move the system architecture toward a place where we had services that modeled our businesses domain, and also lay the groundwork for a potential migration.

The first thing we did was identify the core concepts to our domain that the CRM system currently owned. One of these was the concept of a *project*—that is, something to which a member of staff could be assigned. Multiple other systems needed project information. What we did was instead create a project service. This service exposed projects as RESTful resources, and the external systems could move their integration points over to the new, easier-to-work-with service. Internally, the project service was just a façade, hiding the detail of the underlying integration. You can see this in Figure 4-12.

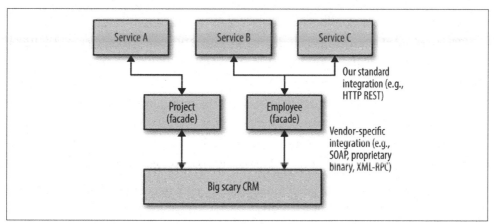

Figure 4-12. Using façade services to mask the underlying CRM

The work, which at the time of this writing was still under way, was to identify other domain concepts that the CRM was handling, and create more façades for them. When the time comes for migration away from the underlying CRM, we could then look at each façade in turn to decide if an internal software solution or something off the shelf could fit the bill.

The Strangler Pattern

When it comes to legacy or even COTS platforms that aren't totally under our control, we also have to deal with what happens when we want to remove them or at least move away from them. A useful pattern here is the Strangler Application Pattern (*http://bit.ly/1v71DOH*). Much like with our example of fronting the CMS system with our own code, with a strangler you capture and intercept calls to the old system. This allows you to decide if you route these calls to existing, legacy code, or direct them to new code you may have written. This allows you to replace functionality over time without requiring a big bang rewrite.

When it comes to microservices, rather than having a single monolithic application intercepting all calls to the existing legacy system, you may instead use a series of microservices to perform this interception. Capturing and redirecting the original calls can become more complex in this situation, and you may require the use of a proxy to do this for you.

Summary

We've looked at a number of different options around integration, and I've shared my thoughts on what choices are most likely to ensure our microservices remain as decoupled as possible from their other collaborators:

- Avoid database integration at all costs.
- Understand the trade-offs between REST and RPC, but strongly consider REST as a good starting point for request/response integration.
- Prefer choreography over orchestration.
- Avoid breaking changes and the need to version by understanding Postel's Law and using tolerant readers.
- Think of user interfaces as compositional layers.

We covered quite a lot here, and weren't able to go into depth on all of these topics. Nonetheless, this should be a good foundation to get you going and point you in the right direction if you want to learn more.

We also spent some time looking at how to work with systems that aren't completely under our control in the form of COTS products. It turns out that this description can just as easily apply to software we wrote!

Some of the approaches outlined here apply equally well to *legacy* software, but what if we want to tackle the often-monumental task of bringing these older systems to heel and decomposing them into more usable parts? We'll discuss that in detail in the next chapter.

CHAPTER 5

Splitting the Monolith

We've discussed what a good service looks like, and why smaller servers may be better for us. We also previously discussed the importance of being able to evolve the design of our systems. But how do we handle the fact that we may already have a large number of codebases lying about that don't follow these patterns? How do we go about decomposing these monolithic applications without having to embark on a big-bang rewrite?

The monolith grows over time. It acquires new functionality and lines of code at an alarming rate. Before long it becomes a big, scary giant presence in our organization that people are scared to touch or change. But all is not lost! With the right tools at our disposal, we can slay this beast.

It's All About Seams

We discussed in Chapter 3 that we want our services to be highly cohesive and loosely coupled. The problem with the monolith is that all too often it is the opposite of both. Rather than tend toward cohesion, and keep things together that tend to change together, we acquire and stick together all sorts of unrelated code. Likewise, loose coupling doesn't really exist: if I want to make a change to a line of code, I may be able to do that easily enough, but I cannot deploy that change without potentially impacting much of the rest of the monolith, and I'll certainly have to redeploy the entire system.

In his book *Working Effectively with Legacy Code* (Prentice-Hall), Michael Feathers defines the concept of a *seam*—that is, a portion of the code that can be treated in isolation and worked on without impacting the rest of the codebase. We also want to identify seams. But rather than finding them for the purpose of cleaning up our codebase, we want to identify seams that can become service boundaries.

So what makes a good seam? Well, as we discussed previously, bounded contexts make excellent seams, because by definition they represent cohesive and yet loosely coupled boundaries in an organization. So the first step is to start identifying these boundaries in our code.

Most programming languages provide namespace concepts that allow us to group similar code together. Java's `package` concept is a fairly weak example, but gives us much of what we need. All other mainstream programming languages have similar concepts built in, with JavaScript very arguably being an exception.

Breaking Apart MusicCorp

Imagine we have a large backend monolithic service that represents a substantial amount of the behavior of MusicCorp's online systems. To start, we should identify the high-level bounded contexts that we think exist in our organization, as we discussed in Chapter 3. Then we want to try to understand what bounded contexts the monolith maps to. Let's imagine that initially we identify four contexts we think our monolithic backend covers:

Catalog
    Everything to do with metadata about the items we offer for sale

Finance
    Reporting for accounts, payments, refunds, etc.

Warehouse
    Dispatching and returning of customer orders, managing inventory levels, etc.

Recommendation
    Our patent-pending, revolutionary recommendation system, which is highly complex code written by a team with more PhDs than the average science lab

The first thing to do is to create packages representing these contexts, and then move the existing code into them. With modern IDEs, code movement can be done automatically via refactorings, and can be done incrementally while we are doing other things. You'll still need tests to catch any breakages made by moving code, however, especially if you're using a dynamically typed language where the IDEs have a harder time of performing refactoring. Over time, we start to see what code fits well, and what code is *left over* and doesn't really fit anywhere. This remaining code will often identify bounded contexts we might have missed!

During this process we can use code to analyze the dependencies between these packages too. Our code should represent our organization, so our packages representing the bounded contexts in our organization should interact in the same way the real-life organizational groups in our domain interact. For example, tools like Structure 101 allow us to see the dependencies between packages graphically. If we spot things that look wrong—for example, the warehouse package depends on code in the finance package when no such dependency exists in the real organization—then we can investigate this problem and try to resolve it.

This process could take an afternoon on a small codebase, or several weeks or months when you're dealing with millions of lines of code. You may not need to sort all code into domain-oriented packages before splitting out your first service, and indeed it can be more valuable to concentrate your effort in one place. There is no need for this to be a big-bang approach. It is something that can be done bit by bit, day by day, and we have a lot of tools at our disposal to track our progress.

So now that we have our codebase organized around these seams, what next?

The Reasons to Split the Monolith

Deciding that you'd like a monolithic service or application to be smaller is a good start. But I would strongly advise you to chip away at these systems. An incremental approach will help you learn about microservices as you go, and will also limit the impact of getting something wrong (and you will get things wrong!). Think of our monolith as a block of marble. We could blow the whole thing up, but that rarely ends well. It makes much more sense to just chip away at it incrementally.

So if we are going to break apart the monolith a piece at a time, where should we start? We have our seams now, but which one should we pull out first? It's best to think about where you are going to get the most benefit from some part of your codebase being separated, rather than just splitting things for the sake of it. Let's consider some drivers that might help guide our chisel.

Pace of Change

Perhaps we know that we have a load of changes coming up soon in how we manage inventory. If we split out the warehouse seam as a service now, we could change that service faster, as it is a separate autonomous unit.

Team Structure

MusicCorp's delivery team is actually split across two geographical regions. One team is in London, the other in Hawaii (some people have it easy!). It would be great if we could split out the code that the Hawaii team works on the most, so it can take full ownership. We'll explore this idea further in Chapter 10.

Security

MusicCorp has had a security audit, and has decided to tighten up its protection of sensitive information. Currently, all of this is handled by the finance-related code. If we split this service out, we can provide additional protections to this individual service in terms of monitoring, protection of data at transit, and protection of data at rest—ideas we'll look at in more detail in Chapter 9.

Technology

The team looking after our recommendation system has been spiking out some new algorithms using a logic programming library in the language Clojure. The team thinks this could benefit our customers by improving what we offer them. If we could split out the recommendation code into a separate service, it would be easy to consider building an alternative implementation that we could test against.

Tangled Dependencies

The other point to consider when you've identified a couple of seams to separate is how entangled that code is with the rest of the system. We want to pull out the seam that is least depended on if we can. If you can view the various seams you have found as a directed acyclical graph of dependencies (something the package modeling tools I mentioned earlier are very good at), this can help you spot the seams that are likely going to be harder to disentangle.

This brings us to what is often the mother of all tangled dependencies: the database.

The Database

We've already discussed at length the challenges of using databases as a method of integrating multiple services. As I made it pretty clear earlier, I am not a fan! This means we need to find seams in our databases too so we can split them out cleanly. Databases, however, are tricky beasts.

Getting to Grips with the Problem

The first step is to take a look at the code itself and see which parts of it read from and write to the database. A common practice is to have a repository layer, backed by some sort of framework like Hibernate, to bind your code to the database, making it easy to map objects or data structures to and from the database. If you have been following along so far, you'll have grouped our code into packages representing our bounded contexts; we want to do the same for our database access code. This may require splitting up the repository layer into several parts, as shown in Figure 5-1.

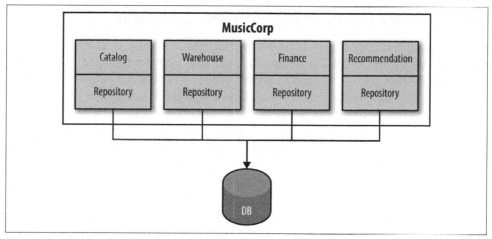

Figure 5-1. Splitting out our repository layers

Having the database mapping code colocated inside the code for a given context can help us understand what parts of the database are used by what bits of code. Hibernate, for example, can make this very clear if you are using something like a mapping file per bounded context.

This doesn't give us the whole story, however. For example, we may be able to tell that the finance code uses the ledger table, and that the catalog code uses the line item table, but it might not be clear that the database enforces a foreign key relationship from the ledger table to the line item table. To see these database-level constraints, which may be a stumbling block, we need to use another tool to visualize the data. A great place to start is to use a tool like the freely available SchemaSpy (*http://sche maspy.sourceforge.net*), which can generate graphical representations of the relationships between tables.

All this helps you understand the coupling between tables that may span what will eventually become service boundaries. But how do you cut those ties? And what about cases where the same tables are used from multiple different bounded contexts? Handling problems like these is not easy, and there are many answers, but it is doable.

Coming back to some concrete examples, let's consider our music shop again. We have identified four bounded contexts, and want to move forward with making them four distinct, collaborating services. We're going to look at a few concrete examples of problems we might face, and their potential solutions. And while some of these examples talk specifically about challenges encountered in standard relational databases, you will find similar problems in other alternative NoSQL stores.

Example: Breaking Foreign Key Relationships

In this example, our catalog code uses a generic line item table to store information about an album. Our finance code uses a ledger table to track financial transactions. At the end of each month we need to generate reports for various people in the organization so they can see how we're doing. We want to make the reports nice and easy to read, so rather than saying, "We sold 400 copies of SKU 12345 and made $1,300," we'd like to add more information about what was sold (i.e., "We sold 400 copies of Bruce Springsteen's *Greatest Hits* and made $1,300"). To do this, our reporting code in the finance package will reach into the line item table to pull out the title for the SKU. It may also have a foreign key constraint from the ledger to the line item table, as we see in Figure 5-2.

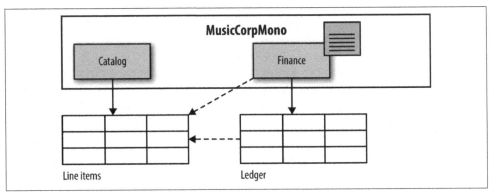

Figure 5-2. Foreign key relationship

So how do we fix things here? Well, we need to make a change in two places. First, we need to stop the finance code from reaching into the line item table, as this table really belongs to the catalog code, and we don't want database integration happening once catalog and finance are services in their own rights. The quickest way to address this is rather than having the code in finance reach into the line item table, we'll expose the data via an API call in the catalog package that the finance code can call. This API call will be the forerunner of a call we will make over the wire, as we see in Figure 5-3.

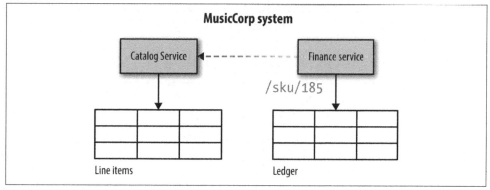

Figure 5-3. Post removal of the foreign key relationship

At this point it becomes clear that we may well end up having to make two database calls to generate the report. This is correct. And the same thing will happen if these are two separate services. Typically concerns around performance are now raised. I have a fairly easy answer to those: how fast does your system need to be? And how fast is it now? If you can test its current performance and know what good performance looks like, then you should feel confident in making a change. Sometimes making one thing slower in exchange for other things is the right thing to do, especially if *slower* is still perfectly acceptable.

But what about the foreign key relationship? Well, we lose this altogether. This becomes a constraint we need to now manage in our resulting services rather than in the database level. This may mean that we need to implement our own consistency check across services, or else trigger actions to clean up related data. Whether or not this is needed is often not a technologist's choice to make. For example, if our order service contains a list of IDs for catalog items, what happens if a catalog item is removed and an order now refers to an invalid catalog ID? Should we allow it? If we do, then how is this represented in the order when it is displayed? If we don't, then how can we check that this isn't violated? These are questions you'll need to get answered by the people who define how your system should behave for its users.

Example: Shared Static Data

I have seen perhaps as many country codes stored in databases (shown in Figure 5-4) as I have written StringUtils classes for in-house Java projects. This seems to imply that we plan to change the countries our system supports way more frequently than we'll deploy new code, but whatever the real reason, these examples of shared static data being stored in databases come up a lot. So what do we do in our music shop if all our potential services read from the same table like this?

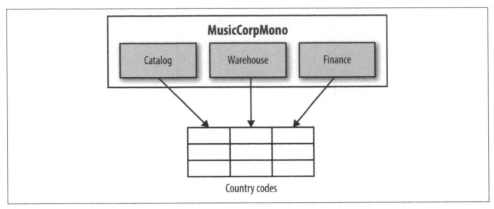

Figure 5-4. Country codes in the database

Well, we have a few options. One is to duplicate this table for each of our packages, with the long-term view that it will be duplicated within each service also. This leads to a potential consistency challenge, of course: what happens if I update one table to reflect the creation of Newmantopia off the east coast of Australia, but not another?

A second option is to instead treat this shared, static data as code. Perhaps it could be in a property file deployed as part of the service, or perhaps just as an enumeration. The problems around the consistency of data remain, although experience has shown that it is far easier to push out changes to configuration files than alter live database tables. This is often a very sensible approach.

A third option, which may well be extreme, is to push this static data into a service of its own right. In a couple of situations I have encountered, the volume, complexity, and rules associated with the static reference data were sufficient that this approach was warranted, but it's probably overkill if we are just talking about country codes!

Personally, in most situations I'd try to push for keeping this data in configuration files or directly in code, as it is the simple option for most cases.

Example: Shared Data

Now let's dive into a more complex example, but one that can be a common problem when you're trying to tease apart systems: shared mutable data. Our finance code tracks payments made by customers for their orders, and also tracks refunds given to them when they return items. Meanwhile, the warehouse code updates records to show that orders for customers have been dispatched or received. All of this data is displayed in one convenient place on the website so that customers can see what is going on with their account. To keep things simple, we have stored all this information in a fairly generic customer record table, as shown in Figure 5-5.

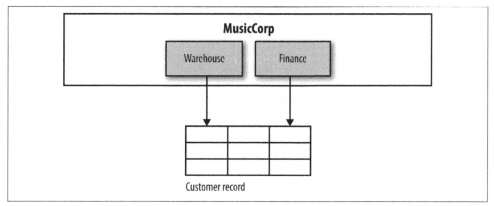

Figure 5-5. Accessing customer data: are we missing something?

So both the finance and the warehouse code are writing to, and probably occasionally reading from, the same table. How can we tease this apart? What we actually have here is something you'll see often—a domain concept that isn't modeled in the code, and is in fact implicitly modeled in the database. Here, the domain concept that is missing is that of Customer.

We need to make the current abstract concept of the customer concrete. As a transient step, we create a new package called Customer. We can then use an API to expose Customer code to other packages, such as finance or warehouse. Rolling this all the way forward, we may now end up with a distinct customer service (Figure 5-6).

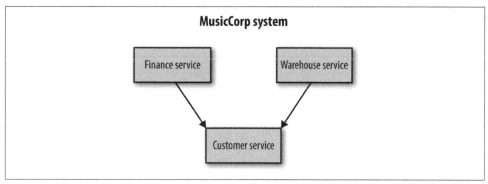

Figure 5-6. Recognizing the bounded context of the customer

Example: Shared Tables

Figure 5-7 shows our last example. Our catalog needs to store the name and price of the records we sell, and the warehouse needs to keep an electronic record of inventory. We decide to keep these two things in the same place in a generic line item table. Before, with all the code merged in together, it wasn't clear that we are actually conflating concerns, but now we can see that in fact we have two separate concepts that could be stored differently.

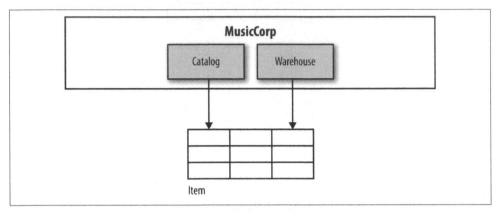

Figure 5-7. Tables being shared between different contexts

The answer here is to split the table in two as we have in Figure 5-8, perhaps creating a stock list table for the warehouse, and a catalog entry table for the catalog details.

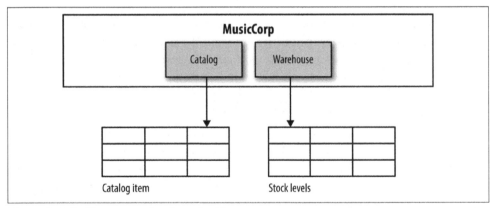

Figure 5-8. Pulling apart the shared table

Refactoring Databases

What we have covered in the preceding examples are a few database refactorings that can help you separate your schemas. For a more detailed discussion of the subject, you may want to take a look at *Refactoring Databases* by Scott J. Ambler and Pramod J. Sadalage (Addison-Wesley).

Staging the Break

So we've found seams in our application code, grouping it around bounded contexts. We've used this to identify seams in the database, and we've done our best to split those out. What next? Do you do a big-bang release, going from one monolithic service with a single schema to two services, each with its own schema? I would actually recommend that you split out the schema but keep the service together before splitting the application code out into separate microservices, as shown in Figure 5-9.

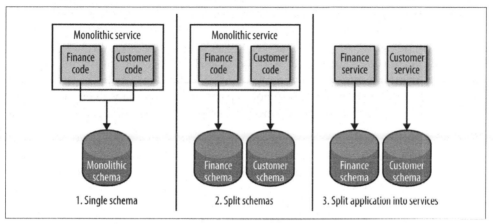

Figure 5-9. Staging a service separation

With a separate schema, we'll be potentially increasing the number of database calls to perform a single action. Where before we might have been able to have all the data we wanted in a single SELECT statement, now we may need to pull the data back from two locations and join in memory. Also, we end up breaking transactional integrity when we move to two schemas, which could have significant impact on our applications; we'll be discussing this next. By splitting the schemas out but keeping the application code together, we give ourselves the ability to revert our changes or continue to tweak things without impacting any consumers of our service. Once we are satisfied that the DB separation makes sense, we can then think about splitting out the application code into two services.

Transactional Boundaries

Transactions are useful things. They allow us to say *these events either all happen together, or none of them happen*. They are very useful when we're inserting data into a database; they let us update multiple tables at once, knowing that if anything fails, everything gets rolled back, ensuring our data doesn't get into an inconsistent state. Simply put, a transaction allows us to group together multiple different activities that take our system from one consistent state to another—everything works, or nothing changes.

Transactions don't just apply to databases, although we most often use them in that context. Message brokers, for example, have long allowed you to post and receive messages within transactions too.

With a monolithic schema, all our create or updates will probably be done within a single transactional boundary. When we split apart our databases, we lose the safety afforded to us by having a single transaction. Consider a simple example in the MusicCorp context. When creating an order, I want to update the order table stating that a customer order has been created, and also put an entry into a table for the warehouse team so it knows there is an order that needs to be picked for dispatch. We've gotten as far as grouping our application code into separate packages, and have also separated the customer and warehouse parts of the schema well enough that we are ready to put them into their own schemas prior to separating the application code.

Within a single transaction in our existing monolithic schema, creating the order and inserting the record for the warehouse team takes place within a single transaction, as shown in Figure 5-10.

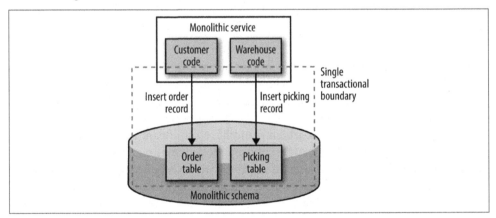

Figure 5-10. Updating two tables in a single transaction

But if we have pulled apart the schema into two separate schemas, one for customer-related data including our order table, and another for the warehouse, we have lost this transactional safety. The order placing process now spans two separate transactional boundaries, as we see in Figure 5-11. If our insert into the order table fails, we can clearly stop everything, leaving us in a consistent state. But what happens when the insert into the order table works, but the insert into the picking table fails?

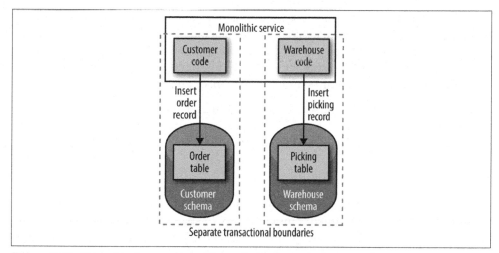

Figure 5-11. Spanning transactional boundaries for a single operation

Try Again Later

The fact that the order was captured and placed might be enough for us, and we may decide to retry the insertion into the warehouse's picking table at a later date. We could queue up this part of the operation in a queue or logfile, and try again later. For some sorts of operations this makes sense, but we have to assume that a retry would fix it.

In many ways, this is another form of what is called *eventual consistency*. Rather than using a transactional boundary to ensure that the system is in a consistent state when the transaction completes, instead we accept that the system will get itself into a consistent state at some point in the future. This approach is especially useful with business operations that might be long-lived. We'll discuss this idea in more depth in Chapter 11 when we cover scaling patterns.

Abort the Entire Operation

Another option is to reject the entire operation. In this case, we have to put the system back into a consistent state. The picking table is easy, as that insert failed, but we have a committed transaction in the order table. We need to unwind this. What we have to do is issue a *compensating transaction*, kicking off a new transaction to wind back what just happened. For us, that could be something as simple as issuing a DELETE statement to remove the order from the database. Then we'd also need to report back via the UI that the operation failed. Our application could handle both aspects within a monolithic system, but we'd have to consider what we could do when we split up the application code. Does the logic to handle the compensating transaction live in the customer service, the order service, or somewhere else?

But what happens if our compensating transaction fails? It's certainly possible. Then we'd have an order in the order table with no matching pick instruction. In this situation, you'd either need to retry the compensating transaction, or allow some backend process to clean up the inconsistency later on. This could be something as simple as a maintenance screen that admin staff had access to, or an automated process.

Now think about what happens if we have not one or two operations we want to be consistent, but three, four, or five. Handling compensating transactions for each failure mode becomes quite challenging to comprehend, let alone implement.

Distributed Transactions

An alternative to manually orchestrating compensating transactions is to use a *distributed transaction*. Distributed transactions try to span multiple transactions within them, using some overall governing process called a *transaction manager* to orchestrate the various transactions being done by underlying systems. Just as with a normal transaction, a distributed transaction tries to ensure that everything remains in a consistent state, only in this case it tries to do so across multiple different systems running in different processes, often communicating across network boundaries.

The most common algorithm for handling distributed transactions—especially short-lived transactions, as in the case of handling our customer order—is to use a *two-phase commit*. With a two-phase commit, first comes the voting phase. This is where each participant (also called a *cohort* in this context) in the distributed transaction tells the transaction manager whether it thinks its local transaction can go ahead. If the transaction manager gets a *yes* vote from all participants, then it tells them all to go ahead and perform their commits. A single *no* vote is enough for the transaction manager to send out a rollback to all parties.

This approach relies on all parties halting until the central coordinating process tells them to proceed. This means we are vulnerable to outages. If the transaction manager goes down, the pending transactions never complete. If a cohort fails to respond during voting, everything blocks. And there is also the case of what happens if a commit fails after voting. There is an assumption implicit in this algorithm that this cannot happen: if a cohort says *yes* during the voting period, then we have to assume it *will* commit. Cohorts need a way of making this commit work at some point. This means this algorithm isn't foolproof—rather, it just tries to catch most failure cases.

This coordination process also mean locks; that is, pending transactions can hold locks on resources. Locks on resources can lead to contention, making scaling systems much more difficult, especially in the context of distributed systems.

Distributed transactions have been implemented for specific technology stacks, such as Java's Transaction API, allowing for disparate resources like a database and a message queue to all participate in the same, overarching transaction. The various algorithms are hard to get right, so I'd suggest you avoid trying to create your own. Instead, do lots of research on this topic if this seems like the route you want to take, and see if you can use an existing implementation.

So What to Do?

All of these solutions add complexity. As you can see, distributed transactions are hard to get right and can actually inhibit scaling. Systems that eventually converge through compensating retry logic can be harder to reason about, and may need other compensating behavior to fix up inconsistencies in data.

When you encounter business operations that currently occur within a single transaction, ask yourself if they really need to. Can they happen in different, local transactions, and rely on the concept of eventual consistency? These systems are much easier to build and scale (we'll discuss this more in Chapter 11).

If you do encounter state that really, really wants to be kept consistent, do everything you can to avoid splitting it up in the first place. Try *really* hard. If you really need to go ahead with the split, think about moving from a purely technical view of the process (e.g., a database transaction) and actually create a concrete concept to represent the transaction itself. This gives you a handle, or a hook, on which to run other operations like compensating transactions, and a way to monitor and manage these more complex concepts in your system. For example, you might create the idea of an "in-process-order" that gives you a natural place to focus all logic around processing the order end to end (and dealing with exceptions).

Reporting

As we've already seen, in splitting a service into smaller parts, we need to also potentially split up how and where data is stored. This creates a problem, however, when it comes to one vital and common use case: reporting.

A change in architecture as fundamental as moving to a microservices architecture will cause a lot of disruption, but it doesn't mean we have to abandon everything we do. The audience of our reporting systems are users like any other, and we need to consider their needs. It would be arrogant to fundamentally change our architecture and just ask them to adapt. While I'm not suggesting that the space of reporting isn't ripe for disruption—it certainly is—there is value in determining how to work with existing processes first. Sometimes we have to pick our battles.

The Reporting Database

Reporting typically needs to group together data from across multiple parts of our organization in order to generate useful output. For example, we might want to enrich the data from our general ledger with descriptions of what was sold, which we get from a catalog. Or we might want to look at the shopping behavior of specific, high-value customers, which could require information from their purchase history and their customer profile.

In a standard, monolithic service architecture, all our data is stored in one big database. This means all the data is in one place, so reporting across all the information is actually pretty easy, as we can simply join across the data via SQL queries or the like. Typically we won't run these reports on the main database for fear of the load generated by our queries impacting the performance of the main system, so often these reporting systems hang on a read replica as shown in Figure 5-12.

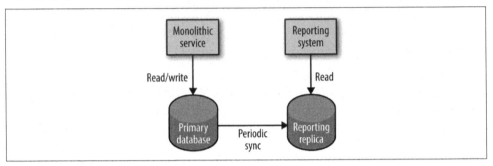

Figure 5-12. Standard read replication

With this approach we have one sizeable upside—that all the data is already in one place, so we can use fairly straightforward tools to query it. But there are also a couple of downsides with this approach. First, the schema of the database is now effectively a shared API between the running monolithic services and any reporting system. So a change in schema has to be carefully managed. In reality, this is another impediment that reduces the chances of anyone wanting to take on the task of making and coordinating such a change.

Second, we have limited options as to how the database can be optimized for either use case—backing the live system or the reporting system. Some databases let us make optimizations on read replicas to enable faster, more efficient reporting; for example, MySQL would allow us to run a different backend that doesn't have the overhead of managing transactions. However, we cannot structure the data differently to make reporting faster if that change in data structure has a bad impact on the running system. What often happens is that the schema either ends up being great for one use case and lousy for the other, or else becomes the lowest common denominator, great for neither purpose.

Finally, the database options available to us have exploded recently. While standard relational databases expose SQL query interfaces that work with many reporting tools, they aren't always the best option for storing data for our running services.

What if our application data is better modeled as a graph, as in Neo4j? Or what if we'd rather use a document store like MongoDB? Likewise, what if we wanted to explore using a column-oriented database like Cassandra for our reporting system, which makes it much easier to scale for larger volumes? Being constrained in having to have one database for both purposes results in us often not being able to make these choices and explore new options.

So it's not perfect, but it works (mostly). Now if our information is stored in multiple different systems, what do we do? Is there a way for us to bring all the data together to run our reports? And could we also potentially find a way to eliminate some of the downsides associated with the standard reporting database model?

It turns out we have a number of viable alternatives to this approach. Which solution makes the most sense to you will depend on a number of factors, but we'll explore a few different options that I have seen in practice.

Data Retrieval via Service Calls

There are many variants of this model, but they all rely on pulling the required data from the source systems via API calls. For a very simple reporting system, like a dashboard that might just want to show the number of orders placed in the last 15 minutes, this might be fine. To report across data from two or more systems, you need to make multiple calls to assemble this data.

This approach breaks down rapidly with use cases that require larger volumes of data, however. Imagine a use case where we want to report on customer purchasing behavior for our music shop over the last 24 months, looking at various trends in customer behavior and how this has impacted on revenue. We need to pull large volumes of data from at least the customer and finance systems. Keeping a local copy of this data in the reporting system is dangerous, as we may not know if it has changed (even historic data may be changed after the fact), so to generate an accurate report we need all of the finance and customer records for the last two years. With even modest numbers of customers, you can see that this quickly will become a very slow operation.

Reporting systems also often rely on third-party tools that expect to retrieve data in a certain way, and here providing a SQL interface is the fastest way to ensure your reporting tool chain is as easy to integrate with as possible. We could still use this approach to pull data periodically into a SQL database, of course, but this still presents us with some challenges.

One of the key challenges is that the APIs exposed by the various microservices may well not be designed for reporting use cases. For example, a customer service may allow us to find a customer by an ID, or search for a customer by various fields, but wouldn't necessarily expose an API to retrieve all customers. This could lead to many calls being made to retrieve all the data—for example, having to iterate through a list of all the customers, making a separate call for each one. Not only could this be inefficient for the reporting system, it could generate load for the service in question too.

While we could speed up some of the data retrieval by adding cache headers to the resources exposed by our service, and have this data cached in something like a reverse proxy, the nature of reporting is often that we access the *long tail* of data. This means that we may well request resources that no one else has requested before (or at least not for a sufficiently long time), resulting in a potentially expensive *cache miss*.

You could resolve this by exposing batch APIs to make reporting easier. For example, our customer service could allow you to pass a list of customer IDs to it to retrieve them in batches, or may even expose an interface that lets you page through all the customers. A more extreme version of this is to model the batch request as a resource in its own right. For example, the customer service might expose something like a `BatchCustomerExport` resource endpoint. The calling system would POST a `BatchRequest`, perhaps passing in a location where a file can be placed with all the data. The customer service would return an HTTP 202 response code, indicating that the request was accepted but has not yet been processed. The calling system could then poll the resource waiting until it retrieves a 201 Created status, indicating that the request has been fulfilled, and then the calling system could go and fetch the data. This would allow potentially large data files to be exported without the overhead of being sent over HTTP; instead, the system could simply save a CSV file to a shared location.

I have seen the preceding approach used for batch insertion of data, where it worked well. I am less in favor of it for reporting systems, however, as I feel that there are other, potentially simpler solutions that can scale more effectively when you're dealing with traditional reporting needs.

Data Pumps

Rather than have the reporting system pull the data, we could instead have the data pushed to the reporting system. One of the downsides of retrieving the data by standard HTTP calls is the overhead of HTTP when we're making a large number of calls, together with the overhead of having to create APIs that may exist only for reporting purposes. An alternative option is to have a standalone program that directly accesses the database of the service that is the source of data, and pumps it into a reporting database, as shown in Figure 5-13.

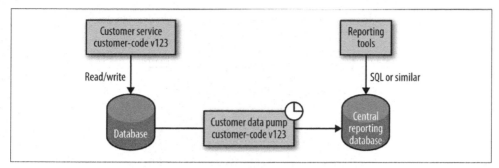

Figure 5-13. Using a data pump to periodically push data to a central reporting database

At this point you'll be saying, "But Sam, you said having lots of programs integrating on the same database is a bad idea!" At least I *hope* you'll be saying that, given how firmly I made the point earlier! This approach, if implemented properly, is a notable exception, where the downsides of the coupling are more than mitigated by making the reporting easier.

To start with, the data pump should be built and managed by the same team that manages the service. This can be something as simple as a command-line program triggered via `Cron`. This program needs to have intimate knowledge of both the internal database for the service, and also the reporting schema. The pump's job is to map one from the other. We try to reduce the problems with coupling to the service's schema by having the same team that manages the service also manage the pump. I would suggest, in fact, that you version-control these together, and have builds of the data pump created as an additional artifact as part of the build of the service itself, with the assumption that whenever you deploy one of them, you deploy them both. As we explicitly state that we deploy these together, and don't open up access to the schema to anyone outside of the service team, many of the traditional DB integration challenges are largely mitigated.

The coupling on the reporting schema itself remains, but we have to treat it as a published API that is hard to change. Some databases give us techniques where we could further mitigate this cost. Figure 5-14 shows an example of this for relational databases, where we could have one schema in the reporting database for each service, using things like materialized views to create the aggregated view. That way, we expose only the reporting schema for the customer data to the customer data pump. Whether this is something that you can do in a performant manner, however, will depend on the capabilities of the database you picked for reporting.

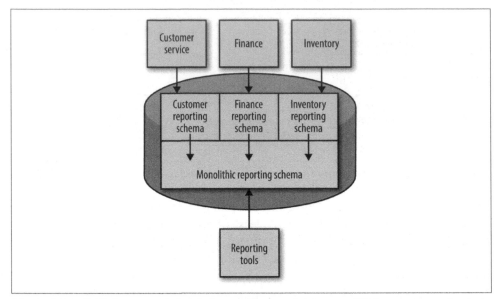

Figure 5-14. Utilizing materialized views to form a single monolithic reporting schema

Here, of course, the complexity of integration is pushed deeper into the schema, and will rely on capabilities in the database to make such a setup performant. While I think data pumps in general are a sensible and workable suggestion, I am less convinced that the complexity of a segmented schema is worthwhile, especially given the challenges in managing change in the database.

Alternative Destinations

On one project I was involved with, we used a series of data pumps to populate JSON files in AWS S3, effectively using S3 to masquerade as a giant data mart! This approach worked very well until we needed to scale our solution, and at the time of writing we are looking to change these pumps to instead populate a cube that can be integrated with standard reporting tools like Excel and Tableau.

Event Data Pump

In Chapter 4, we touched on the idea of microservices emitting events based on the state change of entities that they manage. For example, our customer service may emit an event when a given customer is created, or updated, or deleted. For those microservices that expose such event feeds, we have the option of writing our own event subscriber that pumps data into the reporting database, as shown in Figure 5-15.

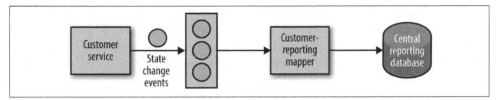

Figure 5-15. An event data pump using state change events to populate a reporting database

The coupling on the underlying database of the source microservice is now avoided. Instead, we are just binding to the events emitted by the service, which are designed to be exposed to external consumers. Given that events are temporal in nature, it also makes it easier for us to be smarter in what data we sent to our central reporting store; we can send data to the reporting system as we see an event, allowing data to flow faster to our reporting system, rather than relying on a regular schedule as with the data pump.

Also, if we store which events have already been processed, we can just process the new events as they arrive, assuming the old events have already been mapped into the reporting system. This means our insertion will be more efficient, as we only need to send deltas. We can do similar things with a data pump, but we have to manage this ourselves, whereas the fundamentally temporal nature of the stream of events (x happens at timestamp y) helps us greatly.

As our event data pump is less coupled to the internals of the service, it is also easier to consider this being managed by a separate group from the team looking after the microservice itself. As long as the nature of our event stream doesn't overly couple subscribers to changes in the service, this event mapper can evolve independently of the service it subscribes to.

The main downsides to this approach are that all the required information must be broadcast as events, and it may not scale as well as a data pump for larger volumes of data that has the benefit of operating directly at the database level. Nonetheless, the looser coupling and fresher data available via such an approach makes it strongly worth considering if you are already exposing the appropriate events.

Backup Data Pump

This option is based on an approach used at Netflix, which takes advantage of existing backup solutions and also resolves some scale issues that Netflix has to deal with. In some ways, you can consider this a special case of a data pump, but it seemed like such an interesting solution that it deserves inclusion.

Netflix has decided to standardize on Cassandra as the backing store for its services, of which there are many. Netflix has invested significant time in building tools to make Cassandra easy to work with, much of which the company has shared with the rest of the world via numerous open source projects. Obviously it is very important that the data Netflix stores is properly backed up. To back up Cassandra data, the standard approach is to make a copy of the data files that back it and store them somewhere safe. Netflix stores these files, known as SSTables, in Amazon's S3 object store, which provides significant data durability guarantees.

Netflix needs to report across all this data, but given the scale involved this is a non-trivial challenge. Its approach is to use Hadoop that uses SSTable backup as the source of its jobs. In the end, Netflix ended up implementing a pipeline capable of processing large amounts of data using this approach, which it then open sourced as the Aegisthus project (*http://bit.ly/1EMC3zf*). Like data pumps, though, with this pattern we still have a coupling to the destination reporting schema (or target system).

It is conceivable that using a similar approach—that is, using mappers that work off backups—would work in other contexts as well. And if you're already using Cassandra, Netflix has already done much of the work for you!

Toward Real Time

Many of the patterns previously outlined are different ways of getting a lot of data from many different places to one place. But does the idea that all our reporting will be done from one location really stack up anymore? We have dashboards, alerting, financial reports, user analytics—all of these use cases have different tolerances for accuracy and timeliness, which may result in different technical options coming to bear. As I will detail in Chapter 8, we are moving more and more toward generic eventing systems capable of routing our data to multiple different places depending on need.

Cost of Change

There are many reasons why, throughout the book, I promote the need to make small, incremental changes, but one of the key drivers is to understand the impact of each alteration we make and change course if required. This allows us to better mitigate the cost of mistakes, but doesn't remove the chance of mistakes entirely. We can—and will—make mistakes, and we should embrace that. What we should also do, though, is understand how best to mitigate the costs of those mistakes.

As we have seen, the cost involved in moving code around within a codebase is pretty small. We have lots of tools that support us, and if we cause a problem, the fix is generally quick. Splitting apart a database, however, is much more work, and rolling back a database change is just as complex. Likewise, untangling an overly coupled integration between services, or having to completely rewrite an API that is used by multiple consumers, can be a sizeable undertaking. The large cost of change means that these operations are increasingly risky. How can we manage this risk? My approach is to try to make mistakes where the impact will be lowest.

I tend to do much of my thinking in the place where the cost of change and the cost of mistakes is as low as it can be: the whiteboard. Sketch out your proposed design. See what happens when you run use cases across what you think your service boundaries will be. For our music shop, for example, imagine what happens when a customer searches for a record, registers with the website, or purchases an album. What calls get made? Do you start seeing odd circular references? Do you see two services that are overly chatty, which might indicate they should be one thing?

A great technique here is to adapt an approach more typically taught for the design of object-oriented systems: class-responsibility-collaboration (CRC) cards. With CRC cards, you write on one index card the name of the class, what its responsibilities are, and who it collaborates with. When working through a proposed design, for each service I list its responsibilities in terms of the capabilities it provides, with the collaborators specified in the diagram. As you work through more use cases, you start to get a sense as to whether all of this hangs together properly.

Understanding Root Causes

We have discussed how to split apart larger services into smaller ones, but why did these services grow so large in the first place? The first thing to understand is that growing a service to the point that it needs to be split is completely OK. We *want* the architecture of our system to change over time in an incremental fashion. The key is knowing it needs to be split before the split becomes too expensive.

But in practice many of us will have seen services grow well beyond the point of sanity. Despite knowing that a smaller set of services would be easier to deal with than the huge monstrosity we currently have, we still plow on with growing the beast. Why?

Part of the problem is knowing where to start, and I'm hoping this chapter has helped. But another challenge is the cost associated with splitting out services. Finding somewhere to run the service, spinning up a new service stack, and so on, are nontrivial tasks. So how do we address this? Well, if doing something is right but difficult, we should strive to make things easier. Investment in libraries and lightweight service frameworks can reduce the cost associated with creating the new service. Giving people access to self-service provision virtual machines or even making a platform as a service (PaaS) available will make it easier to provision systems and test them. Throughout the rest of the book, we'll be discussing a number of ways to help you keep this cost down.

Summary

We decompose our system by finding seams along which service boundaries can emerge, and this can be an incremental approach. By getting good at finding these seams and working to reduce the cost of splitting out services in the first place, we can continue to grow and evolve our systems to meet whatever requirements come down the road. As you can see, some of this work can be painstaking. But the very fact that it can be done incrementally means there is no need to fear this work.

So now we can split our services out, but we've introduced some new problems too. We have many more moving parts to get into production now! So next up we'll dive into the world of deployment.

CHAPTER 6

Deployment

Deploying a monolithic application is a fairly straightforward process. Microservices, with their interdependence, are a different kettle of fish altogether. If you don't approach deployment right, it's one of those areas where the complexity can make your life a misery. In this chapter, we're going to look at some techniques and technology that can help us when deploying microservices into fine-grained architectures.

We're going to start off, though, by taking a look at continuous integration and continuous delivery. These related but different concepts will help shape the other decisions we'll make when thinking about what to build, how to build it, and how to deploy it.

A Brief Introduction to Continuous Integration

Continuous integration (CI) has been around for a number of years at this point. It's worth spending a bit of time going over the basics, however, as especially when we think about the mapping between microservices, builds, and version control repositories, there are some different options to consider.

With CI, the core goal is to keep everyone in sync with each other, which we achieve by making sure that newly checked-in code properly integrates with existing code. To do this, a CI server detects that the code has been committed, checks it out, and carries out some verification like making sure the code compiles and that tests pass.

As part of this process, we often create artifact(s) that are used for further validation, such as deploying a running service to run tests against it. Ideally, we want to build these artifacts once and once only, and use them for all deployments of that version of the code. This is in order to avoid doing the same thing over and over again, and so that we can confirm that the artifact we deployed is the one we tested. To enable these artifacts to be reused, we place them in a repository of some sort, either provided by the CI tool itself or on a separate system.

We'll be looking at what sorts of artifacts we can use for microservices shortly, and we'll look in depth at testing in Chapter 7.

CI has a number of benefits. We get some level of fast feedback as to the quality of our code. It allows us to automate the creation of our binary artifacts. All the code required to build the artifact is itself version controlled, so we can re-create the artifact if needed. We also get some level of traceability from a deployed artifact back to the code, and depending on the capabilities of the CI tool itself, can see what tests were run on the code and artifact too. It's for these reasons that CI has been so successful.

Are You Really Doing It?

I suspect you are probably using continuous integration in your own organization. If not, you should start. It is a key practice that allows us to make changes quickly and easily, and without which the journey into microservices will be painful. That said, I have worked with many teams who, despite saying that they do CI, aren't actually doing it at all. They confuse the use of a CI tool with adopting the practice of CI. The tool is just something that enables the approach.

I really like Jez Humble's three questions he asks people to test if they really understand what CI is about:

Do you check in to mainline once per day?
> You need to make sure your code integrates. If you don't check your code together with everyone else's changes frequently, you end up making future integration harder. Even if you are using short-lived branches to manage changes, integrate as frequently as you can into a single mainline branch.

Do you have a suite of tests to validate your changes?
> Without tests, we just know that syntactically our integration has worked, but we don't know if we have broken the behavior of the system. CI without some verification that our code behaves as expected isn't CI.

When the build is broken, is it the #1 priority of the team to fix it?
> A passing green build means our changes have safely been integrated. A red build means the last change possibly did not integrate. You need to stop all further check-ins that aren't involved in fixing the builds to get it passing again. If you let more changes pile up, the time it takes to fix the build will increase drastically. I've worked with teams where the build has been broken for days, resulting in substantial efforts to eventually get a passing build.

Mapping Continuous Integration to Microservices

When thinking about microservices and continuous integration, we need to think about how our CI builds map to individual microservices. As I have said many times, we want to ensure that we can make a change to a single service and deploy it independently of the rest. With this in mind, how should we map individual microservices to CI builds and source code?

If we start with the simplest option, we could lump everything in together. We have a single, giant repository storing all our code, and have one single build, as we see in Figure 6-1. Any check-in to this source code repository will cause our build to trigger, where we will run all the verification steps associated with all our microservices, and produce multiple artifacts, all tied back to the same build.

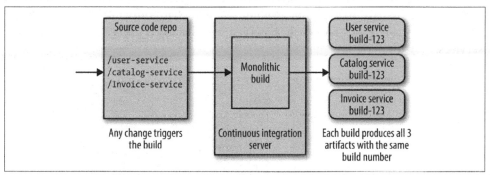

Figure 6-1. Using a single source code repository and CI build for all microservices

This seems much simpler on the surface than other approaches: fewer repositories to worry about, and a conceptually simpler build. From a developer point of view, things are pretty straightforward too. I just check code in. If I have to work on multiple services at once, I just have to worry about one commit.

This model can work perfectly well if you buy into the idea of lock-step releases, where you don't mind deploying multiple services at once. In general, this is absolutely a pattern to avoid, but very early on in a project, especially if only one team is working on everything, this might make sense for short periods of time.

However, there are some significant downsides. If I make a one-line change to a single service—for example, changing the behavior in the user service in Figure 6-1—*all* the other services get verified and built. This could take more time than needed—I'm waiting for things that probably don't need to be tested. This impacts our cycle time, the speed at which we can move a single change from development to live. More troubling, though, is knowing what artifacts should or shouldn't be deployed. Do I now need to deploy all the build services to push my small change into production? It can be hard to tell; trying to guess which services *really* changed just by reading the commit messages is difficult. Organizations using this approach often fall back to just deploying everything together, which we really want to avoid.

Furthermore, if my one-line change to the user service breaks the build, no other changes can be made to the other services until that break is fixed. And think about a scenario where you have multiple teams all sharing this giant build. Who is in charge?

A variation of this approach is to have one single source tree with all of the code in it, with multiple CI builds mapping to parts of this source tree, as we see in Figure 6-2. With well-defined structure, you can easily map the builds to certain parts of the source tree. In general, I am not a fan of this approach, as this model can be a mixed blessing. On the one hand, my check-in/check-out process can be simpler as I have only one repository to worry about. On the other hand, it becomes very easy to get into the habit of checking in source code for multiple services at once, which can make it equally easy to slip into making changes that couple services together. I would greatly prefer this approach, however, over having a single build for multiple services.

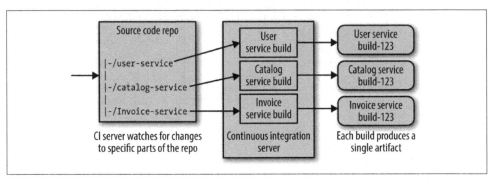

Figure 6-2. A single source repo with subdirectories mapped to independent builds

So is there another alternative? The approach I prefer is to have a single CI build per microservice, to allow us to quickly make and validate a change prior to deployment into production, as shown in Figure 6-3. Here each microservice has its own source code repository, mapped to its own CI build. When making a change, I run only the build and tests I need to. I get a single artifact to deploy. Alignment to team ownership is more clear too. If you own the service, you own the repository and the build. Making changes across repositories can be more difficult in this world, but I'd maintain this is easier to resolve (e.g., by using command-line scripts) than the downside of the monolithic source control and build process.

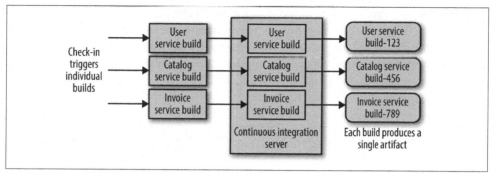

Figure 6-3. Using one source code repository and CI build per microservice

The tests for a given microservice should live in source control with the microservice's source code too, to ensure we always know what tests should be run against a given service.

So, each microservice will live in its own source code repository, and its own CI build process. We'll use the CI build process to create our deployable artifacts too in a fully automated fashion. Now lets look beyond CI to see how continuous delivery fits in.

Build Pipelines and Continuous Delivery

Very early on in using continuous integration, we realized the value in sometimes having multiple stages inside a build. Tests are a very common case where this comes into play. I may have a lot of fast, small-scoped tests, and a small number of large-scoped, slow tests. If we run all the tests together, we may not be able to get fast feedback when our fast tests fail if we're waiting for our long-scoped slow tests to finally finish. And if the fast tests fail, there probably isn't much sense in running the slower tests anyway! A solution to this problem is to have different stages in our build, creating what is known as a *build pipeline*. One stage for the faster tests, one for the slower tests.

This build pipeline concept gives us a nice way of tracking the progress of our software as it clears each stage, helping give us insight into the quality of our software. We build our artifact, and that artifact is used throughout the pipeline. As our artifact moves through these stages, we feel more and more confident that the software will work in production.

Continuous delivery (CD) builds on this concept, and then some. As outlined in Jez Humble and Dave Farley's book of the same name, continuous delivery is the approach whereby we get constant feedback on the production readiness of each and every check-in, and furthermore treat each and every check-in as a release candidate.

To fully embrace this concept, we need to model all the processes involved in getting our software from check-in to production, and know where any given version of the software is in terms of being cleared for release. In CD, we do this by extending the idea of the multistage build pipeline to model each and every stage our software has to go through, both manual and automated. In Figure 6-4, we see a sample pipeline that may be familiar.

Figure 6-4. A standard release process modeled as a build pipeline

Here we really want a tool that embraces CD as a first-class concept. I have seen many people try to hack and extend CI tools to make them do CD, often resulting in complex systems that are nowhere as easy to use as tools that build in CD from the beginning. Tools that fully support CD allow you to define and visualize these pipelines, modeling the entire path to production for your software. As a version of our code moves through the pipeline, if it passes one of these automated verification steps it moves to the next stage. Other stages may be manual. For example, if we have a manual user acceptance testing (UAT) process I should be able to use a CD tool to model it. I can see the next available build ready to be deployed into our UAT environment, deploy it, and if it passes our manual checks, mark that stage as being successful so it can move to the next.

By modeling the entire path to production for our software, we greatly improve visibility of the quality of our software, and can also greatly reduce the time taken between releases, as we have one place to observe our build and release process, and an obvious focal point for introducing improvements.

In a microservices world, where we want to ensure we can release our services independently of each other, it follows that as with CI, we'll want one pipeline per service. In our pipelines, it is an artifact that we want to create and move through our path to production. As always, it turns out our artifacts can come in lots of sizes and shapes. We'll look at some of the most common options available to us in a moment.

And the Inevitable Exceptions

As with all good rules, there are exceptions we need to consider too. The "one microservice per build" approach is absolutely something you should aim for, but are there times when something else makes sense? When a team is starting out with a new project, especially a greenfield one where they are working with a blank sheet of paper, it is quite likely that there will be a large amount of churn in terms of working out where the service boundaries lie. This is a good reason, in fact, for keeping your initial services on the larger side until your understanding of the domain stabilizes.

During this time of churn, changes across service boundaries are more likely, and what is in or not in a given service is likely to change frequently. During this period, having all services in a single build to reduce the cost of cross-service changes may make sense.

It does follow, though, that in this case you need to buy into releasing all the services as a bundle. It also absolutely needs to be a transitionary step. As service APIs stabilize, start moving them out into their own builds. If after a few weeks (or a very small number of months) you are unable to get stability in service boundaries in order to properly separate them, merge them back into a more monolithic service (albeit retaining modular separation within the boundary) and give yourself time to get to grips with the domain. This reflects the experiences of our own SnapCI team, as we discussed in Chapter 3.

Platform-Specific Artifacts

Most technology stacks have some sort of first-class artifact, along with tools to support creating and installing them. Ruby has gems, Java has JAR files and WAR files, and Python has eggs. Developers with experience in one of these stacks will be well versed in working with (and hopefully creating) these artifacts.

From the point of view of a microservice, though, depending on your technology stack, this artifact may not be enough by itself. While a Java JAR file can be made to be executable and run an embedded HTTP process, for things like Ruby and Python applications, you'll expect to use a process manager running inside Apache or Nginx. So we may need some way of installing and configuring other software that we need in order to deploy and launch our artifacts. This is where automated configuration management tools like Puppet and Chef can help.

Another downfall here is that these artifacts are specific to a certain technology stack, which may make deployment more difficult when we have a mix of technologies in play. Think of it from the point of view of someone trying to deploy multiple services together. They could be a developer or tester wanting to test some functionality, or it could be someone managing a production deployment. Now imagine that those services use three completely different deployment mechanisms. Perhaps we have a Ruby Gem, a JAR file, and a Node.JS NPM package. Would they thank you?

Automation can go a long way toward hiding the differences in the deployment mechanisms of the underlying artifacts. Chef, Puppet, and Ansible all support multiple different common technology-specific build artifacts too. But there are different types of artifacts that might be even easier to work with.

Operating System Artifacts

One way to avoid the problems associated with technology-specific artifacts is to create artifacts that are native to the underlying operating system. For example, for a RedHat– or CentOS-based system, I might build RPMs; for Ubuntu, I might build a deb package; or for Windows, an MSI.

The advantage of using OS-specific artifacts is that from a deployment point of view we don't care what the underlying technology is. We just use the tools native to the OS to install the package. The OS tools can also help us uninstall and get information about the packages too, and may even provide package repositories that our CI tools can push to. Much of the work done by the OS package manager can also offset work that you might otherwise do in a tool like Puppet or Chef. On all Linux platforms I have used, for example, you can define dependencies from your packages to other packages you rely on, and the OS tools will automatically install them for you too.

The downside can be the difficulty in creating the packages in the first place. For Linux, the FPM package manager tool (*http://bit.ly/15LaQSb*) gives a nicer abstraction for creating Linux OS packages, and converting from a tarball-based deployment to an OS-based deployment can be fairly straightforward. The Windows space is somewhat trickier. The native packaging system in the form of MSI installers and the like leave a lot to be desired when compared to the capabilities in the Linux space. The NuGet package system has started to help address this, at least in terms of helping manage development libraries. More recently, Chocolatey NuGet has extended these ideas, providing a package manager for Windows designed for deploying tools and services, which is much more like the package managers in the Linux space. This is certainly a step in the right direction, although the fact that the idiomatic style in Windows is still *deploy something in IIS* means that this approach may be unappealing for some Windows teams.

Another downside, of course, could be if you are deploying onto multiple different operating systems. The overhead of managing artifacts for different OSes could be pretty steep. If you're creating software for other people to install, you may not have a choice. If you are installing software onto machines you control, however, I would suggest you look at unifying or at least reducing the number of different operating systems you use. It can greatly reduce variations in behavior from one machine to the next, and simplify deployment and maintenance tasks.

In general, those teams I've seen that have moved to OS-based package management have simplified their deployment approach, and tend to avoid the trap of big, complex deployment scripts. Especially if you're on Linux, this can be a good way to simplify deployment of microservices using disparate technology stacks.

Custom Images

One of the challenges with automated configuration management systems like Puppet, Chef, and Ansible can be the time taken to run the scripts on a machine. Let's take a simple example of a server being provisioned and configured to allow for the deployment of a Java application. Let's assume I'm using AWS to provision the server, using the standard Ubuntu image. The first thing I need to do is install the Oracle JVM to run my Java application. I've seen this simple process take around five minutes, with a couple of minutes taken up by the machine being provisioned, and a few more to install the JVM. Then we can think about actually putting our software on it.

This is actually a fairly trivial example. We will often want to install other common bits of software. For example, we might want to use collectd for gathering OS stats, use logstash for log aggregation, and perhaps install the appropriate bits of nagios for monitoring (we'll talk more about this software in Chapter 8). Over time, more things might get added, leading to longer and longer amounts of time needed for provisioning of these dependencies.

Puppet, Chef, Ansible, and their ilk can be smart and will avoid installing software that is already present. This does not mean that running the scripts on existing machines will always be fast, unfortunately, as running all the checks takes time. We also want to avoid keeping our machines around for too long, as we don't want to allow for too much configuration drift (which we'll explore in more depth shortly). And if we're using an on-demand compute platform we might be constantly shutting down and spinning up new instances on a daily basis (if not more frequently), so the declarative nature of these configuration management tools may be of limited use.

Over time, watching the same tools get installed over and over again can become a real drag. If you are trying to do this multiple times per day—perhaps as part of development or CI—this becomes a real problem in terms of providing fast feedback. It can also lead to increased downtime when deploying in production if your systems don't allow for zero-downtime deployment, as you're waiting to install all the prerequisites on your machines even before you get to installing your software. Models like blue/green deployment (which we'll discuss in Chapter 7) can help mitigate this, as they allow us to deploy a new version of our service without taking the old one offline.

One approach to reducing this spin-up time is to create a virtual machine image that bakes in some of the common dependencies we use, as shown in Figure 6-5. All virtualization platforms I've used allow you to build your own images, and the tools to do so are much more advanced than they were even a few years ago. This shifts things somewhat. Now we could bake the common tools into our own image. When we want to deploy our software, we spin up an instance of this custom image, and all we have to do is install the latest version of our service.

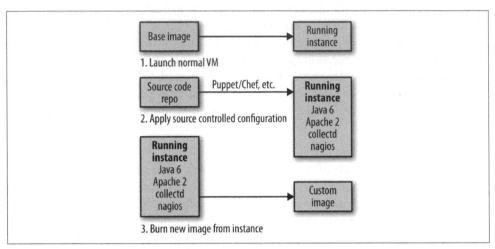

Figure 6-5. Creating a custom VM image

Of course, because you build the image only once, when you subsequently launch copies of this image you don't need to spend time installing your dependencies, as they are already there. This can result in a significant time savings. If your core dependencies don't change, new versions of your service can continue to use the same base image.

There are some drawbacks with this approach, though. Building images can take a long time. This means that for developers you may want to support other ways of deploying services to ensure they don't have to wait half an hour just to create a binary deployment. Second, some of the resulting images can be large. This could be a real problem if you're creating your own VMWare images, for example, as moving a 20GB image around a network isn't always a simple activity. We'll be looking at con‐ tainer technology shortly, and specifically Docker, which can avoid some of these drawbacks.

Historically, one of the challenges is that the tool chain required to build such an image varied from platform to platform. Building a VMWare image is different from building an AWS AMI, a Vagrant image, or a Rackspace image. This may not have been a problem if you had the same platform everywhere, but not all organizations were this lucky. And even if they were, the tools in this space were often difficult to work with, and they didn't play nicely with other tools you might be using for machine configuration.

Packer (*http://www.packer.io/*) is a tool designed to make creation of images much easier. Using configuration scripts of your choice (Chef, Ansible, Puppet, and more are supported), it allows us to create images for different platforms from the same configuration. At the time of writing, it has support for VMWare, AWS, Rackspace Cloud, Digital Ocean, and Vagrant, and I've seen teams use it successfully for building Linux and Windows images. This means you could create an image for deployment on your production AWS environment and a matching Vagrant image for local development and test, all from the same configuration.

Images as Artifacts

So we can create virtual machine images that bake in dependencies to speed up feedback, but why stop there? We could go further, bake our service into the image itself, and adopt the model of our service artifact being an image. Now, when we launch our image, our service is there ready to go. This really fast spin-up time is the reason that Netflix has adopted the model of baking its own services as AWS AMIs.

Just as with OS-specific packages, these VM images become a nice way of abstracting out the differences in the technology stacks used to create the services. Do we care if the service running on the image is written in Ruby or Java, and uses a gem or JAR file? All we care about is that it works. We can focus our efforts, then, on automating the creation and deployment of these images. This also becomes a really neat way to implement another deployment concept, the *immutable server*.

Immutable Servers

By storing all our configuration in source control, we are trying to ensure that we can automatically reproduce services and hopefully entire environments at will. But once we run our deployment process, what happens if someone comes along, logs into the box, and changes things independently of what is in source control? This problem is often called *configuration drift*—the code in source control no longer reflects the configuration of the running host.

To avoid this, we can ensure that no changes are ever made to a running server. Instead, any change, no matter how small, has to go through a build pipeline in order to create a new machine. You can implement this pattern without using image-based deployments, but it is also a logical extension of using images as artifacts. During our image creation, for example, we could actually disable SSH, ensuring that no one could even log onto the box to make a change!

The same caveats we discussed earlier about cycle time still apply, of course. And we also need to ensure that any data we care about that is stored on the box is stored elsewhere. These complexities aside, I've seen adopting this pattern lead to much more straightforward deployments, and easier-to-reason-about environments. And as I've already said, anything we can do to simplify things should be pursued!

Environments

As our software moves through our CD pipeline stages, it will also be deployed into different types of environments. If we think of the example build pipeline in Figure 6-4, we probably have to consider at least four distinct environments: one environment where we run our slow tests, another for UAT, another for performance, and a final one for production. Our microservice should be the same throughout, but the environment will be different. At the very least, they'll be separate, distinct collections of configuration and hosts. But often they can vary much more than that. For example, our production environment for our service might consist of multiple load-balanced hosts spread across two data centers, whereas our test environment might just have everything running on a single host. These differences in environments can introduce a few problems.

I was bitten by this personally many years ago. We were deploying a Java web service into a clustered WebLogic application container in production. This WebLogic cluster replicated session state between multiple nodes, giving us some level of resilience if a single node failed. However, the WebLogic licenses were expensive, as were the machines our software was deployed onto. This meant that in our test environment, our software was deployed on a single machine, in a nonclustered configuration.

This hurt us badly during one release. For WebLogic to be able to copy session state between nodes, the session data needs to be properly serializable. Unfortunately, one of our commits broke this, so when we deployed into production our session replication failed. We ended up resolving this by pushing hard to replicate a clustered setup in our test environment.

The service we want to deploy is the same in all these different environments, but each of the environments serves a different purpose. On my developer laptop I want to quickly deploy the service, potentially against stubbed collaborators, to run tests or carry out some manual validation of behavior, whereas when I deploy into a production environment I may want to deploy multiple copies of my service in a load-balanced fashion, perhaps split across one or more data centers for durability reasons.

As you move from your laptop to build server to UAT environment all the way to production, you'll want to ensure that your environments are more and more production-like to catch any problems associated with these environmental differences sooner. This will be a constant balance. Sometimes the time and cost to reproduce production-like environments can be prohibitive, so you have to make compromises. Additionally, sometimes using a production-like environment can slow down feedback loops; waiting for 25 machines to install your software in AWS might be much slower than simply deploying your service into a local Vagrant instance, for example.

This balance, between production-like environments and fast feedback, won't be static. Keep an eye on the bugs you find further downstream and your feedback times, and adjust this balance as required.

Managing environments for single-artifact monolithic systems can be challenging, especially if you don't have access to systems that are easily automatable. When you think about multiple environments per microservice, this can be even more daunting. We'll look shortly at some different deployment platforms that can make this much easier for us.

Service Configuration

Our services need some configuration. Ideally, this should be a small amount, and limited to those features that change from one environment to another, such as *what username and password should I use to connect to my database?* Configuration that changes from one environment to another should be kept to an absolute minimum. The more your configuration changes fundamental service behavior, and the more that configuration varies from one environment to another, the more you will find problems only in certain environments, which is painful in the extreme.

So if we have some configuration for our service that does change from one environment to another, how should we handle this as part of our deployment process? One option is to build one artifact per environment, with configuration inside the artifact itself. Initially this seems sensible. The configuration is built right in; just deploy it and everything should work fine, right? This is problematic. Remember the concept of continuous delivery. We want to create an artifact that represents our release candidate, and move it through our pipeline, confirming that it is good enough to go into production. Let's imagine I build a Customer-Service-Test and Customer-Service-Prod artifacts. If my Customer-Service-Test artifact passes the tests, but it's the Customer-Service-Prod artifact that I actually deploy, can I be sure that I have verified the software that actually ends up in production?

There are other challenges as well. First, there is the additional time taken to build these artifacts. Next, the fact that you need to know at build time what environments exist. And how do you handle sensitive configuration data? I don't want information about production passwords checked in with my source code, but if it is needed at build time to create all those artifacts, this is often difficult to avoid.

A better approach is to create one single artifact, and manage configuration separately. This could be a properties file that exists for each environment, or different parameters passed in to an install process. Another popular option, especially when dealing with a larger number of microservices, is to use a dedicated system for providing configuration, which we'll explore more in Chapter 11.

Service-to-Host Mapping

One of the questions that comes up quite early on in the discussion around microservices is "How many services per machine?" Before we go on, we should pick a better term than *machine*, or even the more generic *box* that I used earlier. In this era of virtualization, the mapping between a single host running an operating system and the underlying physical infrastructure can vary to a great extent. Thus, I tend to talk about *hosts*, using them as a generic unit of isolation—namely, an operating system onto which I can install and run my services. If you are deploying directly on to physical machines, then one physical server maps to one *host* (which is perhaps not completely correct terminology in this context, but in the absence of better terms may have to suffice). If you're using virtualization, a single physical machine can map to multiple independent hosts, each of which could hold one or more services.

So when thinking of different deployment models, we'll talk about hosts. So, then, how many services per host should we have?

I have a definite view as to which model is preferable, but there are a number of factors to consider when working out which model will be right for you. It's also important to understand that some choices we make in this regard will limit some of the deployment options available to us.

Multiple Services Per Host

Having multiple services per host, as shown in Figure 6-6, is attractive for a number of reasons. First, purely from a host management point of view, it is simpler. In a world where one team manages the infrastructure and another team manages the software, the infrastructure team's workload is often a function of the number of hosts it has to manage. If more services are packed on to a single host, the host management workload doesn't increase as the number of services increases. Second is cost. Even if you have access to a virtualization platform that allows you to provision and resize virtual hosts, the virtualization can add an overhead that reduces the underlying resources available to your services. In my opinion, both these problems can be addressed with new working practices and technology, and we'll explore that shortly.

This model is also familiar to those who deploy into some form of an application container. In some ways, the use of an application container is a special case of the multiple-services-per-host model, so we'll look into that separately. This model can also simplify the life of the developer. Deploying multiple services to a single host in production is synonymous with deploying multiple services to a local dev workstation or laptop. If we want to look at an alternative model, we want to find a way to keep this conceptually simple for developers.

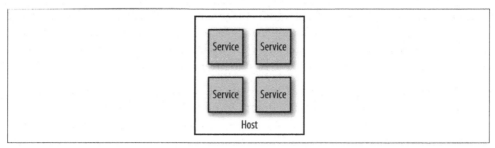

Figure 6-6. Multiple microservices per host

There are some challenges with this model, though. First, it can make monitoring more difficult. For example, when tracking CPU, do I need to track the CPU of one service independent of the others? Or do I care about the CPU of the box as a whole? Side effects can also be hard to avoid. If one service is under significant load, it can end up reducing the resources available to other parts of the system. Gilt, when scaling out the number of services it ran, hit this problem. Initially it coexisted many services on a single box, but uneven load on one of the services would have an adverse impact on everything else running on that host. This makes impact analysis of host failures more complex as well—taking a single host out of commission can have a large ripple effect.

Deployment of services can be somewhat more complex too, as ensuring one deployment doesn't affect another leads to additional headaches. For example, if I use Puppet to prepare a host, but each service has different (and potentially contradictory) dependencies, how can I make that work? In the worst-case scenario, I have seen people tie multiple service deployments together, deploying multiple different services to a single host in one step, to try to simplify the deployment of multiple services to one host. In my opinion, the small upside in improving simplicity is more than outweighed by the fact that we have given up one of the key benefits of microservices: striving for independent release of our software. If you do adopt the multiple-services-per-host model, make sure you keep hold of the idea that each service should be deployed independently.

This model can also inhibit autonomy of teams. If services for different teams are installed on the same host, who gets to configure the host for their services? In all likelihood, this ends up getting handled by a centralized team, meaning it takes more coordination to get services deployed.

Another issue is that this option can limit our deployment artifact options. Image-based deployments are out, as are immutable servers unless you tie multiple different services together in a single artifact, which we really want to avoid.

The fact that we have multiple services on a single host means that efforts to target scaling to the service most in need of it can be complicated. Likewise, if one microservice handles data and operations that are especially sensitive, we might want to set up the underlying host differently, or perhaps even place the host itself in a separate network segment. Having everything on one host means we might end up having to treat all services the same way even if their needs are different.

As my colleague Neal Ford puts it, many of our working practices around deployment and host management are an attempt to optimize for scarcity of resources. In the past, the only option if we wanted another host was to buy or rent another physical machine. This often had a large lead time to it and resulted in a long-term financial commitment. It wasn't uncommon for clients I have worked with to provision new servers only every two to three years, and trying to get additional machines outside of these timelines was difficult. But on-demand computing platforms have drastically reduced the costs of computing resources, and improvements in virtualization technology mean even for in-house hosted infrastructure there is more flexibility.

Application Containers

If you're familiar with deploying .NET applications behind IIS or Java applications into a servlet container, you will be well acquainted with the model where multiple distinct services or applications sit inside a single application container, which in turn sits on a single host, as we see in Figure 6-7. The idea is that the application container your services live in gives you benefits in terms of improved manageability, such as clustering support to handle grouping multiple instances together, monitoring tools, and the like.

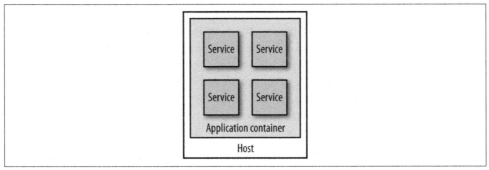

Figure 6-7. Multiple microservices per host

This setup can also yield benefits in terms of reducing overhead of language runtimes. Consider running five Java services in a single Java servlet container. I only have the overhead of one single JVM. Compare this with running five independent JVMs on the same host when using embedded containers. That said, I still feel that these application containers have enough downsides that you should challenge yourself to see if they are really required.

First among the downsides is that they inevitably constrain technology choice. You have to buy into a technology stack. This can limit not only the technology choices for the implementation of the service itself, but also the options you have in terms of automation and management of your systems. As we'll discuss shortly, one of the ways we can address the overhead of managing multiple hosts is around automation, and so constraining our options for resolving this may well be doubly damaging.

I would also question some of the value of the container features. Many of them tout the ability to manage clusters to support shared in-memory session state, something we absolutely want to avoid in any case due to the challenges this creates when scaling our services. And the monitoring capabilities they provide won't be sufficient when we consider the sorts of joined-up monitoring we want to do in a microservices world, as we'll see in Chapter 8. Many of them also have quite slow spin-up times, impacting developer feedback cycles.

There are other sets of problems too. Attempting to do proper lifecycle management of applications on top of platforms like the JVM can be problematic, and more complex than simply restarting a JVM. Analyzing resource use and threads is also much more complex, as you have multiple applications sharing the same process. And remember, even if you do get value from a technology-specific container, they aren't free. Aside from the fact that many of them are commercial and so have a cost implication, they add a resource overhead in and of themselves.

Ultimately, this approach is again an attempt to optimize for scarcity of resources that simply may not hold up anymore. Whether you decide to have multiple services per host as a deployment model, I would strongly suggest looking at self-contained deployable microservices as artifacts. For .NET, this is possible with things like Nancy, and Java has supported this model for years. For example, the venerable Jetty embedded container makes for a very lightweight self-contained HTTP server, which is the core of the Dropwizard stack. Google has been known to quite happily use embedded Jetty containers for serving static content directly, so we know these things can operate at scale.

Single Service Per Host

With a single-service-per-host model shown in Figure 6-8, we avoid side effects of multiple hosts living on a single host, making monitoring and remediation much simpler. We have potentially reduced our single points of failure. An outage to one host should impact only a single service, although that isn't always clear when you're using a virtualized platform. We'll cover designing for scale and failure more in Chapter 11. We also can more easily scale one service independent from others, and deal with security concerns more easily by focusing our attention only on the service and host that requires it.

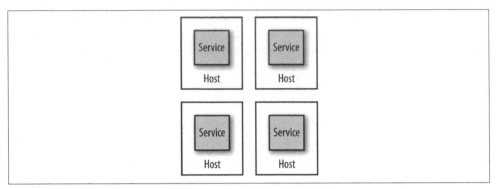

Figure 6-8. A single microservice per host

Just as important is that we have opened up the potential to use alternative deployment techniques such as image-based deployments or the immutable server pattern, which we discussed earlier.

We've added a lot of complexity in adopting a microservice architecture. The last thing we want to do is go looking for more sources of complexity. In my opinion, if you don't have a viable PaaS available, then this model does a very good job of reducing a system's overall complexity. Having a single-service-per-host model is significantly easier to reason about and can help reduce complexity. If you can't embrace this model yet, I won't say microservices aren't for you. But I would suggest that you look to move toward this model over time as a way of reducing the complexity that a microservice architecture can bring.

Having an increased number of hosts has potential downsides, though. We have more servers to manage, and there might also be a cost implication of running more distinct hosts. Despite these problems, this is still the model I prefer for microservice architectures. And we'll talk about a few things we can do to reduce the overhead of handling large numbers of hosts shortly.

Platform as a Service

When using a platform as a service (PaaS), you are working at a higher-level abstraction than at a single host. Most of these platforms rely on taking a technology-specific artifact, such as a Java WAR file or Ruby gem, and automatically provisioning and running it for you. Some of these platforms will transparently attempt to handle scaling the system up and down for you, although a more common (and in my experience less error-prone) way will allow you some control over how many nodes your service might run on, but it handles the rest.

At the time of writing, most of the best, most polished PaaS solutions are hosted. Heroku comes to mind as being probably the gold class of PaaS. It doesn't just handle running your service, it also supports services like databases in a very simple fashion.

Self-hosted solutions do exist in this space, although they are more immature than the hosted solutions.

When PaaS solutions work well, they work very well indeed. However, when they don't quite work for you, you often don't have much control in terms of getting under the hood to fix things. This is part of the trade-off you make. I would say that in my experience the smarter the PaaS solutions try to be, the more they go wrong. I've used more than one PaaS that attempts to autoscale based on application use, but does it badly. Invariably the heuristics that drive these smarts tend to be tailored for the average application rather than your specific use case. The more nonstandard your application, the more likely it is that it might not play nicely with a PaaS.

As the good PaaS solutions handle so much for you, they can be an excellent way of handling the increased overhead we get with having many more moving parts. That said, I'm still not sure that we have all the models right in this space yet, and the limited self-hosted options mean that this approach might not work for you. In the coming decade though I expect we'll be targeting PaaS for deployment more than having to self-manage hosts and deployments of individual services.

Automation

The answer to so many problems we have raised so far comes down to automation. With a small number of machines, it is possible to manage everything manually. I used to do this. I remember running a small set of production machines, and I would collect logs, deploy software, and check processes by manually logging in to the box. My productivity seemed to be constrained by the number of terminal windows I could have open at once—a second monitor was a huge step up. This breaks down really fast, though.

One of the pushbacks against the single-service-per-host setup is the perception that the amount of overhead to manage these hosts will increase. This is certainly true if you are doing everything manually. Double the servers, double the work! But if we automate control of our hosts, and deployment of the services, then there is no reason why adding more hosts should increase our workload in a linear fashion.

But even if we keep the number of hosts small, we still are going to have lots of services. That means multiple deployments to handle, services to monitor, logs to collect. Automation is essential.

Automation is also how we can make sure that our developers still remain productive. Giving them the ability to self-service-provision individual services or groups of services is key to making developers' lives easier. Ideally, developers should have access to exactly the same tool chain as is used for deployment of our production services so as to ensure that we can spot problems early on. We'll be looking at a lot of technology in this chapter that embraces this view.

Picking technology that enables automation is highly important. This starts with the tools used to manage hosts. Can you write a line of code to launch a virtual machine, or shut one down? Can you deploy the software you have written automatically? Can you deploy database changes without manual intervention? Embracing a culture of automation is key if you want to keep the complexities of microservice architectures in check.

Two Case Studies on the Power of Automation

It is probably helpful to give you a couple of concrete examples that explain the power of good automation. One of our clients in Australia is RealEstate.com.au (REA). Among other things, the company provides real estate listings for retail and commercial customers in Australia and elsewhere in the Asia-Pacific region. Over a number of years, it has been moving its platform toward a distributed, microservices design. When it started on this journey it had to spend a lot of time getting the tooling around the services just right—making it easy for developers to provision machines, to deploy their code, or monitor them. This caused a front-loading of work to get things started.

In the first three months of this exercise, REA was able to move just two new microservices into production, with the development team taking full responsibility for the entire build, deployment, and support of the services. In the next three months, between 10–15 services went live in a similar manner. By the end of the 18-month period, REA had over 60–70 services.

This sort of pattern is also borne out by the experiences of Gilt (*http://bit.ly/ 1z1WR3T*), an online fashion retailer that started in 2007. Gilt's monolithic Rails application was starting to become difficult to scale, and the company decided in 2009 to start decomposing the system into microservices. Again automation, especially tooling to help developers, was given as a key reason to drive Gilt's explosion in the use of microservices. A year later, Gilt had around 10 microservices live; by 2012, over 100; and in 2014, over 450 microservices by Gilt's own count—in other words, around three services for every developer in Gilt.

From Physical to Virtual

One of the key tools available to us in managing a large number of hosts is finding ways of chunking up existing physical machines into smaller parts. Traditional virtualization like VMWare or that used by AWS has yielded huge benefits in reducing the overhead of host management. However, there have been some new advances in this space that are well worth exploring, as they can open up even more interesting possibilities for dealing with our microservice architecture.

Traditional Virtualization

Why is having lots of hosts expensive? Well, if you need a physical server per host, the answer is fairly obvious. If this is the world you are operating in, then the multiple-service-per-host model is probably right for you, although don't be surprised if this becomes an ever more challenging constraint. I suspect, however, that most of you are using virtualization of some sort. Virtualization allows us to slice up a physical server into separate hosts, each of which can run different things. So if we want one service per host, can't we just slice up our physical infrastructure into smaller and smaller pieces?

Well, for some people, you can. However, slicing up the machine into ever increasing VMs isn't free. Think of our physical machine as a sock drawer. If we put lots of wooden dividers into our drawer, can we store more socks or fewer? The answer is fewer: the dividers themselves take up room too! Our drawer might be easier to deal with and organize, and perhaps we could decide to put T-shirts in one of the spaces now rather than just socks, but more dividers means less overall space.

In the world of virtualization, we have a similar overhead as our sock drawer dividers. To understand where this overhead comes from, let's look at how most virtualization is done. Figure 6-9 shows a comparison of two types of virtualization. On the left, we see the various layers involved in what is called *type 2 virtualization*, which is the sort implemented by AWS, VMWare, VSphere, Xen, and KVM. (Type 1 virtualization refers to technology where the VMs run directly on hardware, not on top of another operating system.) On our physical infrastructure we have a host operating system. On this OS we run something called a *hypervisor*, which has two key jobs. First, it maps resources like CPU and memory from the virtual host to the physical host. Second, it acts as a control layer, allowing us to manipulate the virtual machines themselves.

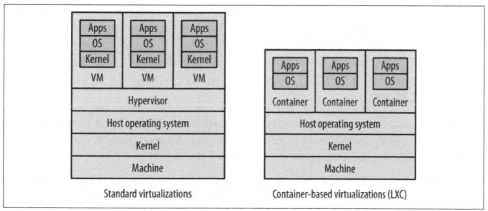

Figure 6-9. A comparison of standard Type 2 virtualization, and lightweight containers

Inside the VMs, we get what looks like completely different hosts. They can run their own operating systems, with their own kernels. They can be considered almost hermetically sealed machines, kept isolated from the underlying physical host and the other virtual machines by the hypervisor.

The problem is that the hypervisor here needs to set aside resources to do its job. This takes away CPU, I/O, and memory that could be used elsewhere. The more hosts the hypervisor manages, the more resources it needs. At a certain point, this overhead becomes a constraint in slicing up your physical infrastructure any further. In practice, this means that there are often diminishing returns in slicing up a physical box into smaller and smaller parts, as proportionally more and more resources go into the overhead of the hypervisor.

Vagrant

Vagrant is a very useful deployment platform, which is normally used for dev and test rather than production. Vagrant provides you with a virtual cloud on your laptop. Underneath, it uses a standard virtualization system (typically VirtualBox, although it can use other platforms). It allows you to define a set of VMs in a text file, along with how the VMs are networked together and which images the VMs should be based on. This text file can be checked in and shared between team members.

This makes it easier for you to create production-like environments on your local machine. You can spin up multiple VMs at a time, shut individual ones to test failure modes, and have the VMs mapped through to local directories so you can make changes and see them reflected immediately. Even for teams using on-demand cloud platforms like AWS, the faster turnaround of using Vagrant can be a huge boon for development teams.

One of the downsides, though, is that running lots of VMs can tax the average development machine. If we have one service to one VM, you may not be able to bring up your entire system on your local machine. This can result in the need to stub out some dependencies to make things manageable, which is one more thing you'll have to handle to ensure that the development and test experience is a good one.

Linux Containers

For Linux users, there is an alternative to virtualization. Rather than having a hypervisor to segment and control separate virtual hosts, Linux containers instead create a separate process space in which other processes live.

On Linux, processes are run by a given user, and have certain capabilities based on how the permissions are set. Processes can spawn other processes. For example, if I launch a process in a terminal, that child process is generally considered a child of the terminal process. The Linux kernel's job is maintaining this tree of processes.

Linux containers extend this idea. Each container is effectively a subtree of the overall system process tree. These containers can have physical resources allocated to them, something the kernel handles for us. This general approach has been around in many forms, such as Solaris Zones and OpenVZ, but it is LXC that has become most popular. LXC is now available out of the box in any modern Linux kernel.

If we look at a stack diagram for a host running LXC in Figure 6-9, we see a few differences. First, we don't need a hypervisor. Second, although each container can run its own operating system distribution, it has to share the same kernel (because the kernel is where the process tree lives). This means that our host operating system could run Ubuntu, and our containers CentOS, as long as they could both share the same kernel.

We don't just benefit from the resources saved by not needing a hypervisor. We also gain in terms of feedback. Linux containers are *much* faster to provision than full-fat virtual machines. It isn't uncommon for a VM to take many minutes to start—but with Linux containers, startup can take a few seconds. You also have finer-grained control over the containers themselves in terms of assigning resources to them, which makes it much easier to tweak the settings to get the most out of the underlying hardware.

Due to the lighter-weight nature of containers, we can have many more of them running on the same hardware than would be possible with VMs. By deploying one service per container, as in Figure 6-10, we get a degree of isolation from other containers (although this isn't perfect), and can do so much more cost effectively than would be possible if we wanted to run each service in its own VM.

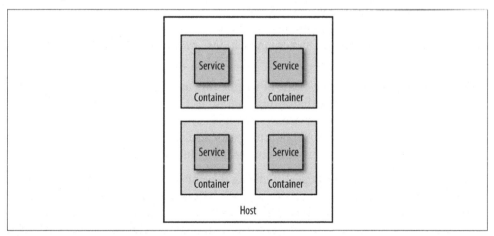

Figure 6-10. Running services in separate containers

Containers can be used well with full-fat virtualization too. I've seen more than one project provision a large AWS EC2 instance and run LXC containers on it to get the best of both worlds: an on-demand ephemeral compute platform in the form of EC2, coupled with highly flexible and fast containers running on top of it.

Linux containers aren't without some problems, however. Imagine I have lots of microservices running in their own containers on a host. How does the outside world see them? You need some way to route the outside world through to the underlying containers, something many of the hypervisors do for you with normal virtualization. I've seen many a person sink inordinate amounts of time into configuring port forwarding using IPTables to expose containers directly. Another point to bear in mind is that these containers cannot be considered completely sealed from each other. There are many documented and known ways in which a process from one container can bust out and interact with other containers or the underlying host. Some of these problems are by design and some are bugs that are being addressed, but either way if you don't trust the code you are running, don't expect that you can run it in a container and be safe. If you need that sort of isolation, you'll need to consider using virtual machines instead.

Docker

Docker is a platform built on top of lightweight containers. It handles much of the work around handling containers for you. In Docker, you create and deploy *apps*, which are synonymous with images in the VM world, albeit for a container-based platform. Docker manages the container provisioning, handles some of the networking problems for you, and even provides its own registry concept that allows you to store and version Docker applications.

The Docker app abstraction is a useful one for us, because just as with VM images the underlying technology used to implement the service is hidden from us. We have our builds for our services create Docker applications, and store them in the Docker registry, and away we go.

Docker can also alleviate some of the downsides of running lots of services locally for dev and test purposes. Rather than using Vagrant to host multiple independent VMs, each one containing its own service, we can host a single VM in Vagrant that runs a Docker instance. We then use Vagrant to set up and tear down the Docker platform itself, and use Docker for fast provisioning of individual services.

A number of different technologies are being developed to take advantage of Docker. CoreOS is a very interesting operating system designed with Docker in mind. It is a stripped-down Linux OS that provides only the essential services to allow Docker to run. This means it consumes fewer resources than other operating systems, making it possible to dedicate even more resources of the underlying machine to our containers. Rather than using a package manager like debs or RPMs, all software is installed as independent Docker apps, each running in its own container.

Docker itself doesn't solve all problems for us. Think of it as a simple PaaS that works on a single machine. If you want tools to help you manage services across multiple Docker instances across multiple machines, you'll need to look at other software that adds these capabilities. There is a key need for a scheduling layer that lets you request a container and then finds a Docker container that can run it for you. In this space, Google's recently open sourced Kubernetes and CoreOS's cluster technology can help, and it seems every month there is a new entrant in this space. Deis (*http://deis.io/*) is another interesting tool based on Docker, which is attempting to provide a Heroku-like PaaS on top of Docker.

I talked earlier about PaaS solutions. My struggle with them has always been that they often get the abstraction level wrong, and that self-hosted solutions lag significantly behind hosted solutions like Heroku. Docker gets much more of this right, and the explosion of interest in this space means I suspect it will become a much more viable platform for all sorts of deployments over the next few years for all sorts of different use cases. In many ways, Docker with an appropriate scheduling layer sits between IaaS and PaaS solutions—the term *containers as a service (CaaS)* is already being used to describe it.

Docker is being used in production by multiple companies. It provides many of the benefits of lightweight containers in terms of efficiency and speed of provisioning, together with the tools to avoid many of the downsides. If you are interested in looking at alternative deployment platforms, I'd strongly suggest you give Docker a look.

A Deployment Interface

Whatever underlying platform or artifacts you use, having a uniform interface to deploy a given service is vital. We'll want to trigger deployment of a microservice on demand in a variety of different situations, from deployments locally for dev and test to production deployments. We'll also want to keep our deployment mechanisms as similar as possible from dev to production, as the last thing we want is to find ourselves hitting problems in production because deployment uses a completely different process!

After many years of working in this space, I am convinced that the most sensible way to trigger any deployment is via a single, parameterizable command line call. This can be triggered by scripts, launched by your CI tool, or typed in by hand. I've built wrapper scripts in a variety of technology stacks to make this work, from Windows batch, to bash, to Python Fabric scripts, and more, but all of the command lines share the same basic format.

We need to know what we are deploying, so we need to provide the name of a known entity, or in our case a microservice. We also need to know what version of the entity we want. The answer to *what version* tends to be one of three possibilities. When you're working locally, it'll be whatever version is on your local machine. When testing, you'll want the latest *green* build, which could just be the most recent blessed artifact in our artifact repository. Or when testing/diagnosing issues, we may want to deploy an exact build.

The third and final thing we'll need to know is what environment we want the microservice deployed into. As we discussed earlier, our microservice's topology may differ from one environment to the next, but that should be hidden from us here.

So, imagine we create a simple `deploy` script that takes these three parameters. Say we're developing locally and want to deploy our catalog service into our local environment. I might type:

```
$ deploy artifact=catalog environment=local version=local
```

Once I've checked in, our CI build service picks up the change and creates a new build artifact, giving it the build number b456. As is standard in most CI tools, this value gets passed along the pipeline. When our test stage gets triggered, the CI stage will run:

```
$ deploy artifact=catalog environment=ci version=b456
```

Meanwhile, our QA wants to pull the latest version of the catalog service into an integrated test environment to do some exploratory testing, and to help with a showcase. That team runs:

```
$ deploy artifact=catalog environment=integrated_qa version=latest
```

The tool I've used the most for this is Fabric, a Python library designed to map command-line calls to functions, along with good support for handling tasks like SSH into remote machines. Pair it with an AWS client library like Boto, and you have everything you need to fully automate very large AWS environments. For Ruby, Capistrano is similar in some ways to Fabric, and on Windows you could go a long way using PowerShell.

Environment Definition

Clearly, for this to work, we need to have some way of defining what our environments look like, and what our service looks like in a given environment. You can think of an environment definition as a mapping from a microservice to compute, network, and storage resources. I've done this with YAML files before, and used my scripts to pull this data in. Example 6-1 is a simplified version of some work I did a couple of years ago for a project that used AWS.

Example 6-1. An example environment definition

```
development:
  nodes:
  - ami_id: ami-e1e1234
    size:    t1.micro ❶
    credentials_name: eu-west-ssh ❷
    services: [catalog-service]
    region: eu-west-1

production:
  nodes:
  - ami_id: ami-e1e1234
    size:    m3.xlarge ❶
    credentials_name: prod-credentials ❷
    services: [catalog-service]
    number: 5  ❸
```

❶ We varied the size of the instances we used to be more cost effective. You don't need a 16-core box with 64GB of RAM for exploratory testing!

❷ Being able to specify different credentials for different environments is key. Credentials for sensitive environments were stored in different source code repos that only select people would have access to.

❸ We decided that by default if a service had more than one node configured, we would automatically create a load balancer for it.

I have removed some detail for the sake of brevity.

The catalog-service information was stored elsewhere. It didn't differ from one environment to the next, as you can see in Example 6-2.

Example 6-2. An example environment definition

```
catalog-service:
  puppet_manifest : catalog.pp ❶
  connectivity:
    - protocol: tcp
      ports: [ 8080, 8081 ]
      allowed: [ WORLD ]
```

❶ This was the name of the Puppet file to run—we happened to use Puppet solo in this situation, but theoretically could have supported alternative configuration systems.

Obviously, a lot of the behavior here was convention based. For example, we decided to normalize which ports services used wherever they ran, and automatically configured load balancers if a service had more than one instance (something that AWS's ELBs make fairly easy).

Building a system like this required a significant amount of work. The effort is often front-loaded, but can be essential to manage the deployment complexity you have. I hope in the future you won't have to do this yourself. Terraform is a very new tool from Hashicorp, which works in this space. I'd generally shy away from mentioning such a new tool in a book that is more about ideas than technology, but it is attempting to create an open source tool along these lines. It's early days yet, but already its capabilities seem really interesting. With the ability to target deployments on a number of different platforms, in the future it could be just the tool for the job.

Summary

We've covered a lot of ground here, so a recap is in order. First, focus on maintaining the ability to release one service independently from another, and make sure that whatever technology you select supports this. I greatly prefer having a single repository per microservice, but am firmer still that you need one CI build per microservice if you want to deploy them separately.

Next, if possible, move to a single-service per host/container. Look at alternative technologies like LXC or Docker to make managing the moving parts cheaper and easier, but understand that whatever technology you adopt, a culture of automation is key to managing everything. Automate everything, and if the technology you have doesn't allow this, get some new technology! Being able to use a platform like AWS will give you huge benefits when it comes to automation.

Make sure you understand the impact your deployment choices have on developers, and make sure they feel the love too. Creating tools that let you self-service-deploy any given service into a number of different environments is really important, and will help developers, testers, and operations people alike.

Finally, if you want to go deeper into this topic, I thoroughly recommend you read Jez Humble and David Farley's *Continuous Delivery* (Addison-Wesley), which goes into much more detail on subjects like pipeline design and artifact management.

In the next chapter, we'll be going deeper into a topic we touched on briefly here. Namely, how do we test our microservices to make sure they actually work?

CHAPTER 7

Testing

The world of automated testing has advanced significantly since I first started writing code, and every month there seems to be some new tool or technique to make it even better. But challenges remain as how to effectively and efficiently test our functionality when it spans a distributed system. This chapter breaks down the problems associated with testing finer-grained systems and presents some solutions to help you make sure you can release your new functionality with confidence.

Testing covers a lot of ground. Even when we are *just* talking about automated tests, there are a large number to consider. With microservices, we have added another level of complexity. Understanding what different types of tests we can run is important to help us balance the sometimes-opposing forces of getting our software into production as quickly as possible versus making sure our software is of sufficient quality.

Types of Tests

As a consultant, I like pulling out the odd quadrant as a way of categorizing the world, and I was starting to worry this book wouldn't have one. Luckily, Brian Marick came up with a fantastic categorization system for tests that fits right in. Figure 7-1 shows a variation of Marick's quadrant from Lisa Crispin and Janet Gregory's book *Agile Testing* (Addison-Wesley) that helps categorize the different types of tests.

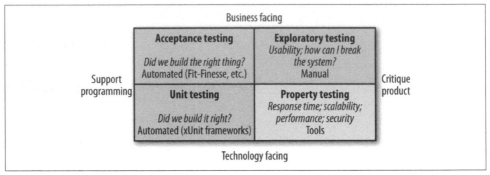

Figure 7-1. Brian Marick's testing quadrant. Crispin, Lisa; Gregory, Janet, Agile Testing: A Practical Guide for Testers and Agile Teams, 1st Edition, © 2009. Adapted by permission of Pearson Education, Inc., Upper Saddle River, NJ.

At the bottom, we have tests that are *technology-facing*—that is, tests that aid the developers in creating the system in the first place. Performance tests and small-scoped *unit* tests fall into this category—all typically automated. This is compared with the top half of the quadrant, where tests help the nontechnical stakeholders understand how your system works. These could be large-scoped, end-to-end tests, as shown in the top-left Acceptance Test square, or manual testing as typified by user testing done against a UAT system, as shown in the Exploratory Testing square.

Each type of test shown in this quadrant has a place. Exactly how much of each test you want to do will depend on the nature of your system, but the key point to understand is that you have multiple choices in terms of how to test your system. The trend recently has been away from any large-scale manual testing, in favor of automating as much as possible, and I certainly agree with this approach. If you currently carry out large amounts of manual testing, I would suggest you address that before proceeding too far down the path of microservices, as you won't get many of their benefits if you are unable to validate your software quickly and efficiently.

For the purposes of this chapter, we will ignore manual testing. Although this sort of testing can be very useful and certainly has its part to play, the differences with testing a microservice architecture mostly play out in the context of various types of automated tests, so that is where we will focus our time.

But when it comes to automated tests, how many of each test do we want? Another model will come in very handy to help us answer this question, and understand what the different trade-offs might be.

Test Scope

In his book *Succeeding with Agile* (Addison-Wesley), Mike Cohn outlines a model called the Test Pyramid to help explain what types of automated tests you need. The pyramid helps us think about the scopes the tests should cover, but also the proportions of different types of tests we should aim for. Cohn's original model split automated tests into Unit, Service, and UI, which you can see in Figure 7-2.

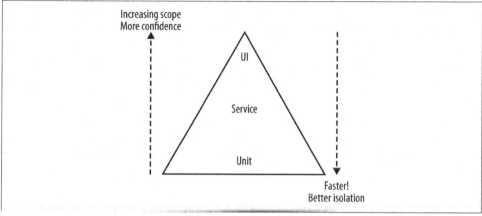

Figure 7-2. Mike Cohn's Test Pyramid. Cohn, Mike, Succeeding with Agile: Software Development Using Scrum, 1st Edition, © 2010. Adapted by permission of Pearson Education, Inc., Upper Saddle River, NJ.

The problem with this model is that all these terms mean different things to different people. "Service" is especially overloaded, and there are many definitions of a unit test out there. Is a test a unit test if I only test one line of code? I'd say yes. Is it still a unit test if I test multiple functions or classes? I'd say no, but many would disagree! I tend to stick with the Unit and Service names despite their ambiguity, but much prefer calling *UI* tests *end-to-end* tests, which we'll do from now on.

Given the confusion, it's worth us looking at what these different layers mean.

Let's look at a worked example. In Figure 7-3, we have our helpdesk application and our main website, both of which are interacting with our customer service to retrieve, review, and edit customer details. Our customer service in turn is talking to our loyalty points bank, where our customers accrue points by buying Justin Bieber CDs. Probably. This is obviously a sliver of our overall music shop system, but it is a good enough slice for us to dive into a few different scenarios we may want to test.

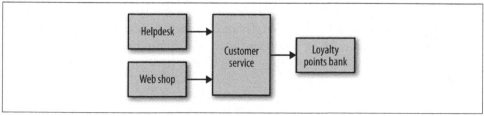

Figure 7-3. Part of our music shop under test

Unit Tests

These are tests that typically test a single function or method call. The tests generated as a side effect of *test-driven design* (TDD) will fall into this category, as do the sorts of tests generated by techniques such as property-based testing. We're not launching services here, and are limiting the use of external files or network connections. In general, you want a large number of these sorts of tests. Done right, they are very, very fast, and on modern hardware you could expect to run many thousands of these in less than a minute.

These are tests that help us developers and so would be *technology-facing*, not *business-facing*, in Marick's terminology. They are also where we hope to catch most of our bugs. So, in our example, when we think about the customer service, unit tests would cover small parts of the code in isolation, as shown in Figure 7-4.

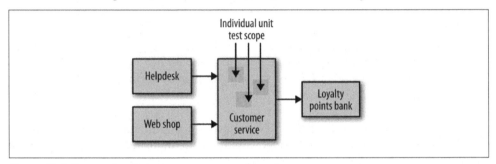

Figure 7-4. Scope of unit tests on our example system

The prime goal of these tests is to give us very fast feedback about whether our functionality is good. Tests can be important to support refactoring of code, allowing us to restructure our code as we go, knowing that our small-scoped tests will catch us if we make a mistake.

Service Tests

Service tests are designed to bypass the user interface and test services directly. In a monolithic application, we might just be testing a collection of classes that provide a *service* to the UI. For a system comprising a number of services, a service test would test an individual service's capabilities.

The reason we want to test a single service by itself is to improve the isolation of the test to make finding and fixing problems faster. To achieve this isolation, we need to stub out all external collaborators so only the service itself is in scope, as Figure 7-5 shows.

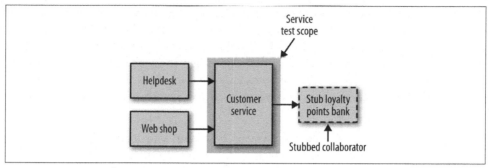

Figure 7-5. Scope of service tests on our example system

Some of these tests could be as fast as small tests, but if you decide to test against a real database, or go over networks to stubbed downstream collaborators, test times can increase. They also cover more scope than a simple unit test, so that when they fail it can be harder to detect what is broken than with a unit test. However, they have much fewer moving parts and are therefore less brittle than larger-scoped tests.

End-to-End Tests

End-to-end tests are tests run against your entire system. Often they will be driving a GUI through a browser, but could easily be mimicking other sorts of user interaction, like uploading a file.

These tests cover a lot of production code, as we see in Figure 7-6. So when they pass, you feel good: you have a high degree of confidence that the code being tested will work in production. But this increased scope comes with downsides, and as we'll see shortly, they can be very tricky to do well in a microservices context.

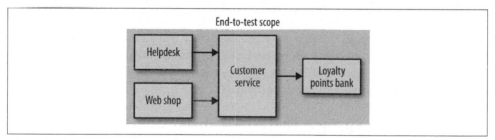

Figure 7-6. Scope of end-to-end tests on our example system

Trade-Offs

When you're reading the pyramid, the key thing to take away is that as you go up the pyramid, the test scope increases, as does our confidence that the functionality being tested works. On the other hand, the feedback cycle time increases as the tests take longer to run, and when a test fails it can be harder to determine which functionality has broken. As you go down the pyramid, in general the tests become much faster, so we get much faster feedback cycles. We find broken functionality faster, our continuous integration builds are faster, and we are less likely to move on to a new task before finding out we have broken something. When those smaller-scoped tests fail, we also tend to know what broke, often exactly what line of code. On the flipside, we don't get a lot of confidence that our system as a whole works if we've only tested one line of code!

When broader-scoped tests like our service or end-to-end tests fail, we will try to write a fast unit test to catch that problem in the future. In that way, we are constantly trying to improve our feedback cycles.

Virtually every team I've worked on has used different names than the ones that Cohn uses in the pyramid. Whatever you call them, the key takeaway is that you will want tests of different scope for different purposes.

How Many?

So if these tests all have trade-offs, how many of each type do you want? A good rule of thumb is that you probably want an order of magnitude more tests as you descend the pyramid, but the important thing is knowing that you do have different types of automated tests and understanding if your current balance gives you a problem!

I worked on one monolithic system, for example, where we had 4,000 unit tests, 1,000 service tests, and 60 end-to-end tests. We decided that from a feedback point of view we had way too many service and end-to-end tests (the latter of which were the worst offenders in impacting feedback loops), so we worked hard to replace the test coverage with smaller-scoped tests.

A common anti-pattern is what is often referred to as a *test snow cone*, or inverted pyramid. Here, there are little to no small-scoped tests, with all the coverage in large-scoped tests. These projects often have glacially slow test runs, and very long feedback cycles. If these tests are run as part of continuous integration, you won't get many builds, and the nature of the build times means that the build can stay broken for a long period when something does break.

Implementing Service Tests

Implementing unit tests is a fairly simple affair in the grand scheme of things, and there is plenty of documentation out there explaining how to write them. The service and end-to-end tests are the ones that are more interesting.

Our service tests want to test a slice of functionality across the whole service, but to isolate ourselves from other services we need to find some way to stub out all of our collaborators. So, if we wanted to write a test like this for the customer service from

Figure 7-3, we would deploy an instance of the customer service, and as discussed earlier we would want to stub out any downstream services.

One of the first things our continuous integration build will do is create a binary artifact for our service, so deploying that is pretty straightforward. But how do we handle faking the downstream collaborators?

Our service test suite needs to launch stub services for any downstream collaborators (or ensure they are running), and configure the service under test to connect to the stub services. We then need to configure the stubs to send responses back to mimic the real-world services. For example, we might configure the stub for the loyalty points bank to return known points balances for certain customers.

Mocking or Stubbing

When I talk about stubbing downstream collaborators, I mean that we create a stub service that responds with canned responses to known requests from the service under test. For example, I might tell my stub points bank that when asked for the balance of customer 123, it should return 15,000. The test doesn't care if the stub is called 0, 1, or 100 times. A variation on this is to use a mock instead of a stub.

When using a mock, I actually go further and make sure the call was made. If the expected call is not made, the test fails. Implementing this approach requires more smarts in the fake collaborators that we create, and if overused can cause tests to become brittle. As noted, however, a stub doesn't care if it is called 0, 1, or many times.

Sometimes, though, mocks can be very useful to ensure that the expected side effects happen. For example, I might want to check that when I create a customer, a new points balance is set up for that customer. The balance between stubbing and mocking calls is a delicate one, and is just as fraught in service tests as in unit tests. In general, though, I use stubs far more than mocks for service tests. For a more in-depth discussion of this trade-off, take a look at *Growing Object-Oriented Software, Guided by Tests*, by Steve Freeman and Nat Pryce (Addison-Wesley).

In general, I rarely use mocks for this sort of testing. But having a tool that can do both is useful.

While I feel that stubs and mocks are actually fairly well differentiated, I know the distinction can be confusing to some, especially when some people throw in other terms like *fakes*, *spies*, and *dummies*. Martin Fowler calls all of these things, including stubs and mocks, test doubles (*http://bit.ly/1C7atPb*).

A Smarter Stub Service

Normally for stub services I've rolled them myself. I've used everything from Apache or Nginx to embedded Jetty containers or even command-line-launched Python web servers used to launch stub servers for such test cases. I've probably reproduced the same work time and time again in creating these stubs. My ThoughtWorks colleague Brandon Bryars has potentially saved many of us a chunk of work with his stub/mock server called Mountebank (*http://www.mbtest.org/*).

You can think of Mountebank as a small software appliance that is programmable via HTTP. The fact that it happens to be written in NodeJS is completely opaque to any calling service. When it launches, you send it commands telling it what port to stub on, what protocol to handle (currently TCP, HTTP, and HTTPS are supported, with more planned), and what responses it should send when requests are sent. It also supports setting expectations if you want to use it as a mock. You can add or remove these stub endpoints at will, making it possible for a single Mountebank instance to stub more than one downstream dependency.

So, if we want to run our service tests for just our customer service we can launch the customer service, and a Mountebank instance that acts as our loyalty points bank. And if those tests pass, I can deploy the customer service straightaway! Or can I? What about the services that call the customer service—the helpdesk and the web shop? Do we know if we have made a change that may break them? Of course, we have forgotten the important tests at the top of the pyramid: the end-to-end tests.

Those Tricky End-to-End Tests

In a microservice system, the capabilities we expose via our user interfaces are delivered by a number of services. The point of the end-to-end tests as outlined in Mike Cohn's pyramid is to drive functionality through these user interfaces against everything underneath to give us an overview of a large amount of our system.

So, to implement an end-to-end test we need to deploy multiple services together, then run a test against all of them. Obviously, this test has much more scope, resulting in more confidence that our system works! On the other hand, these tests are liable to be slower and make it harder to diagnose failure. Let's dig into them a bit more using our previous example to see how these tests can fit in.

Imagine we want to push out a new version of the customer service. We want to deploy our changes into production as soon as possible, but are concerned that we may have introduced a change that could break either the helpdesk or the web shop. No problem—let's deploy all of our services together, and run some tests against the helpdesk and web shop to see if we've introduced a bug. Now a naive approach would be to just add these tests onto the end of our customer service pipeline, as in Figure 7-7.

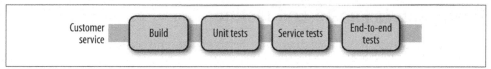

Figure 7-7. Adding our end-to-end tests stage: the right approach?

So far, so good. But the first question we have to ask ourselves is which version of the other services should we use? Should we run our tests against the versions of help-desk and web shop that are in production? It's a sensible assumption, but what if there is a new version of either the helpdesk or web shop queued up to go live; what should we do then?

Another problem: if we have a set of customer service tests that deploy lots of services and run tests against them, what about the end-to-end tests that the other services run? If they are testing the same thing, we may find ourselves covering lots of the same ground, and may duplicate a lot of the effort to deploy all those services in the first place.

We can deal with both of these problems elegantly by having multiple pipelines *fan in* to a single, end-to-end test stage. Here, whenever a new build of one of our services is triggered, we run our end-to-end tests, an example of which we can see in Figure 7-8. Some CI tools with better build pipeline support will enable fan-in models like this out of the box.

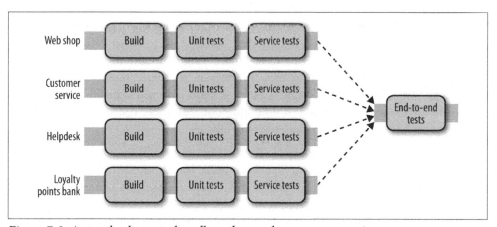

Figure 7-8. A standard way to handle end-to-end tests across services

So any time any of our services changes, we run the tests local to that service. If those tests pass, we trigger our integration tests. Great, eh? Well, there are a few problems.

Downsides to End-to-End Testing

There are, unfortunately, many disadvantages to end-to-end testing.

Flaky and Brittle Tests

As test scope increases, so too does the number of moving parts. These moving parts can introduce test failures that do not show that the functionality under test is broken, but that some other problem has occurred. As an example, if we have a test to verify that we can place an order for a single CD, but we are running that test against four or five services, if any of them is down we could get a failure that has nothing to do with the nature of the test itself. Likewise, a temporary network glitch could cause a test to fail without saying anything about the functionality under test.

The more moving parts, the more brittle our tests may be, and the less deterministic they are. If you have tests that *sometimes* fail, but everyone just re-runs them because they may pass again later, then you have flaky tests. It isn't only tests covering lots of different process that are the culprit here. Tests that cover functionality being exercised on multiple threads are often problematic, where a failure could mean a race condition, a timeout, or that the functionality is actually broken. Flaky tests are the enemy. When they fail, they don't tell us much. We re-run our CI builds in the hope that they will pass again later, only to see check-ins pile up, and suddenly we find ourselves with a load of broken functionality.

When we detect flaky tests, it is essential that we do our best to remove them. Otherwise, we start to lose faith in a test suite that "always fails like that." A test suite with flaky tests can become a victim of what Diane Vaughan calls the *normalization of deviance*—the idea that over time we can become so accustomed to things being wrong that we start to accept them as being normal and not a problem.[1] This very human tendency means we need to find and eliminate these tests as soon as we can before we start to assume that failing tests are OK.

In "Eradicating Non-Determinism in Tests" (*http://bit.ly/1Daos3Q*), Martin Fowler advocates the approach that if you have flaky tests, you should track them down and if you can't immediately fix them, remove them from the suite so you can treat them. See if you can rewrite them to avoid testing code running on multiple threads. See if you can make the underlying environment more stable. Better yet, see if you can replace the flaky test with a smaller-scoped test that is less likely to exhibit problems. In some cases, changing the software under test to make it easier to test can also be the right way forward.

---

1 Diane Vaughan, *The Challenger Launch Decision: Risky Technology, Culture, and Deviance at NASA* (Chicago: University of Chicago Press, 1996).

Who Writes These Tests?

With the tests that run as part of the pipeline for a specific service, the sensible starting point is that the team that owns that service should write those tests (we'll talk more about service ownership in Chapter 10). But if we consider that we might have multiple teams involved, and the end-to-end-tests step is now effectively shared between the teams, who writes and looks after these tests?

I have seen a number of anti-patterns caused here. These tests become a free-for-all, with all teams granted access to add tests without any understanding of the health of the whole suite. This can often result in an explosion of test cases, sometimes resulting in the test snow cone we talked about earlier. I have seen situations where, because there was no real obvious ownership of these tests, their results get ignored. When they break, everyone assumes it is someone else's problem, so they don't care whether the tests are passing.

Sometimes organizations react by having a dedicated team write these tests. This can be disastrous. The team developing the software becomes increasingly distant from the tests for its code. Cycle times increase, as service owners end up waiting for the test team to write end-to-end tests for the functionality they just wrote. Because another team writes these tests, the team that wrote the service is less involved with, and therefore less likely to know, how to run and fix these tests. Although it is unfortunately still a common organizational pattern, I see significant harm done whenever a team is distanced from writing tests for the code it wrote in the first place.

Getting this aspect right is really hard. We don't want to duplicate effort, nor do we want to completely centralize this to the extent that the teams building services are too far removed from things. The best balance I have found is to treat the end-to-end test suite as a shared codebase, but with joint ownership. Teams are free to check in to this suite, but the ownership of the health of the suite has to be shared between the teams developing the services themselves. If you want to make extensive use of end-to-end tests with multiple teams I think this approach is essential, and yet I have seen it done very rarely, and never without issue.

How Long?

These end-to-end tests can take a while. I have seen them take up to a day to run, if not more, and on one project I worked on, a full regression suite took six weeks! I rarely see teams actually curate their end-to-end test suites to reduce overlap in test coverage, or spend enough time in making them fast.

This slowness, combined with the fact that these tests can often be flaky, can be a major problem. A test suite that takes all day and often has breakages that have nothing to do with broken functionality are a disaster. Even if your functionality *is* broken, it could take you many hours to find out—at which point many of us would already have moved on to other activities, and the context switch in shifting our brains back to fix the issue is painful.

We can ameliorate some of this by running tests in parallel—for example, making use of tools like Selenium Grid. However, this approach is not a substitute for actually understanding what needs to be tested and actively *removing* tests that are no longer needed.

Removing tests is sometimes a fraught exercise, and I suspect shares much in common with people who want to remove certain airport security measures. No matter how ineffective the security measures might be, any conversation about removing them is often countered with knee-jerk reactions about not caring about people's safety or wanting terrorists to win. It is hard to have a balanced conversation about the value something adds versus the burden it entails. It can also be a difficult risk/reward trade-off. Do you get thanked if you remove a test? Maybe. But you'll certainly get blamed if a test you removed lets a bug through. When it comes to the larger-scoped test suites, however, this is exactly what we need to be able to do. If the same feature is covered in 20 different tests, perhaps we can get rid of half of them, as those 20 tests take 10 minutes to run! What this requires is a better understanding of risk, which something humans are famously bad at. As a result, this intelligent curation and management of larger-scoped, high-burden tests happens incredibly infrequently. Wishing people did this more isn't the same thing as making it happen.

The Great Pile-up

The long feedback cycles associated with end-to-end tests aren't just a problem when it comes to developer productivity. With a long test suite, any breaks take a while to fix, which reduces the amount of time that the end-to-end tests can be expected to be passing. If we deploy only software that has passed through all our tests successfully (which we should!), this means fewer of our services get through to the point of being deployable into production.

This can lead to a pile-up. While a broken integration test stage is being fixed, more changes from upstream teams can pile in. Aside from the fact that this can make fixing the build harder, it means the scope of changes to be deployed increases. One way to resolve this is to not let people check in if the end-to-end tests are failing, but given a long test suite time this is often impractical. Try saying, "You 30 developers: no check-ins til we fix this seven-hour-long build!"

The larger the scope of a deployment and the higher the risk of a release, the more likely we are to break something. A key driver to ensuring we can release our software frequently is based on the idea that we release small changes as soon as they are ready.

The Metaversion

With the end-to-end test step, it is easy to start thinking, *So, I know all these services at these versions work together, so why not deploy them all together?* This very quickly becomes a conversation along the lines of, *So why not use a version number for the whole system?* To quote Brandon Bryars (*http://bit.ly/15BPCVE*), "Now you have 2.1.0 problems."

By versioning together changes made to multiple services, we effectively embrace the idea that changing and deploying multiple services at once is acceptable. It becomes the norm, it becomes OK. In doing so, we cede one of the main advantages of microservices: the ability to deploy one service by itself, independently of other services.

All too often, the approach of accepting multiple services being deployed together drifts into a situation where services become coupled. Before long, nicely separate services become increasingly tangled with others, and you never notice as you never try to deploy them by themselves. You end up with a tangled mess where you have to orchestrate the deployment of multiple services at once, and as we discussed previously, this sort of coupling can leave us in a worse place than we would be with a single, monolithic application.

This is bad.

Test Journeys, Not Stories

Despite the disadvantages just outlined, for many users end-to-end tests can still be manageable with one or two services, and in these situations still make a lot of sense. But what happens with 3, 4, 10, or 20 services? Very quickly these test suites become hugely bloated, and in the worst case can result in Cartesian-like explosion in the scenarios under test.

This situation worsens if we fall into the trap of adding a new end-to-end test for every piece of functionality we add. Show me a codebase where every new story results in a new end-to-end test, and I'll show you a bloated test suite that has poor feedback cycles and huge overlaps in test coverage.

The best way to counter this is to focus on a *small* number of core journeys to test for the whole system. Any functionality not covered in these core journeys needs to be covered in tests that analyze services in isolation from each other. These journeys need to be mutually agreed upon, and jointly owned. For our music shop, we might focus on actions like ordering a CD, returning a product, or perhaps creating a new customer—high-value interactions and very few in number.

By focusing on a small number (and I mean *small*: very low double digits even for complex systems) of tests we can reduce the downsides of integration tests, but we cannot avoid all of them. Is there a better way?

Consumer-Driven Tests to the Rescue

What is one of the key problems we are trying to address when we use the integration tests outlined previously? We are trying to ensure that when we deploy a new service to production, our changes won't break consumers. One way we can do this without requiring testing against the real consumer is by using a *consumer-driven contract (CDC)*.

With CDCs, we are defining the expectations of a consumer on a service (or producer). The expectations of the consumers are captured in code form as tests, which are then run against the producer. If done right, these CDCs should be run as part of the CI build of the producer, ensuring that it never gets deployed if it breaks one of these contracts. Very importantly from a test feedback point of view, these tests need to be run only against a single producer in isolation, so can be faster and more reliable than the end-to-end tests they might replace.

As an example, let's revisit our customer service scenario. The customer service has two separate consumers: the helpdesk and web shop. Both these consuming services have expectations for how the customer service will behave. In this example, you create two sets of tests: one for each consumer representing the helpdesk's and web shop's use of the customer service. A good practice here is to have someone from the producer and consumer teams collaborate on creating the tests, so perhaps people from the web shop and helpdesk teams pair with people from the customer service team.

Because these CDCs are expectations on how the customer service should behave, they can be run against the customer service by itself with any of its downstream dependencies stubbed out, as Figure 7-9 shows. From a scope point of view, they sit at the same level in the test pyramid as service tests, albeit with a very different focus, as shown in Figure 7-10. These tests are focused on how a consumer will use the service, and the trigger if they break is very different when compared with service tests. If one of these CDCs breaks during a build of the customer service, it becomes obvious which consumer would be impacted. At this point, you can either fix the problem or else start the discussion about introducing a breaking change in the manner we discussed in Chapter 4. So with CDCs, we can identify a breaking change prior to our software going into production without having to use a potentially expensive end-to-end test.

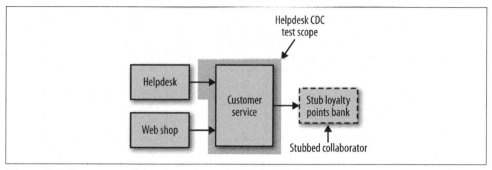

Figure 7-9. Consumer-driven testing in the context of our customer service example

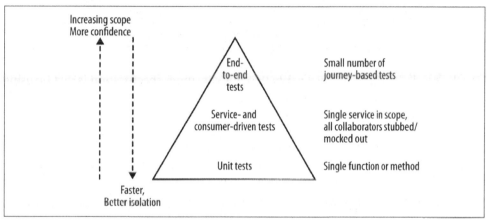

Figure 7-10. Integrating consumer-driven tests into the test pyramid

Pact

Pact (*http://bit.ly/1GZwceN*) is a consumer-driven testing tool that was originally developed in-house at RealEstate.com.au, but is now open source, with Beth Skurrie driving most of the development. Originally just for Ruby, Pact now includes JVM and .NET ports.

Pact works in a very interesting way, as summarized in Figure 7-11. The consumer starts by defining the expectations of the producer using a Ruby DSL. Then, you launch a local mock server, and run this expectation against it to create the Pact specification file. The Pact file is just a formal JSON specification; you could obviously handcode these, but using the language API is much easier. This also gives you a running mock server that can be used for further isolated tests of the consumer.

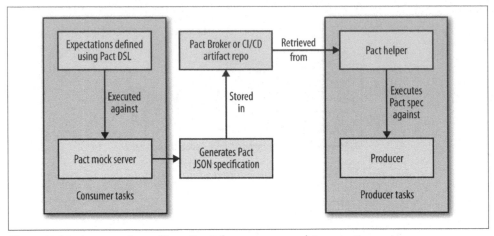

Figure 7-11. An overview of how Pact does consumer-driven testing

On the producer side, you then verify that this consumer specification is met by using the JSON Pact specification to drive calls against your API and verify responses. For this to work, the producer codebase needs access to the Pact file. As we discussed earlier in Chapter 6, we expect both the consumer and producer to be in different builds. The use of a language-agnostic JSON specification is an especially nice touch. It means that you can generate the consumer's specification using a Ruby client, but use it to verify a Java producer by using the JVM port of Pact.

As the JSON Pact specification is created by the consumer, this needs to become an artifact that the producer build has access to. You could store this in your CI/CD tool's artifact repository, or else use the Pact Broker, which allows you to store multiple versions of your Pact specifications. This could let you run your consumer-driven contract tests against multiple different versions of the consumers, if you wanted to test against, say, the version of the consumer in production and the version of the consumer that was most recently built.

Confusingly, there is a ThoughtWorks open source project called Pacto (*http://bit.ly/ 1ylH0t8*), which is also a Ruby tool used for consumer-driven testing. It has the ability to record interactions between client and server to generate the expectations. This makes writing consumer-driven contracts for existing services fairly easy. With Pacto, once generated these expectations are more or less static, whereas with Pact you regenerate the expectations in the consumer with every build. The fact that you can define expectations for capabilities the producer may not even have yet also better fits into a workflow where the producing service is still being (or has yet to be) developed.

It's About Conversations

In agile, stories are often referred to as a placeholder for a conversation. CDCs are just like that. They become the codification of a set of discussions about what a service API should look like, and when they break, they become a trigger point to have conversations about how that API should evolve.

It is important to understand that CDCs require good communication and trust between the consumer and producing service. If both parties are in the same team (or the same person!), then this shouldn't be hard. However, if you are consuming a service provided with a third party, you may not have the frequency of communication, or trust, to make CDCs work. In these situations, you may have to make do with limited larger-scoped integration tests just around the *untrusted* component. Alternatively, if you are creating an API for thousands of potential consumers, such as with a publicly available web service API, you may have to play the role of the consumer yourself (or perhaps work with a subset of your consumers) in defining these tests. Breaking huge numbers of external consumers is a pretty bad idea, so if anything the importance of CDCs is increased!

So Should You Use End-to-End Tests?

As outlined in detail earlier in the chapter, end-to-end tests have a large number of disadvantages that grow significantly as you add more moving parts under test. From speaking to people who have been implementing microservices at scale for a while now, I have learned that most of them over time remove the need entirely for end-to-end tests in favor of tools like CDCs and improved monitoring. But they do not necessarily throw those tests away. They end up using many of those end-to-end journey tests to monitor the production system using a technique called *semantic monitoring*, which we will discuss more in Chapter 8.

You can view running end-to-end tests prior to production deployment as training wheels. While you are learning how CDCs work, and improving your production monitoring and deployment techniques, these end-to-end tests may form a useful safety net, where you are trading off cycle time for decreased risk. But as you improve those other areas, you can start to reduce your reliance on end-to-end tests to the point where they are no longer needed.

Similarly, you may work in an environment where the appetite to *learn in production* is low, and people would rather work as hard as they can to eliminate any defects before production, even if that means software takes longer to ship. As long as you understand that you cannot be certain that you have eliminated all sources of defects, and that you will still need to have effective monitoring and remediation in place in production, this may be a sensible decision.

Obviously you'll have a better understanding of your own organization's risk profile than me, but I would challenge you to think long and hard about how much end-to-end testing you really need to do.

Testing After Production

Most testing is done before the system is in production. With our tests, we are defining a series of models with which we hope to prove whether our system works and behaves as we would like, both functionally and nonfunctionally. But if our models are not perfect, then we will encounter problems when our systems are used in anger. Bugs slip into production, new failure modes are discovered, and our users use the system in ways we could never expect.

One reaction to this is often to define more and more tests, and refine our models, to catch more issues early and reduce the number of problems we encounter with our running production system. However, at a certain point we have to accept that we hit diminishing returns with this approach. With testing prior to deployment, we cannot reduce the chance of failure to zero.

Separating Deployment from Release

One way in which we can catch more problems before they occur is to extend where we run our tests beyond the traditional predeployment steps. Instead, if we can deploy our software, and test it in situ prior to directing production loads against it, we can detect issues specific to a given environment. A common example of this is the *smoke test suite*, a collection of tests designed to be run against newly deployed software to confirm that the deployment worked. These tests help you pick up any local environmental issues. If you're using a single command-line command to deploy any given microservice (and you should), this command should run the smoke tests automatically.

Another example of this is what is called *blue/green deployment*. With blue/green, we have two copies of our software deployed at a time, but only one version of it is receiving real requests.

Let's consider a simple example, seen in Figure 7-12. In production, we have v123 of the customer service live. We want to deploy a new version, v456. We deploy this alongside v123, but do not direct any traffic to it. Instead, we perform some testing in situ against the newly deployed version. Once the tests have worked, we direct the production load to the new v456 version of the customer service. It is common to keep the old version around for a short period of time, allowing for a fast fallback if you detect any errors.

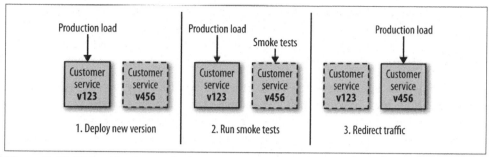

Figure 7-12. Using blue/green deployments to separate deployment from release

Implementing blue/green deployment requires a few things. First, you need to be able to direct production traffic to different hosts (or collections of hosts). You could do this by changing DNS entries, or updating load-balancing configuration. You also need to be able to provision enough hosts to have both versions of the microservice running at once. If you're using an elastic cloud provider, this could be straightforward. Using blue/green deployments allows you to reduce the risk of deployment, as well as gives you the chance to revert should you encounter a problem. If you get good at this, the entire process can be completely automated, with either the full roll-out or revert happening without any human intervention.

Quite aside from the benefit of allowing us to test our services in situ prior to sending them production traffic, by keeping the old version running while we perform our release we greatly reduce the downtime associated with releasing our software. Depending on what mechanism is used to implement the traffic redirection, the switchover between versions can be completely invisible to the customer, giving us zero-downtime deployments.

There is another technique worth discussing briefly here too, which is sometimes confused with blue/green deployments, as it can use some of the same technical implementations. It is known as *canary releasing*.

Canary Releasing

With canary releasing, we are verifying our newly deployed software by directing amounts of production traffic against the system to see if it performs as expected. "Performing as expected" can cover a number of things, both functional and non-functional. For example, we could check that a newly deployed service is responding to requests within 500ms, or that we see the same proportional error rates from the new and the old service. But you could go deeper than that. Imagine we've released a new version of the recommendation service. We might run both of them side by side but see if the recommendations generated by the new version of the service result in as many expected sales, making sure that we haven't released a suboptimal algorithm.

If the new release is bad, you get to revert quickly. If it is good, you can push increasing amounts of traffic through the new version. Canary releasing differs from blue/green in that you can expect versions to coexist for longer, and you'll often vary the amounts of traffic.

Netflix uses this approach extensively. Prior to release, new service versions are deployed alongside a baseline cluster that represents the same version as production. Netflix then runs a subset of the production load over a number of hours against both the new version and the baseline, scoring both. If the canary passes, the company then proceeds to a full roll-out into production.

When considering canary releasing, you need to decide if you are going to divert a portion of production requests to the canary or just copy production load. Some teams are able to shadow production traffic and direct it to their canary. In this way, the existing production and canary versions can see exactly the same requests, but only the results of the production requests are seen externally. This allows you to do a side-by-side comparison while eliminating the chance that a failure in the canary can be seen by a customer request. The work to shadow production traffic can be complex, though, especially if the events/requests being replayed aren't idempotent.

Canary releasing is a powerful technique, and can help you verify new versions of your software with real traffic, while giving you tools to manage the risk of pushing out a bad release. It does require a more complex setup, however, than blue/green deployment, and a bit more thought. You could expect to coexist different versions of your services for longer than with blue/green, so you may be tying up more hardware for longer than before. You'll also need more sophisticated traffic routing, as you may want to ramp up or down the percentages of the traffic to get more confidence that your release works. If you already handle blue/green deployments, you may have some of the building blocks already.

Mean Time to Repair Over Mean Time Between Failures?

So by looking at techniques like blue/green deployment or canary releasing, we find a way to test closer to (or even in) production, and we also build tools to help us manage a failure if it occurs. Using these approaches is a tacit acknowledgment that we cannot spot and catch all problems before we actually release our software.

Sometimes expending the same effort into getting better at remediation of a release can be significantly more beneficial than adding more automated functional tests. In the web operations world, this is often referred to as the trade-off between optimizing for *mean time between failures (MTBF)* and *mean time to repair (MTTR)*.

Techniques to reduce the time to recovery can be as simple as very fast rollbacks coupled with good monitoring (which we'll discuss in Chapter 8), like blue/green deployments. If we can spot a problem in production early, and roll back early, we reduce the impact to our customers. We can also use techniques like blue/green deployment, where we deploy a new version of our software and test it in situ prior to directing our users to the new version.

For different organizations, this trade-off between MTBF and MTTR will vary, and much of this lies with understanding the true impact of failure in a production environment. However, most organizations that I see spending time creating functional test suites often expend little to no effort at all on better monitoring or recovering from failure. So while they may reduce the number of defects that occur in the first place, they can't eliminate all of them, and are unprepared for dealing with them if they pop up in production.

Trade-offs other than MTBF and MTTR exist. For example, if you are trying to work out if anyone will actually use your software, it may make much more sense to get something out now, to prove the idea or the business model before building robust software. In an environment where this is the case, testing may be overkill, as the impact of not knowing if your idea works is much higher than having a defect in production. In these situations, it can be quite sensible to avoid testing prior to production altogether.

Cross-Functional Testing

The bulk of this chapter has been focused on testing specific pieces of functionality, and how this differs when you are testing a microservice-based system. However, there is another category of testing that is important to discuss. *Nonfunctional requirements* is an umbrella term used to describe those characteristics your system exhibits that cannot simply be implemented like a normal feature. They include aspects like the acceptable latency of a web page, the number of users a system should support, how accessible your user interface should be to people with disabilities, or how secure your customer data should be.

The term *nonfunctional* never sat well with me. Some of the things that get covered by this term seem very functional in nature! One of my colleagues, Sarah Taraporewalla, coined the phrase *cross-functional requirements (CFR)* instead, which I greatly prefer. It speaks more to the fact that these system behaviors really only emerge as the result of lots of cross-cutting work.

Many, if not most, CFRs can really only be met in production. That said, we can define test strategies to help us see if we are at least moving toward meeting these goals. These sorts of tests fall into the *Property Testing* quadrant. A great example of this is the performance test, which we'll discuss in more depth shortly.

For some CFRs, you may want to track them at an individual service level. For example, you may decide that the durability of service you require from your payment service is significantly higher, but you are happy with more downtime for your music recommendation service, knowing that your core business can survive if you are unable to recommend artists similar to Metallica for 10 minutes or so. These trade-offs will end up having a large impact on how you design and evolve your system, and once again the fine-grained nature of a microservice-based system gives you many more chances to make these trade-offs.

Tests around CFRs should follow the pyramid too. Some tests will have to be end-to-end, like load tests, but others won't. For example, once you've found a performance bottleneck in an end-to-end load test, write a smaller-scoped test to help you catch the problem in the future. Other CFRs fit faster tests quite easily. I remember working on a project where we had insisted on ensuring our HTML markup was using proper accessibility features to help people with disabilities use our website. Checking the generated markup to make sure that the appropriate controls were there could be done very quickly without the need for any networking roundtrips.

All too often, considerations about CFRs come far too late. I strongly suggest looking at your CFRs as early as possible, and reviewing them regularly.

Performance Tests

Performance tests are worth calling out explicitly as a way of ensuring that some of our cross-functional requirements can be met. When decomposing systems into smaller microservices, we increase the number of calls that will be made across network boundaries. Where previously an operation might have involved one database call, it may now involve three or four calls across network boundaries to other services, with a matching number of database calls. All of this can decrease the speed at which our systems operate. Tracking down sources of latency is especially important. When you have a call chain of multiple synchronous calls, if any part of the chain starts acting slowly, everything is affected, potentially leading to a significant impact. This makes having some way to performance test your applications even more important than it might be with a more monolithic system. Often the reason this sort of testing gets delayed is because initially there isn't enough of the system there to test. I understand this problem, but all too often it leads to kicking the can down the road, with performance testing often only being done just before you go live for the first time, if at all! Don't fall into this trap.

As with functional tests, you may want a mix. You may decide that you want performance tests that isolate individual services, but start with tests that check core journeys in your system. You may be able to take end-to-end journey tests and simply run these at volume.

To generate worthwhile results, you'll often need to run given scenarios with gradually increasing numbers of simulated customers. This allows you to see how latency of calls varies with increasing load. This means that performance tests can take a while to run. In addition, you'll want the system to match production as closely as possible, to ensure that the results you see will be indicative of the performance you can expect on the production systems. This can mean that you'll need to acquire a more production-like volume of data, and may need more machines to match the infrastructure—tasks that can be challenging. Even if you struggle to make the performance environment truly production-like, the tests may still have value in tracking down bottlenecks. Just be aware that you may get false negatives, or even worse, false positives.

Due to the time it takes to run performance tests, it isn't always feasible to run them on every check-in. It is a common practice to run a subset every day, and a larger set every week. Whatever approach you pick, make sure you run them as regularly as you can. The longer you go without running performance tests, the harder it can be to track down the culprit. Performance problems are especially difficult to resolve, so if you can reduce the number of commits you need to look at in order to see a newly introduced problem, your life will be much easier.

And make sure you also look at the results! I've been very surprised by the number of teams I have encountered who have spent a lot of work implementing tests and running them, and never check the numbers. Often this is because people don't know what a *good* result looks like. You really need to have targets. This way, you can make the build go *red* or *green* based on the results, with a red (failing) build being a clear call to action.

Performance testing needs to be done in concert with monitoring the real system performance (which we'll discuss more in Chapter 8), and ideally should use the same tools in your performance test environment for visualizing system behavior as those you use in production. This can make it much easier to compare like with like.

Summary

Bringing this all together, what I have outlined here is a holistic approach to testing that hopefully gives you some general guidance on how to proceed when testing your own systems. To reiterate the basics:

- Optimize for fast feedback, and separate types of tests accordingly.
- Avoid the need for end-to-end tests wherever possible by using consumer-driven contracts.
- Use consumer-driven contracts to provide focus points for conversations between teams.
- Try to understand the trade-off between putting more effort into testing and detecting issues faster in production (optimizing for MTBF versus MTTR).

If you are interested in reading more about testing, I recommend *Agile Testing* by Lisa Crispin and Janet Gregory (Addison-Wesley), which among other things covers the use of the testing quadrant in more detail.

This chapter focused mostly on making sure our code works before it hits production, but we also need to know how to make sure our code works once it's deployed. In the next chapter, we'll take a look at how to monitor our microservice-based systems.

CHAPTER 8

Monitoring

As I've hopefully shown so far, breaking our system up into smaller, fine-grained microservices results in multiple benefits. It also, however, adds complexity when it comes to monitoring the system in production. In this chapter, we'll look at the challenges associated with monitoring and identifying problems in our fine-grained systems, and I'll outline some of the things you can do to have your cake and eat it too!

Picture the scene. It's a quiet Friday afternoon, and the team is looking forward to sloping off early to the pub as a way to start a weekend away from work. Then suddenly the emails arrive. The website is misbehaving! Twitter is ablaze with your company's failings, your boss is chewing your ear off, and the prospects of a quiet weekend vanish.

What's the first thing you need to know? What the hell has gone wrong?

In the world of the monolithic application, we at least have a very obvious place to start our investigations. Website slow? It's the monolith. Website giving odd errors? It's the monolith. CPU at 100%? Monolith. Smell of burning? Well, you get the idea. Having a single point of failure also makes failure investigation somewhat simpler!

Now let's think about our own, microservice-based system. The capabilities we offer our users are served from multiple small services, some of which communicate with yet more services to accomplish their tasks. There are lots of advantages to such an approach (which is good, as otherwise this book would be a waste of time), but in the world of monitoring, we have a more complex problem on our hands.

We now have multiple servers to monitor, multiple logfiles to sift through, and multiple places where network latency could cause problems. So how do we approach this? We need to make sense of what otherwise might be a chaotic, tangled mess—the last thing any of us wants to deal with on a Friday afternoon (or at any time, come to that!).

The answer here is pretty straightforward: monitor the small things, and use aggregation to see the bigger picture. To see how, we'll start with the simplest system we can: a single node.

Single Service, Single Server

Figure 8-1 presents a very simple setup: one host, running one service. Now we need to monitor it in order to know when something goes wrong, so we can fix it. So what should we look for?

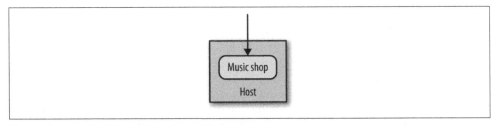

Figure 8-1. A single service on a single host

First, we'll want to monitor the host itself. CPU, memory—all of these things are useful. We'll want to know what they should be when things are healthy, so we can alert when they go out of bounds. If we want to run our own monitoring software, we could use something like Nagios to do so, or else use a hosted service like New Relic.

Next, we'll want to have access to the logs from the server itself. If a user reports an error, these logs should pick it up and hopefully tell us when and where the error is. At this point, with our single host we can probably get by with just logging on to the host and using command-line tools to scan the log. We may even get advanced and use `logrotate` to move old logs out of the way and avoid them taking up all our disk space.

Finally, we might want to monitor the application itself. At a bare minimum, monitoring the response time of the service is a good idea. You'll probably be able to do this by looking at the logs coming either from a web server fronting your service, or perhaps from the service itself. If we get very advanced, we might want to track the number of errors we are reporting.

Time passes, loads increase, and we find ourselves needing to scale…

Single Service, Multiple Servers

Now we have multiple copies of the service running on separate hosts, as shown in Figure 8-2, with requests to the different service instances distributed via a load balancer. Things start to get a bit trickier now. We still want to monitor all the same things as before, but need to do so in such a way that we can isolate the problem.

When the CPU is high, is it a problem we are seeing on all hosts, which would point to an issue with the service itself, or is it isolated to a single host, implying that the host itself has the problem—perhaps a rogue OS process?

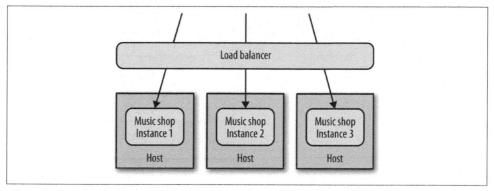

Figure 8-2. A single service distributed across multiple hosts

So at this point, we still want to track the host-level metrics, and alert on them. But now we want to see what they are across all hosts, as well as individual hosts. In other words, we want to aggregate them up, and still be able to drill down. Nagios lets us group our hosts like this—so far, so good. A similar approach will probably suffice for our application.

Then we have our logs. With our service running on more than one server, we'll probably get tired of logging into each box to look at it. With just a few hosts, though, we can use tools like ssh-multiplexers, which allow us to run the same commands on multiple hosts. A big monitor and a `grep "Error" app.log` later, and we can find our culprit.

For tasks like response time tracking, we can get some of the aggregation for free by tracking at the load balancer itself. But we need to track the load balancer as well, of course; if that misbehaves, we have a problem. At this point, we also probably care a lot more about what a healthy service looks like, as we'll configure our load balancer to remove unhealthy nodes from our application. Hopefully by the time we get here we have at least some idea of that...

Multiple Services, Multiple Servers

In Figure 8-3, things get much more interesting. Multiple services are collaborating to provide capabilities to our users, and those services are running on multiple hosts—be they physical or virtual. How do you find the error you're looking for in thousands of lines of logs on multiple hosts? How do you determine if one server is misbehaving, or if it is a systematic issue? And how do you track back an error found deep down in a call chain between multiple hosts and work out what caused it?

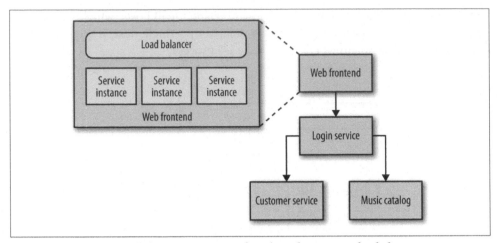

Figure 8-3. Multiple collaborating services distributed across multiple hosts

The answer is collection and central aggregation of as much as we can get our hands on, from logs to application metrics.

Logs, Logs, and Yet More Logs...

Now the number of hosts we are running on is becoming a challenge. SSH-multiplexing to retrieve logs probably isn't going to cut it now, and there isn't a screen big enough for you to have terminals open on every host. Instead, we're looking to use specialized subsystems to grab our logs and make them available centrally. One example of this is logstash (*http://logstash.net*), which can parse multiple logfile formats and can send them to downstream systems for further investigation.

Kibana (*http://bit.ly/1BrIp6a*) is an ElasticSearch-backed system for viewing logs, illustrated in Figure 8-4. You can use a query syntax to search through logs, allowing you to do things like restrict time and date ranges or use regular expressions to find matching strings. Kibana can even generate graphs from the logs you send it, allowing you to see at a glance how many errors have been generated over time, for example.

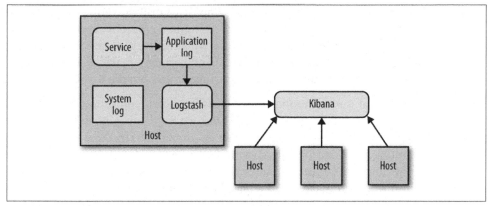

Figure 8-4. Using Kibana to view aggregated logs

Metric Tracking Across Multiple Services

As with the challenge of looking at logs for different hosts, we need to look at better ways to gather and view our metrics. It can be hard to know what *good* looks like when we're looking at metrics for a more complex system. Our website is seeing nearly 50 4XX HTTP error codes per second. Is that bad? The CPU load on the catalog service has increased by 20% since lunch; has something gone wrong? The secret to knowing when to panic and when to relax is to gather metrics about how your system behaves over a long-enough period of time that clear patterns emerge.

In a more complex environment, we'll be provisioning new instances of our services pretty frequently, so we want the system we pick to make it very easy to collect metrics from new hosts. We'll want to be able to look at a metric aggregated for the whole system—for example, the average CPU load—but we'll also want to aggregate that metric for all the instances of a given service, or even for a single instance of that service. That means we'll need to be able to associate metadata with the metric to allow us to infer this structure.

Graphite is one such system that makes this very easy. It exposes a very simple API and allows you to send metrics in real time. It then allows you to query those metrics to produce charts and other displays to see what is happening. The way it handles volume is also interesting. Effectively, you configure it so that you reduce the resolution of older metrics to ensure the volumes don't get too large. So, for example, I might record the CPU for my hosts once every 10 seconds for the last 10 minutes, then an aggregated sample every minute for the last day, down to perhaps one sample every 30 minutes for the last several years. In this way, you can store information about how your system has behaved over a long period of time without needing huge amounts of storage.

Graphite also enables you to aggregate across samples, or drill down to a single series, so you can see the response time for your whole system, a group of services, or a single instance. If Graphite doesn't work for you for whatever reason, make sure you get similar capabilities in any other tool you select. And certainly make sure you can get access to the raw data to provide your own reporting or dashboards if you need to.

Another key benefit of understanding your trends is when it comes to capacity planning. Are we reaching our limit? How long until we need more hosts? In the past when we brought physical hosts, this was often an annual job. In the new age of on-demand computing provided by infrastructure as a service (IaaS) vendors, we can now scale up or down in minutes, if not seconds. This means that if we understand our usage patterns, we can make sure we have just enough infrastructure to serve our needs. The smarter we are in tracking our trends and knowing what to do with them, the more cost effective and responsive our systems can be.

Service Metrics

The operating systems we run on generate a large number of metrics for us, as you'll find the moment you install collectd on a Linux box and point it at Graphite. Likewise, supporting subsystems like Nginx or Varnish exposes useful information like response times or cache hit rates. But what about your own service?

I would strongly suggest having your services expose basic metrics themselves. At a bare minimum, for a web service you should probably expose metrics like response times and error rates—vital if your server isn't fronted by a web server that is doing this for you. But you should really go further. For example, our accounts service may want to expose the number of times customers view their past orders, or your web shop might want to capture how much money has been made during the last day.

Why do we care about this? Well, for a number of reasons. First, there is an old adage that 80% of software features are never used. Now I can't comment on how accurate that figure is, but as someone who has been developing software for nearly 20 years, I *know* that I have spent a lot of time on features that never actually get used. Wouldn't it be nice to know what they are?

Second, we are getting better than ever at reacting to how our users are using our system to work out how to improve it. Metrics that inform us of how our systems behave can only help us here. We push out a new version of the website, and find that the number of searches by genre has gone up significantly on the catalog service. Is that a problem, or expected?

Finally, we can never know what data will be useful! More times than I can count I've wanted to capture data to help me understand something only after the chance to do so has long passed. I tend to err toward exposing everything and relying on my metrics system to handle this later.

Libraries exist for a number of different platforms that allow our services to send metrics to standard systems. Codahale's Metrics library (*http://metrics.codahale.com/*) is one such example library for the JVM. It allows you to store metrics as counters, timers, or gauges; supports time-boxing metrics (so you can specify metrics like "number of orders in the last five minutes"); and also comes out of the box with support for sending data to Graphite and other aggregating and reporting systems.

Synthetic Monitoring

We can try to work out if a service is *healthy* by, for example, deciding what a good CPU level is, or what makes for an acceptable response time. If our monitoring system detects that the actual values fall outside this safe level, we can trigger an alert—something that a tool like Nagios is more than capable of.

However, in many ways, these values are one step removed from what we actually want to track—namely, *is the system working?* The more complex the interactions between the services, the further removed we are from actually answering that question. So what if our monitoring systems were programmed to act a bit like our users, and could report back if something goes wrong?

I first did this back in 2005. I was part of a small ThoughtWorks team that was building a system for an investment bank. Throughout the trading day, lots of events came in representing changes in the market. Our job was to react to these changes, and look at the impact on the bank's portfolio. We were working under some fairly tight deadlines, as the goal was to have done all our calculations in less than 10 seconds after the event arrived. The system itself consisted of around five discrete services, at least one of which was running on a computing grid that, among other things, was scavenging unused CPU cycles on around 250 desktop hosts in the bank's disaster recovery center.

The number of moving parts in the system meant a lot of noise was being generated from many of the lower-level metrics we were gathering. We didn't have the benefit of scaling gradually or having the system run for a few months to understand what *good* looked like for metrics like our CPU rate or even the latencies of some of the individual components. Our approach was to generate fake events to price part of the portfolio that was not booked into the downstream systems. Every minute or so, we had Nagios run a command-line job that inserted a fake event into one of our queues. Our system picked it up and ran all the various calculations just like any other job, except the results appeared in the *junk* book, which was used only for testing. If a repricing wasn't seen within a given time, Nagios reported this as an issue.

This fake event we created is an example of *synthetic transaction*. We used this synthetic transaction to ensure the system was behaving semantically, which is why this technique is often called *semantic monitoring*.

In practice, I've found the use of synthetic transactions to perform semantic monitoring like this to be a far better indicator of issues in systems than alerting on the lower-level metrics. They don't replace the need for the lower-level metrics, though—we'll still want that detail when we need to find out *why* our semantic monitoring is reporting a problem.

Implementing Semantic Monitoring

Now in the past, implementing semantic monitoring was a fairly daunting task. But the world has moved on, and the means to do this is at our fingertips! You are running tests for your systems, right? If not, go read Chapter 7 and come back. All done? Good!

If we look at the tests we have that test a given service end to end, or even our whole system end to end, we have much of what we need to implement semantic monitoring. Our system already exposes the hooks needed to launch the test and check the result. So why not just run a subset of these tests, on an ongoing basis, as a way of monitoring our system?

There are some things we need to do, of course. First, we need to be careful about the data requirements of our tests. We may need to find a way for our tests to adapt to different live data if this changes over time, or else set a different source of data. For example, we could have a set of fake users we use in production with a known set of data.

Likewise, we have to make sure we don't accidentally trigger unforeseen side effects. A friend told me a story about an ecommerce company that accidentally ran its tests against its production ordering systems. It didn't realize its mistake until a large number of washing machines arrived at the head office.

Correlation IDs

With a large number of services interacting to provide any given end-user capability, a single initiating call can end up generating multiple more downstream service calls. For example, consider the example of a customer being registered. The customer fills in all her details in a form and clicks submit. Behind the scenes, we check validity of the credit card details with our payment service, talk to our postal service to send out a welcome pack in the post, and send a welcome email using our email service. Now what happens if the call to the payment service ends up generating an odd error? We'll talk at length about handling the failure in Chapter 11, but consider the difficulty of diagnosing what happened.

If we look at the logs, the only service registering an error is our payment service. If we are lucky, we can work out what request caused the problem, and we may even be able to look at the parameters of the call. Now consider that this is a simple example, and that one initiating request could generate a chain of downstream calls and maybe events being fired off that are handled in an asynchronous manner. How can we reconstruct the flow of calls in order to reproduce and fix the problem? Often what we need is to see that error in the wider context of the initiating call; in other words, we'd like to trace the call chain upstream, just like we do with a stack trace.

One approach that can be useful here is to use correlation IDs. When the first call is made, you generate a GUID for the call. This is then passed along to all subsequent calls, as seen in Figure 8-5, and can be put into your logs in a structured way, much as you'll already do with components like the log level or date. With the right log aggregation tooling, you'll then be able to trace that event all the way through your system:

```
15-02-2014 16:01:01 Web-Frontend INFO [abc-123] Register
15-02-2014 16:01:02 RegisterService INFO [abc-123] RegisterCustomer ...
15-02-2014 16:01:03 PostalSystem INFO [abc-123] SendWelcomePack ...
15-02-2014 16:01:03 EmailSystem INFO [abc-123] SendWelcomeEmail ...
15-02-2014 16:01:03 PaymentGateway ERROR [abc-123] ValidatePayment ...
```

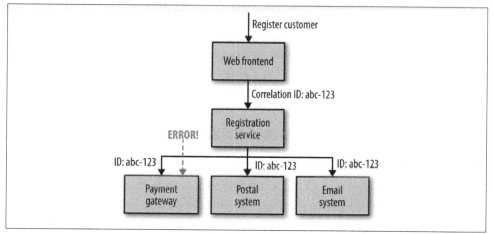

Figure 8-5. Using correlation IDs to track call chains across multiple services

You will, of course, need to ensure that each service knows to pass on the correlation ID. This is where you need to standardize and be stronger in enforcing this across your system. But once you have done this, you can actually create tooling to track all sorts of interactions. Such tooling can be useful in tracking down event storms, odd corner cases, or even identifying especially costly transactions, as you can picture the whole cascade of calls.

Software such as Zipkin (*http://twitter.github.io/zipkin/*) can also trace calls across multiple system boundaries. Based on the ideas from Google's own tracing system, Dapper, Zipkin can provide very detailed tracing of interservice calls, along with a UI to help present the data. Personally, I've found the requirements of Zipkin to be somewhat heavyweight, requiring custom clients and supporting collection systems.

Given that you'll already want log aggregation for other purposes, it feels much simpler to instead make use of data you're already collecting than have to plumb in additional sources of data. That said, if you find that you need a more advanced tool to track interservice calls like this, you might want to give them a look.

One of the real problems with correlation IDs is that you often don't know you need one until *after* you already have a problem that could be diagnosed only if you had the ID at the beginning! This is especially problematic, as retrofitting correlation IDs in is very difficult; you need to handle them in a standardized way to be able to easily reconsititute call chains. Although it might seem like additional work up front, I would strongly suggest you consider putting them in as soon as you can, especially if your system will make use of event-driven architecture patterns, which can lead to some odd emergent behavior.

Needing to handle tasks like consistently passing through correlation IDs can be a strong argument for the use of thin shared client wrapper libraries. At a certain scale, it becomes difficult to ensure that everyone is calling downstream services in the right way and collecting the right sort of data. It only takes one service partway through the chain to forget to do this for you to lose critical information. If you do decide to create an in-house client library to make things like this work out of the box, do make sure you keep it very thin and not tied to any particular producing service. For example, if you are using HTTP as the underlying protocol for communication, just wrap a standard HTTP client library, adding in code to make sure you propogate the correlation IDs in the headers.

The Cascade

Cascading failures can be especially perilous. Imagine a situation where the network connection between our music shop website and the catalog service goes down. The services themselves appear healthy, but they can't talk to each other. If we just looked at the health of the individual service, we wouldn't know there is a problem. Using synthetic monitoring—for example, to mimic a customer searching for a song—would pick up the problem. But we'd also need to report on the fact that one service cannot see another in order to determine the cause of the problem.

Therefore, monitoring the integration points between systems is key. Each service instance should track and expose the health of its downstream dependencies, from the database to other collaborating services. You should also allow this information to be aggregated to give you a rolled-up picture. You'll want to see the response time of the downstream calls, and also detect if it is erroring.

As we'll discuss more in Chapter 11, you can use libraries to implement a circuit breaker around network calls to help you handle cascading failures in a more elegant fashion, allowing you to more gracefully degrade your system. Some of these libraries, such as Hystrix for the JVM, also do a good job of providing these monitoring capabilities for you.

Standardization

As we've covered previously, one of the ongoing balancing acts you'll need to pull off is where to allow for decisions to be made narrowly for a single service versus where you need to standardize across your system. In my opinion, monitoring is one area where standardization is incredibly important. With services collaborating in lots of different ways to provide capabilities to users using multiple interfaces, you need to view the system in a holistic way.

You should try to write your logs out in a standard format. You definitely want to have all your metrics in one place, and you may want to have a list of standard names for your metrics too; it would be very annoying for one service to have a metric called ResponseTime, and another to have one called RspTimeSecs, when they mean the same thing.

As always with standardization, tools can help. As I've said before, the key is making it easy to do the right thing—so why not provide preconfigured virtual machine images with logstash and collectd ready to go, along with application libraries that let you talk to Graphite really easily?

Consider the Audience

All this data we are gathering is for a purpose. More specifically, we are gathering all this data for different people to help them do their jobs; this data becomes a call to action. Some of this data needs to trigger an immediate call to action for our support team—for example, in the case of one of our synthetic monitoring tests failing. Other data, like the fact that our CPU load has increased by 2% over the last week, is potentially only of interest when we're doing capacity planning. Likewise, your boss is probably going to want to know right away that revenue dipped 25% after the last release, but probably doesn't need to be woken up because searches for "Justin Bieber" have gone up 5% in the last hour.

What our people want to see and react to *right now* is different than what they need when drilling down. So, for the type of person who will be looking at this data, consider the following:

- What they need to know right now
- What they might want later
- How they like to consume data

Alert on the things they need to know right now. Create big visible displays with this information that sit in the corner of the room. Give them easy access to the data they need to know later. And spend time with them to know how they want to consume data. A discussion about all the nuances involved in the graphical display of quantitative information is certainly outside the scope of this book, but a great place to start is Stephen Few's excellent book *Information Dashboard Design: Displaying Data for At-a-Glance Monitoring* (Analytics Press).

The Future

I have seen many organizations where metrics are siloed into different systems. Application-level metrics, like the number of orders placed, end up in a proprietary analytics system like Omniture, which is often available only to select parts of *the business*, or else ends up in the dreaded data warehouse, aka where data goes to die. Reporting from such systems is often not available in real time, although that is starting to change. Meanwhile, *system* metrics like response times, error rates, and CPU load are stored in systems that the operations teams can access. These systems typically allow for real-time reporting, as normally the point of them is to provoke an immediate call to action.

Historically, the idea that we can find out about key business metrics a day or two later was fine, as typically we were unable to react fast enough to this data to do anything about it anyway. Now, though, we operate in a world in which many of us can and do push out multiple releases per day. Teams now measure themselves not in terms of how many *points* they complete, but instead optimize for how long it takes for code to get from laptop to live. In such an environment, we need all our metrics at our fingertips to take the right action. Ironically, the very systems that store business metrics are often not tuned for immediate access to data, but our operational systems are.

So why handle operational and business metrics in the same way? Ultimately, both types of things break down to events that say *something happened at X*. So, if we can unify the systems we use to gather, aggregate, and store these events, and make them available for reporting, we end up with a much simpler architecture.

Riemann (*http://riemann.io/*) is an event server that allows for fairly advanced aggregation and routing of events and can form part of such a solution. Suro (*https://github.com/Netflix/suro*) is Netflix's *data pipeline* and operates in a similar space. Suro is explicitly used to handle both metrics associated with user behavior, and more operational data like application logs. This data can then be dispatched to a variety of systems, like Storm for real-time analysis, Hadoop for offline batch processing, or Kibana for log analysis.

Many organizations are moving in a fundamentally different direction: away from having specialized tool chains for different types of metrics and toward more generic event routing systems capable of significant scale. These systems manage to provide much more flexibility, while at the same time actually simplifying our architecture.

Summary

So, we've covered a lot here! I'll attempt to summarize this chapter into some easy-to-follow advice.

For each service:

- Track inbound response time at a bare minimum. Once you've done that, follow with error rates and then start working on application-level metrics.
- Track the health of all downstream responses, at a bare minimum including the response time of downstream calls, and at best tracking error rates. Libraries like Hystrix can help here.
- Standardize on how and where metrics are collected.
- Log into a standard location, in a standard format if possible. Aggregation is a pain if every service uses a different layout!
- Monitor the underlying operating system so you can track down rogue processes and do capacity planning.

For the system:

- Aggregate host-level metrics like CPU together with application-level metrics.
- Ensure your metric storage tool allows for aggregation at a system or service level, and drill down to individual hosts.
- Ensure your metric storage tool allows you to maintain data long enough to understand trends in your system.
- Have a single, queryable tool for aggregating and storing logs.
- Strongly consider standardizing on the use of correlation IDs.
- Understand what requires a call to action, and structure alerting and dashboards accordingly.
- Investigate the possibility of unifying how you aggregate all of your various metrics by seeing if a tool like Suro or Riemann makes sense for you.

I've also attempted to outline the direction in which monitoring is moving: away from systems specialized to do just one thing, and toward generic event processing systems that allow you to look at your system in a more holistic way. This is an exciting and emerging space, and while a full investigation is outside the scope of this book, hopefully I've given you enough to get started with. If you want to know more, I go into some of these ideas and more in my earlier publication *Lightweight Systems for Realtime Monitoring* (O'Reilly).

In the next chapter, we'll take a different holistic view of our systems to consider some of the unique advantages—and challenges—that fine-grained architectures can provide in the area of security.

CHAPTER 9

Security

We've become familiar with stories about security breaches of large-scale systems resulting in our data being exposed to all sorts of dodgy characters. But more recently, events like the Edward Snowden revelations have made us even more aware of the value of data that companies hold about us, and the value of data that we hold for our customers in the systems we build. This chapter will give a brief overview of some aspects of security you should consider when designing your systems. While not meant to be exhaustive, it will lay out some of the main options available to you and give you a starting point for your own further research.

We need to think about what protection our data needs while in transit from one point to another, and what protection it needs at rest. We need to think about the security of our underlying operating systems, and our networks too. There is so much to think about, and so much we could do! So how much security do we need? How can we work out what is *enough* security?

But we also need to think of the human element. How do we know who a person is, and what he can do? And how does this relate to how our servers talk to each other? Let's start there.

Authentication and Authorization

Authentication and authorization are core concepts when it comes to people and things that interact with our system. In the context of security, *authentication* is the process by which we confirm that a party is who she says she is. For a human, you typically authenticate a user by having her type in her username and password. We assume that only she has access to this information, and therefore that the person entering this information must be her. Other, more complex systems exist as well, of course. My phone now lets me use my fingerprint to confirm that I am who I say I am. Generally, when we're talking abstractly about who or what is being authenticated, we refer to that party as the *principal*.

Authorization is the mechanism by which we map from a principal to the action we are allowing her to do. Often, when a principal is authenticated, we will be given information about her that will help us decide what we should let her do. We might, for example, be told what department or office she works in—pieces of information that our systems can use to decide what she can and cannot do.

For single, monolithic applications, it is common for the application itself to handle authentication and authorization for you. Django, the Python web framework, comes out of the box with user management, for example. When it comes to distributed systems, though, we need to think of more advanced schemes. We don't want everyone to have to log in separately for different systems, using a different username and password for each. The aim is to have a single identity that we can authenticate once.

Common Single Sign-On Implementations

A common approach to authentication and authorization is to use some sort of *single sign-on (SSO)* solution. SAML, which is the reigning implementation in the enterprise space, and OpenID Connect both provide capabilities in this area. More or less they use the same core concepts, although the terminology differs slightly. The terms used here are from SAML.

When a principal tries to access a resource (like a web-based interface), she is directed to authenticate with an *identity provider*. This may ask her to provide a username and password, or might use something more advanced like two-factor authentication. Once the identity provider is satisfied that the principal has been authenticated, it gives information to the *service provider*, allowing it to decide whether to grant her access to the resource.

This identity provider could be an externally hosted system, or something inside your own organization. Google, for example, provides an OpenID Connect identity provider. For enterprises, though, it is common to have your own identity provider, which may be linked to your company's *directory service*. A directory service could be something like the Lightweight Directory Access Protocol (LDAP) or Active Directory. These systems allow you to store information about principals, such as what roles they play in the organization. Often, the directory service and the identity provider are one and the same, while sometimes they are separate but linked. Okta, for example, is a hosted SAML identity provider that handles tasks like two-factor authentication, but can link to your company's directory services as the source of truth.

SAML is a SOAP-based standard, and is known for being fairly complex to work with despite the libraries and tooling available to support it. OpenID Connect is a standard that has emerged as a specific implementation of OAuth 2.0, based on the way Google and others handle SSO. It uses simpler REST calls, and in my opinion is likely to make inroads into enterprises due to its improved ease of use. Its biggest stumbling block right now is the lack of identity providers that support it. For a public-facing website, you might be OK using Google as your provider, but for internal systems or systems where you want more control over and visibility into how and where your data is installed, you'll want your own in-house identity provider. At the time of writing, OpenAM and Gluu are two of the very few options available in this space, compared to a wealth of options for SAML (including Active Directory, which seems to be everywhere). Until and unless existing identity providers start supporting OpenID Connect, its growth may be limited to those situations where people are happy using a public identity provider.

So while I think OpenID Connect is the future, it's quite possible it'll take a while to reach widespread adoption.

Single Sign-On Gateway

Within a microservice setup, each service could decide to handle the redirection to, and handshaking with, the identity provider. Obviously, this could mean a lot of duplicated work. A shared library could help, but we'd have to be careful to avoid the coupling that can come from shared code. This also wouldn't help if you had multiple different technology stacks.

Rather than having each service manage handshaking with your identity provider, you can use a gateway to act as a proxy, sitting between your services and the outside world (as shown in Figure 9-1). The idea is that we can centralize the behavior for redirecting the user and perform the handshake in only one place.

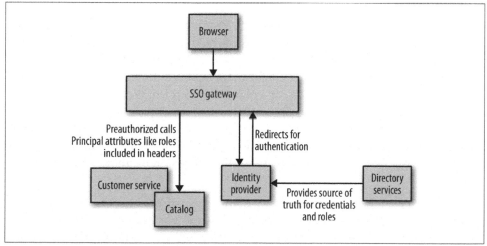

Figure 9-1. Using a gateway to handle SSO

However, we still need to solve the problem of how the downstream service receives information about principals, such as their username or what roles they play. If you're using HTTP, it could populate headers with this information. Shibboleth is one tool that can do this for you, and I've seen it used with Apache to great effect to handle integration with SAML-based identity providers.

Another problem is that if we have decided to offload responsibility for authentication to a gateway, it can be harder to reason about how a microservice behaves when looking at it in isolation. Remember in Chapter 7 where we explored some of the challenges in reproducing production-like environments? If you go the gateway route, make sure your developers can launch their services behind one without too much work.

One final problem with this approach is that it can lull you into a false sense of security. I like the idea of defense in depth—from network perimeter, to subnet, to firewall, to machine, to operating system, to the underlying hardware. You have the ability to implement security measures at all of these points, some of which we'll get into shortly. I have seen some people put all their eggs in one basket, relying on the gateway to handle every step for them. And we all know what happens when we have a single point of failure…

Obviously you could use this gateway to do other things. If using a layer of Apache instances running Shibboleth, for example, you could also decide to terminate HTTPS at this level, run intrusion detection, and so on. Do be careful, though. Gateway layers tend to take on more and more functionality, which itself can end up being a giant coupling point. And the more functionality something has, the greater the attack surface.

Fine-Grained Authorization

A gateway may be able to provide fairly effective coarse-grained authentication. For example, it could prevent access to any non-logged-in user to the helpdesk application. Assuming our gateway can extract attributes about the principal as a result of the authentication, it may be able to make more nuanced decisions. For example, it is common to place people in groups, or assign them to roles. We can use this information to understand what they can do. So for the helpdesk application, we might allow access only to principals with a specific role (e.g., STAFF). Beyond allowing (or disallowing) access to specific resources or endpoints, though, we need to leave the rest to the microservice itself; it will need to make further decisions about what operations to allow.

Back to our helpdesk application: do we allow any staff members to see any and all details? More likely, we'll have different roles at work. For example, a principal in the CALL_CENTER group might be allowed to view any piece of information about a customer except his payment details. The principal might also be able to issue refunds, but that amount might be capped. Someone who has the CALL_CEN-TER_TEAM_LEADER role, however, might be able to issue larger refunds.

These decisions need to be local to the microservice in question. I have seen people use the various attributes supplied by identity providers in horrible ways, using really fine-grained roles like CALL_CENTER_50_DOLLAR_REFUND, where they end up putting information specific to one part of one of our system's behavior into their directory services. This is a nightmare to maintain and gives very little scope for our services to have their own independent lifecycle, as suddenly a chunk of information about how a service behaves lives elsewhere, perhaps in a system managed by a different part of the organization.

Instead, favor coarse-grained roles, modeled around how your organization works. Going all the way back to the early chapters, remember that we are building software to match how our organization works. So use your roles in this way too.

Service-to-Service Authentication and Authorization

Up to this point we've been using the term *principal* to describe anything that can authenticate and be authorized to do things, but our examples have actually been about humans using computers. But what about programs, or other services, authenticating with each other?

Allow Everything Inside the Perimeter

Our first option could be to just assume that any calls to a service made from inside our perimeter are implicitly trusted.

Depending on the sensitivity of the data, this might be fine. Some organizations attempt to ensure security at the perimeter of their networks, and therefore assume they don't need to do anything else when two services are talking together. However, should an attacker penetrate your network, you will have little protection against a typical *man-in-the-middle* attack. If the attacker decides to intercept and read the data being sent, change the data without you knowing, or even in some circumstances pretend to be the thing you are talking to, you may not know much about it.

This is by far the most common form of inside-perimeter trust I see in organizations. They may decide to run this traffic over HTTPS, but they don't do much else. I'm not saying that is a good thing! For most of the organizations I see using this model, I worry that the implicit trust model is not a conscious decision, but more that people are unaware of the risks in the first place.

HTTP(S) Basic Authentication

HTTP Basic Authentication allows for a client to send a username and password in a standard HTTP header. The server can then check these details and confirm that the client is allowed to access the service. The advantage here is that this is an extremely well-understood and well-supported protocol. The problem is that doing this over HTTP is highly problematic, as the username and password are not sent in a secure manner. Any intermediate party can look at the information in the header and see the data. Thus, HTTP Basic Authentication should normally be used over HTTPS.

When using HTTPS, the client gains strong guarantees that the server it is talking to is who the client thinks it is. It also gives us additional protection against people eavesdropping on the traffic between the client and server or messing with the payload.

The server needs to manage its own SSL certificates, which can become problematic when it is managing multiple machines. Some organizations take on their own certificate issuing process, which is an additional administrative and operational burden. Tools around managing this in an automated fashion are nowhere near as mature as they could be, and it isn't just the issuing process you have to handle. Self-signed certificates are not easily revokable, and thus require a lot more thought around disaster scenarios. See if you can dodge all this work by avoiding self-signing altogether.

Another downside is that traffic sent via SSL cannot be cached by reverse proxies like Varnish or Squid. This means that if you need to cache traffic, it will have to be done either inside the server or inside the client. You can fix this by having a load balancer terminate the SSL traffic, and having the cache sit behind the load balancer.

We also have to think about what happens if we are using an existing SSO solution, like SAML, that already has access to usernames and passwords. Do we want our basic service auth to use the same set of credentials, allowing us one process for issuing and revoking them? We could do this by having the service talk to the same directory service that backs our SSO solution. Alternatively, we could store the usernames and passwords ourselves inside the service, but then we run the risk of duplicating behavior.

One note: in this approach, all the server knows is that the client has the username and password. We have no idea if this information is coming from a machine we expect; it could be coming from anyone on our network.

Use SAML or OpenID Connect

If you are already using SAML or OpenID Connect as your authentication and authorization scheme, you could just use that for service-to-service interactions too. If you're using a gateway, you'll need to route all in-network traffic via the gateway too, but if each service is handling the integration itself, this approach should just work out of the box. The advantage here is that you're making use of existing infrastructure, and get to centralize all your service access controls in a central directory server. We'd still need to route this over HTTPS if we wanted to avoid man-in-the-middle attacks.

Clients have a set of credentials they use to authenticate themselves with the identity provider, and the service gets the information it needs to decide on any fine-grained authentication.

This does mean you'll need an account for your clients, sometimes referred to as a *service account*. Many organizations use this approach quite commonly. A word of warning, though: if you are going to create service accounts, try to keep their use narrow. So consider each microservice having its own set of credentials. This makes revoking/changing access easier if the credentials become compromised, as you only need to revoke the set of credentials that have been affected.

There are a couple of other downsides, though. First, just as with Basic Auth, we need to securely store our credentials: where do the username and password live? The client will need to find some secure way to store this data. The other problem is that some of the technology in this space to do the authentication is fairly tedious to code for. SAML, in particular, makes implementing a client a painful affair. OpenID Connect has a simpler workflow, but as we discussed earlier it isn't that well supported yet.

Client Certificates

Another approach to confirm the identity of a client is to make use of capabilities in Transport Layer Security (TLS), the successor to SSL, in the form of client certificates. Here, each client has an X.509 certificate installed that is used to establish a link between client and server. The server can verify the authenticity of the client certificate, providing strong guarantees that the client is valid.

The operational challenges here in certificate management are even more onerous than with just using server-side certificates. It isn't just some of the basic issues of creating and managing a greater number of certificates; rather, it's that with all the complexities around the certificates themselves, you can expect to spend a lot of time trying to diagnose why a service won't accept what you believe to be a completely valid client certificate. And then we have to consider the difficulty of revoking and reissuing certificates should the worst happen. Using wildcard certificates can help, but won't solve all problems. This additional burden means you'll be looking to use this technique when you are especially concerned about the sensitivity of the data being sent, or if you are sending data via networks you don't fully control. So you might decide to secure communication of very important data between parties that is sent over the Internet, for example.

HMAC Over HTTP

As we discussed earlier, the use of Basic Authentication over plain HTTP is not terribly sensible if we are worried about the username and password being compromised. The traditional alternative is route traffic HTTPS, but there are some downsides. Aside from managing the certificates, the overhead of HTTPS traffic can place additional strain on servers (although, to be honest, this has a lower impact than it did several years ago), and the traffic cannot easily be cached.

An alternative approach, as used extensively by Amazon's S3 APIs for AWS and in parts of the OAuth specification, is to use a *hash-based messaging code (HMAC)* to sign the request.

With HMAC the body request along with a private key is hashed, and the resulting hash is sent along with the request. The server then uses its own copy of the private key and the request body to re-create the hash. If it matches, it allows the request. The nice thing here is that if a man in the middle messes with the request, then the hash won't match and the server knows the request has been tampered with. And the private key is never sent in the request, so it cannot be compromised in transit! The added benefit is that this traffic can then more easily be cached, and the overhead of generating the hashes may well be lower than handling HTTPS traffic (although your mileage may vary).

There are three downsides to this approach. First, both the client and server need a shared secret that needs to be communicated somehow. How do they share it? It could be hardcoded at both ends, but then you have the problem of revoking access if the secret becomes compromised. If you communicate this key over some alternative protocol, then you need to make sure that that protocol is also very secure!

Second, this is a pattern, not a standard, and thus there are divergent ways of implementing it. As a result, there is a dearth of good, open, and usable implementations of this approach. In general, if this approach interests you, then do some more reading to understand the different ways it is done. I'd go as far as to say just look at how Amazon does this for S3 and copy its approach, especially using a sensible hashing function with a suitably long key like SHA-256. JSON web tokens (JWT) (*http://bit.ly/T7BMED*) are also worth looking at, as they implement a very similar approach and seem to be gaining traction. But be aware of the difficulty of getting this stuff right. My colleague was working with a team that was implementing its own JWT implementation, omitted a single Boolean check, and invalidated its entire authentication code! Hopefully over time we'll see more reusable library implementations.

Finally, understand that this approach ensures only that no third party has manipulated the request and that the private key itself remains private. The rest of the data in the request will still be visible to parties snooping on the network.

API Keys

All public APIs from services like Twitter, Google, Flickr, and AWS make use of API keys. API keys allow a service to identify who is making a call, and place limits on what they can do. Often the limits go beyond simply giving access to a resource, and can extend to actions like rate-limiting specific callers to protect quality of service for other people.

When it comes to using API keys to handle your own microservice-to-microservice approach, the exact mechanics of how it works will depend on the technology you use. Some systems use a single API key that is shared, and use an approach similar to HMAC as just described. A more common approach is to use a public and private key pair. Typically, you'll manage keys centrally, just as we would manage identities of people centrally. The gateway model is very popular in this space.

Part of their popularity stems from the fact that API keys are focused on ease of use for programs. Compared to handling a SAML handshake, API key–based authentication is much simpler and more straightforward.

The exact capabilities of the systems vary, and you have multiple options in both the commercial and open source space. Some of the products just handle the API key exchange and some basic key management. Other tools offer everything up to and including rate limiting, monetization, API catalogs, and discovery systems.

Some API systems allow you to bridge API keys to existing directory services. This would allow you to issue API keys to principals (representing people or systems) in your organization, and control the lifecycle of those keys in the same way you'd manage their normal credentials. This opens up the possibility of allowing access to your services in different ways but keeping the same source of truth—for example, using SAML to authenticate humans for SSO, and using API keys for service-to-service communication, as shown in Figure 9-2.

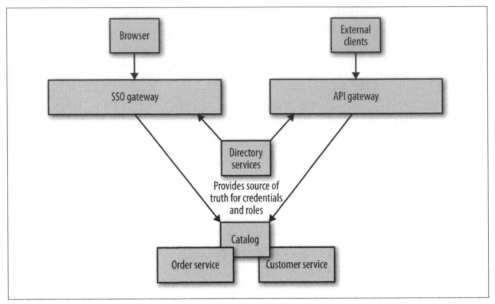

Figure 9-2. Using directory services to synchronize principal information between an SSO and an API gateway

The Deputy Problem

Having a principal authenticate with a given microservice is simple enough. But what happens if that service then needs to make additional calls to complete an operation? Take a look at Figure 9-3, which illustrates MusicCorp's online shopping site. Our online shop is a browser-based JavaScript UI. It makes calls to a server-side shop application, using the backends-for-frontends pattern we described in Chapter 4. Calls made between the browser and server can be authenticated using SAML or OpenID Connect or similar. So far, so good.

When I am logged in, I can click on a link to view details of an order. To display the information, we need to pull back the original order from the order service, but we also want to look up shipping information for the order. So clicking the link to */orderStatus/12345* causes the online shop to initiate a call from the online shop service to both the order service and shipping service asking for those details. But should these downstream services accept the calls from the online shop? We could adopt a stance of implicit trust—that because the call came from within our perimeter, it is OK. We could even use certificates or API keys to confirm that yes, it really is the online shop asking for this information. But is this enough?

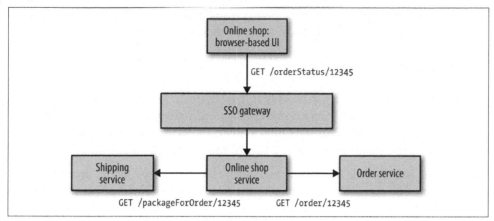

Figure 9-3. An example where a confused deputy could come into play

There is a type of vulnerability called the *confused deputy problem*, which in the context of service-to-service communication refers to a situation where a malicious party can trick a deputy service into making calls to a downstream service on his behalf that he shouldn't be able to. For example, as a customer, when I log in to the online shopping system, I can see my account details. What if I could trick the online shopping UI into making a request for someone else's details, maybe by making a call with my logged-in credentials?

In this example, what is to stop me from asking for orders that are not mine? Once logged in, I could start sending requests for other orders that aren't mine to see if I could get useful information. We could try to protect against this inside the online shop itself, by checking who the order is for and rejecting it if someone's asking for things he shouldn't. If we have lots of different applications that surface this information, though, we could potentially be duplicating this logic in lots of places.

We could route requests directly from the UI to the order service and allow it to validate the request, but then we hit the various downsides we discussed in Chapter 4. Alternatively, when the online shop sends the request to the order service, it could state not just what order it wants, but also on whose behalf it is asking. Some authentication schemes allow us to pass in the original principal's credentials downstream, although with SAML this is a bit of a nightmare, involving nested SAML assertions that are technically achievable—but so difficult that no one ever does this. This can become even more complex, of course. Imagine if the services the online shop talks to in turn make more downstream calls. How far do we have to go in validating trust for all those deputies?

This problem, unfortunately, has no simple answer, because it isn't a simple problem. Be aware that it exists, though. Depending on the sensitivity of the operation in question, you might have to choose between implicit trust, verifying the identity of the caller, or asking the caller to provide the credentials of the original principal.

Securing Data at Rest

Data lying about is a liability, especially if it is sensitive. Hopefully we've done everything we can to ensure attackers cannot breach our network, and also that they cannot breach our applications or operating systems to get access to the underlying close up. However, we need to be prepared in case they do—defense in depth is key.

Many of the high-profile security breaches involve data at rest being acquired by an attacker, and that data being readable by the attacker. This is either because the data was stored in an unencrypted form, or because the mechanism used to protect the data had a fundamental flaw.

The mechanisms by which secure information can be protected are many and varied, but whichever approach you pick there are some general things to bear in mind.

Go with the Well Known

The easiest way you can mess up data encryption is to try to implement your own encryption algorithms, or even try to implement someone else's. Whatever programming language you use, you'll have access to reviewed, regularly patched implementations of well-regarded encryption algorithms. Use those! And subscribe to the mailing lists/advisory lists for the technology you choose to make sure you are aware of vulnerabilities as they are found so you can keep them patched and up to date.

For encryption at rest, unless you have a very good reason for picking something else, pick a well-known implementation of AES-128 or AES-256 for your platform.[1] Both the Java and .NET runtimes include implementations of AES that are highly likely to be well tested (and well patched), but separate libraries exist for most platforms too—for example, the Bouncy Castle libraries (*http://www.bouncycastle.org/*) for Java and C#.

For passwords, you should consider using a technique called *salted password hashing* (*http://bit.ly/1BrIKpi*).

Badly implemented encryption could be worse than having none, as the false sense of security (pardon the pun) can lead you to take your eye off the ball.

---

[1] In general, key length increases the amount of work required to brute-force-break a key. Therefore you can assume the longer the key, the more secure your data. However, some minor concerns have been raised about the implementation of AES-256 for certain types of keys by respected security expert Bruce Schneier (*http://bit.ly/1tgAx7j*). This is one of those areas where you need to do more research on what the current advice is at the time of reading!

It's All About the Keys

As has been covered so far, encryption relies on an algorithm taking the data to be encrypted and a key and then producing the encrypted data. So, where is your key stored? Now if I am encrypting my data because I am worried about someone stealing my whole database, and I store the key I use in the same database, then I haven't really achieved much! Therefore, we need to store the keys somewhere else. But where?

One solution is to use a separate security appliance to encrypt and decrypt data. Another is to use a separate key vault that your service can access when it needs a key. The lifecycle management of the keys (and access to change them) can be a vital operation, and these systems can handle this for you.

Some databases even include built-in support for encryption, such as SQL Server's Transparent Data Encryption, that aim to handle this in a transparent fashion. Even if your database of choice does, research how the keys are handled and understand if the threat you are protecting against is actually being mitigated.

Again, this stuff is complex. Avoid implementing your own, and do some good research!

Pick Your Targets

Assuming everything should be encrypted can simplify things somewhat. There is no guesswork about what should or should not be protected. However, you'll still need to think about what data can be put into logfiles to help problem identification, and the computational overhead of encrypting everything can become pretty onerous, needing more powerful hardware as a result. This is even more challenging when you're applying database migrations as part of refactoring schemas. Depending on the changes being made, the data may need to be decrypted, migrated, and re-encrypted.

By subdividing your system into more fine-grained services, you might identify an entire data store that can be encrypted wholesale, but even then it is unlikely. Limiting this encryption to a known set of tables is a sensible approach.

Decrypt on Demand

Encrypt data when you first see it. Only decrypt on demand, and ensure that data is never stored anywhere.

Encrypt Backups

Backups are good. We want to back up our important data, and almost by definition data we are worried enough about that we want to encrypt it is important enough to back up! So it may seem like an obvious point, but we need to make sure that *our backups are also encrypted*. This also means that we need to know which keys are needed to handle which version of data, especially if the keys change. Having clear key management becomes fairly important.

Defense in Depth

As I've mentioned earlier, I dislike putting all our eggs in one basket. It's all about defence in depth. We've talked already about securing data in transit, and securing data at rest. But are there other protections we could put in place to help?

Firewalls

Having one or more firewalls is a very sensible precaution to take. Some are very simple, able only to restrict access to certain types of traffic on certain ports. Others are more sophisticated. ModSecurity, for example, is a type of application firewall that can help throttle connections from certain IP ranges and detect other sorts of malicious attacks.

There is value in having more than one firewall. For example, you may decide to use IPTables locally on a host to secure that host, setting up the allowable ingress and egress. These rules could be tailored to the locally running services, with a firewall at the perimeter for controlling general access.

Logging

Good logging, and specifically the ability to aggregate logs from multiple systems, is not about prevention, but can help with detecting and recovering from bad things happening. For example, after applying security patches you can often see in logs if people have been exploiting certain vulnerabilities. Patching makes sure it won't happen again, but if it already *has* happened, you may need to go into recovery mode. Having logs available allows you to see if something bad happened after the fact.

Note, however, that we need to be careful about what information we store in our logs! Sensitive information needs to be culled to ensure we aren't leaking important data into our logs, which could end up being a great target for attackers.

Intrusion Detection (and Prevention) System

Intrusion detection systems (IDS) can monitor networks or hosts for suspicious behavior, reporting problems when it sees them. *Intrusion prevention systems (IPS)*, as well as monitoring for suspicious activity, can step in to stop it from happening. Unlike a firewall, which is primarily looking outward to stop bad things from getting in, IDS and IPS are actively looking inside the perimeter for suspect behavior. When you're starting from scratch, IDS may make most sense. These systems are heuristic-based (as are many application firewalls), and it is possible that the generic starting set of rules will either be too lenient or not lenient enough for how your service behaves.

Using a more passive IDS to alert you to problems is a good way to tune your rules before using it in a more active capacity.

Network Segregation

With a monolithic system, we have limits to how we can structure our networks to provide additional protections. With microservices, though, you can put them into different network segments to further control how services talk to each other. AWS, for example, provides the ability to automatically provision a *virtual private cloud (VPC)*, which allow hosts to live in separate subnets. You can then specify which VPCs can see each other by defining peering rules, and even route traffic through gateways to proxy access, giving you in effect multiple perimeters at which additional security measures can be put into place.

This could allow you to segment networks based on team ownership, or perhaps by risk level.

Operating System

Our systems rely on a large amount of software that we didn't write, and may have security vulnerabilities that could expose our application, namely our operating systems and the other supporting tools we run on them. Here, basic advice can get you a long way. Start with only running services as OS users that have as few permissions as possible, to ensure that if such an account is compromised it will do minimal damage.

Next, patch your software. Regularly. This needs to be automated, and you need to know if your machines are out of sync with the latest patch levels. Tools like Microsoft's SCCM or RedHat's Spacewalk can be beneficial here, as they can help you see if machines are up to date with the latest patches and initiate updates if required. If you are using tools like Ansible, Puppet, or Chef, chances are you are already fairly happy with pushing out changes automatically—these tools can get you a long way too, but won't do everything for you.

This really is basic stuff, but it is surprising how often I see critical software running on unpatched, old operating systems. You can have the most well-defined and protected application-level security in the world, but if you have an old version of a web server running on your machine as root that has an unpatched buffer overflow vulnerability, then your system could still be extremely vulnerable.

Another thing to look at if you are using Linux is the emergence of security modules for the operating system itself. AppArmor, for example, allows you to define how your application is expected to behave, with the kernel keeping an eye on it. If it starts doing something it shouldn't, the kernel steps in. AppArmor has been around for a while, as has SELinux. Although technically either of them should work on any modern Linux system, in practice some distributions support one better than the other. AppArmor is used by default in Ubuntu and SuSE, for example, whereas SELinux has traditionally been well supported by RedHat. A newer option is Grsecurity, which aims to be simpler to use than either AppArmor or SELinux while also trying to expand on their capabilities, but it requires a custom kernel to work. I'd suggest taking a look at all three to see which fits your use cases best, but I like the idea of having another layer of protection and prevention at work.

A Worked Example

Having a finer-grained system architecture gives us much more freedom in how we implement our security. For those parts that deal with the most sensitive information or expose the most valuable capabilities, we can adopt the strictest security provisions. But for other parts of the system, we can afford to be much more lax in what we worry about.

Let's consider MusicCorp once again, and pull some of the preceding concepts together to see where and how we might use some of these security techniques. We're looking primarily at the security concerns of data in transit and at rest. Figure 9-4 shows a subset of the overall system that we'll be analyzing, which currently shows a crushing lack of regard for security concerns. Everything is sent over plain old HTTP.

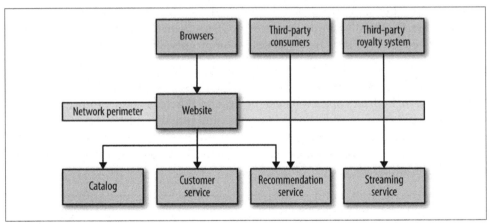

Figure 9-4. A subset of MusicCorp's unfortunately insecure architecture

Here we have standard web browsers that are used by our customers to shop on the site. We also introduce the concept of a third-party royalty gateway: we've started working with a third-party company that will handle royalty payments for our new streaming service. It contacts us occasionally to pull down records of what music has been streamed when—information we jealously protect as we are worried about competition from rival companies. Finally, we expose our catalog data to other third parties—for example, allowing the metadata about artist or song to be embedded in music review sites. Inside our network perimeter, we have some collaborating services, which are only ever used internally.

For the browser, we'll use a mix of standard HTTP traffic for nonsecure content, to allow for it to be cached. For secure, logged-in pages, all secure content will be sent over HTTPS, giving our customers extra protection if they are doing things like running on public WiFi networks.

When it comes to the third-party royalty payment system, we are concerned not only about the nature of the data we are exposing, but also about making sure the requests we're getting are legitimate. Here, we insist that our third party uses client certificates. All the data is sent over a secure, cryptographic channel, increasing our ability to ensure we're being asked for this data by the right person. We do, of course, have to think about what happens when the data leaves our control. Will our partner care about the data as much as we will?

For the feeds of catalog data, we want this information shared as widely as possible to allow people to easily buy music from us! However, we don't want this abused, and we'd like some idea of who is using our data. Here, API keys make perfect sense.

Inside the network perimeter, things are a bit more nuanced. How worried are we about people compromising our internal networks? Ideally, we'd like to use HTTPS at a minimum, but managing it is somewhat painful. We decide instead to put the work (initially, at least) into hardening our network perimeter, including having a properly configured firewall and selecting an appropriate hardware or software security appliance to check for malicious traffic (e.g., port scanning or denial-of-service attacks).

That said, we are concerned about *some* of our data and where it lives. We aren't worried about the catalog service; after all, we want that data shared and have provided an API for it! But we are very concerned about our customers' data. Here, we decide to encrypt the data held by the customer service, and decrypt data on read. If attackers do penetrate our network, they could still run requests against the customer service's API, but the current implementation does not allow for the bulk retrieval of customer data. If it did, we would likely consider the use of client certificates to protect this information. Even if attackers compromise the machine the database is running on and manage to download the entire contents, they would need access to the key used to encrypt and decrypt the data to make use if it.

Figure 9-5 shows the final picture. As you can see, the choices we made about what technology to use were based on an understanding of the nature of the information being secured. Your own architecture's security concerns are likely to be very different, and so you may end up with a different-looking solution.

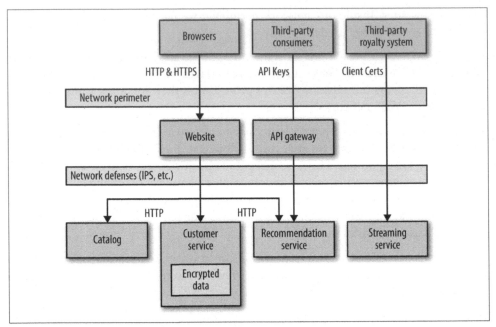

Figure 9-5. MusicCorp's more secure system

Be Frugal

As disk space becomes cheaper and the capabilities of the databases improve, the ease with which bulk amounts of information can be captured and stored is improving rapidly. This data is valuable—not only to businesses themselves, which increasingly see data as a valuable asset, but equally to the users who value their own privacy. The data that pertains to an individual, or could be used to derive information about an individual, must be the data we are most careful about.

However, what if we made our lives a bit easier? Why not scrub as much information as possible that can be personally identifiable, and do it as soon as possible? When logging a request from a user, do we need to store the entire IP address forever, or could we replace the last few digits with *x*? Do we need to store someone's name, age, gender, and date of birth in order to provide her with product offers, or is her age range and postcode enough information?

The advantages here are manifold. First, if you don't store it, no one can steal it. Second, if you don't store it, no one (e.g., a governmental agency) can ask for it either!

The German phrase *Datensparsamkeit* represents this concept. Originating from German privacy legislation, it encapsulates the concept of only storing as much information as is *absolutely required* to fulfill business operations or satisfy local laws.

This is obviously in direct tension with the move toward storing more and more information, but it is a start to realize that this tension even exists!

The Human Element

Much of what we have covered here is the basics of how to implement technological safeguards to protect your systems and data from malicious, external attackers. However, you may also need processes and policies in place to deal with the human element in your organization. How do you revoke access to credentials when someone leaves the organization? How can you protect yourself against social engineering? As a good mental exercise, consider what damage a disgruntled ex-employee could do to your systems if she wanted to. Putting yourself in the mindset of a malicious party is often a good way to reason about the protections you may need, and few malicious parties have as much inside information as a recent employee!

The Golden Rule

If there is nothing else you take away from this chapter, let it be this: don't write your own crypto. Don't invent your own security protocols. Unless you are a cryptographic expert with years of experience, if you try inventing your own encoding or elaborate cryptographic protections, you will get it wrong. And even *if* you are a cryptographic expert, you may still get it wrong.

Many of the tools previously outlined, like AES, are industry-hardened technologies whose underlying algorithms have been peer reviewed, and whose software implementation has been rigorously tested and patched over many years. They are good enough! Reinventing the wheel in many cases is often just a waste of time, but when it comes to security it can be outright dangerous.

Baking Security In

Just as with automated functional testing, we don't want security to be left to a different set of people, nor do we want to leave everything to the last minute. Helping educate developers about security concerns is key, as raising everyone's general awareness of security issues can help reduce them in the first place. Getting people familar with the OWASP Top Ten list and OWASP's Security Testing Framework can be a great place to start. Specialists absolutely have their place, though, and if you have access to them, use them to help you.

There are automated tools that can probe our systems for vulnerabilities, such as by looking for cross-site scripting attacks. The Zed Attack Proxy (aka ZAP) is a good example. Informed by the work of OWASP, ZAP attempts to re-create malicious attacks on your website. Other tools exist that use static analysis to look for common coding mistakes that can open up security holes, such as Brakeman (*http://brakeman scanner.org/*) for Ruby. Where these tools can be easily integrated into normal CI builds, integrate them into your standard check-ins. Other sorts of automated tests are more involved. For example, using something like Nessus to scan for vulnerabilities is a bit more involved and it may require a human to interpret the results. That said, these tests are still automatable, and it may make sense to run them with the same sort of cadence as load testing.

Microsoft's Security Development Lifecycle (*http://bit.ly/1nYsK6v*) also has some good models for how delivery teams can bake security in. Some aspects of it feel overly waterfall, but take a look and see what aspects can fit into your current workflow.

External Verification

With security, I think there is great value in having an external assessment done. Exercises like penetration testing, when done by an outside party, really do mimic real-world attempts. They also sidestep the issue that teams aren't always able to see the mistakes they have made themselves, as they are too close to the problem. If you're a big enough company, you may have a dedicated infosec team that can help you. If not, find an external party who can. Reach out to them early, understand how they like to work, and find out how much notice they need to do a test.

You'll also need to consider how much verification you require before each release. Generally, doing a full penetration test, for example, isn't needed for small incremental releases, but may be for larger changes. What you need depends on your own risk profile.

Summary

So again we return to a core theme of the book—that having a system decomposed into finer-grained services gives us many more options as to how to solve a problem. Not only can having microservices potentially reduce the impact of any given breach, but it also gives us more ability to trade off the overhead of more complex and secure approaches where data is sensitive, and a lighter-weight approach when the risks are lower.

Once you understand the threat levels of different parts of your system, you should start to get a sense of when to consider security during transit, at rest, or not at all.

Finally, understand the importance of defense in depth, make sure you patch your operating systems, and even if you consider yourself a rock star, don't try to implement your own cryptography!

If you want a general overview of security for browser-based applications, a great place to start is the excellent Open Web Application Security Project (OWASP) nonprofit (*https://www.owasp.org/*), whose regularly updated *Top 10 Security Risk* document should be considered essential reading for any developer. Finally, if you want a more general discussion of cryptography, check out the book *Cryptography Engineering* by Niels Ferguson, Bruce Schneier, and Tadayoshi Kohno (Wiley).

Getting to grips with security is often about understanding people and how they work with our systems. One human-related aspect we haven't yet discussed in terms of microservices is the interplay between organizational structures and the architectures themselves. But as with security, we'll see that ignoring the human element can be a grave mistake.

CHAPTER 10

Conway's Law and System Design

Much of the book so far has focused on the technical challenges in moving toward a fine-grained architecture. But there are other, organizational issues to consider as well. As we'll learn in this chapter, you ignore your company's organization chart at your peril!

Our industry is young, and seems to be constantly reinventing itself. And yet a few key *laws* have stood the test of time. Moore's law, for example, which states that the density of transistors on integrated circuits doubles every two years, has proved to be uncannily accurate (although some people predict that this trend is already slowing). One law that I have found to be almost universally true, and far more useful in my day-to-day work, is Conway's law.

Melvin Conway's paper *How Do Committees Invent*, published in *Datamation* magazine in April 1968, observed that:

> Any organization that designs a system (defined more broadly here than just information systems) will inevitably produce a design whose structure is a copy of the organization's communication structure.

This statement is often quoted, in various forms, as Conway's law. Eric S. Raymond summarized this phenomenon in *The New Hacker's Dictionary* (MIT Press) by stating "If you have four groups working on a compiler, you'll get a 4-pass compiler."

Evidence

The story goes that when Melvin Conway submitted his paper on this topic to the Harvard Business Review, they rejected it, claiming he hadn't proved his thesis. I've seen this theory borne out in so many different situations that I've accepted it as true. But you don't have to take my word for it: since Conway's original submission, a lot of work has been done in this area. A number of studies have been carried out to explore the interrelation of organizational structure and the systems they create.

Loose and Tightly Coupled Organizations

In *Exploring the Duality Between Product and Organizational Architectures* (Harvard Business School), the authors Alan MacCormack, John Rusnak, and Carliss Baldwin look at a number of different software systems, loosely categorized as being created either by *loosely coupled organizations* or *tightly coupled organizations*. For tightly coupled organizations, think commercial product firms that are typically colocated with strongly aligned visions and goals, while loosely coupled organizations are well represented by distributed open source communities.

In their study, in which they matched similar product pairs from each type of organization, the authors found that the more loosely coupled organizations actually created more modular, less coupled systems, whereas the more tightly focused organization's software was less modularized.

Windows Vista

Microsoft carried out an empirical study (*http://bit.ly/1Bfbdwb*) where it looked at how its own organizational structure impacted the software quality of a specific product, Windows Vista. Specifically, the researchers looked at multiple factors to determine how error-prone a component in the system would be.[1] After looking at multiple metrics, including commonly used software quality metrics like code complexity, they found that the metrics associated with organizational structures proved to be the most statistically relevant measures.

So here we have another example of the organizational structure impacting the nature of the system that organization creates.

Netflix and Amazon

Probably the two poster children for the idea that organizations and architecture should be aligned are Amazon and Netflix. Early on, Amazon started to understand the benefits of teams owning the whole lifecycle of the systems they managed. It wanted teams to own and operate the systems they looked after, managing the entire lifecycle. But Amazon also knew that small teams can work faster than large teams. This led famously to its *two-pizza teams*, where no team should be so big that it could not be fed with two pizzas. This driver for small teams owning the whole lifecycle of

---

1 And we all know Windows Vista was quite error-prone!

their services is a major reason why Amazon developed Amazon Web Services. It needed to create the tooling to allow its teams to be self-sufficient.

Netflix learned from this example, and ensured that from the beginning it structured itself around small, independent teams, so that the services they created would also be independent from each other. This ensured that the architecture of the system was optimized for speed of change. Effectively, Netflix designed the organizational structure for the system architecture it wanted.

What Can We Do with This?

So evidence, anecdotal and empirical, points to our organizational structure being a strong influence on the nature (and quality) of the systems we provide. So how does this understanding help us? Let's look at a few different organizational situations and understand what impact each might have on our system design.

Adapting to Communication Pathways

Let's first consider a simple, single team. It's in charge of all aspects of the system design and implementation. It can have frequent, fine-grained communication. Imagine that this team is in charge of a single service—say, our music shop's catalog service. Now consider the inside of a service: lots of fine-grained method or function calls. As we've discussed before, we aim to ensure our services are decomposed such that the pace of change inside a service is much higher than the pace of change between services. This single team, with its ability for fine-grained communication, matches nicely with the communication pathways of the code within the service.

This single team finds it easy to communicate about proposed changes and refactorings, and typically has a good sense of ownership.

Now let's imagine a different scenario. Instead of a single, geolocated team owning our catalog service, suppose that teams in the UK and India both are actively involved in changing a service—effectively having joint ownership of the service. Geographical and time zone boundaries here make fine-grained communication between those teams difficult. Instead, they rely on more coarse-grained communication via video conferencing and email. How easy is it for a team member in the UK to make a simple refactoring with confidence? The cost of communications in a geographically distributed team is higher, and therefore the cost of coordinating changes is higher.

When the cost of coordinating change increases, one of two things happen. Either people find ways to reduce the coordination/communication costs, or they stop making changes. The latter is exactly how we end up with large, hard-to-maintain codebases.

I recall one client project I worked on where ownership of a single service was shared between two geographical locations. Eventually, each site started specializing what work it handled. This allowed it to take ownership of part of the codebase, within which it could have an easier cost of change. The teams then had more coarse-grained communication about how the two parts interrelated; effectively, the communication pathways made possible within the organizational structure matched the coarse-grained API that formed the boundary between the two halves of the codebase.

So where does this leave us when considering evolving our own service design? Well, I would suggest that geographical boundaries between people involved with the development of a system can be a great way to drive when services should be decomposed, and that in general, you should look to assign ownership of a service to a single, colocated team who can keep the cost of change low.

Perhaps your organization decides that it wants to increase the number of people working on your project by opening up an office in another country. At this point, think actively about what parts of your system can be moved over. Perhaps this is what drives your decisions about what seams to split out next.

It is also worth noting at this point that, at least based on the observations of the authors of the *Exploring the Duality Between Product and Organizational Architectures* report previously referenced, if the organization building the system is more loosely coupled (e.g., consisting of geographically distributed teams), the systems being built tend toward the more modular, and therefore hopefully less coupled. The tendency of a single team that owns many services to lean toward tighter integration is very hard to maintain in a more distributed organization.

Service Ownership

What do I mean by *service ownership*? In general, it means that the team owning a service is responsible for making changes to that service. The team should feel free to restructure the code however it wants, as long as that change doesn't break consuming services. For many teams, *ownership* extends to all aspects of the service, from sourcing requirements to building, deploying, and maintaining the application. This model is especially prevalent with microservices, where it is easier for a small team to own a small service. This increased level of ownership leads to increased autonomy and speed of delivery. Having one team responsible for deploying and maintaining the application means it has an incentive to create services that are *easy* to deploy; that is, concerns about "throwing something over the wall" dissipate when there is no one to throw it to!

This model is certainly one I favor. It pushes the decisions to the people best able to make them, giving the team both increased power and autonomy, but also making it accountable for its work. I've seen far too many developers hand their system over for testing or deployment phases and think that their work is done at that point.

Drivers for Shared Services

I have seen many teams adopt a model of shared service ownership. I find this approach suboptimal, for reasons already discussed. However, the drivers that cause people to pick shared services are important to understand, especially as we may be able to find some compelling alternative models that can address people's underlying concerns.

Too Hard to Split

Obviously, one of the reasons you may find yourself with a single service owned by more than one team is that the cost of splitting the service is too high, or perhaps your organization might not see the point of it. This is a common occurrence with large monolithic systems. If this is the main challenge you face, then I hope some of the advice given in Chapter 5 will be of use. You could also consider merging teams together, to align more closely with the architecture itself.

Feature Teams

The idea of feature teams (aka feature-based teams) is that a small team drives the development of a set of features, implementing all functionality required even if it cuts across component (or even service) boundaries. The goals of feature teams are sensible enough. This structure allows the team to retain a focus on the end result and ensures that the work is joined up, avoiding some of the challenges of trying to coordinate changes across multiple different teams.

In many situations, the feature team is a reaction to traditional IT organizations where team structure is aligned around technical boundaries. For example, you might have a team that is responsible for the UI, another that is responsible for the application logic, and a third handling the database. In this environment, a feature team is a significant step up, as it works across all these layers to deliver the functionality.

With wholesale adoption of feature teams, all services can be considered shared. Everyone can change every service, every piece of code. The role of the service custodians here becomes much more complex, if the role exists at all. Unfortunately, I rarely see functioning custodians at all where this pattern is adopted, leading to the sorts of issues we discussed earlier.

But let's again consider what microservices are: services modeled after a business domain, not a technical one. And if our team that owns any given service is similarly aligned along the business domain, it is much more likely that the team will be able to retain a customer focus, and see more of the feature development through, because it has a holistic understanding and ownership of all the technology associated with a service.

Cross-cutting changes can occur, of course, but their likelihood is significantly reduced by our avoiding technology-oriented teams.

Delivery Bottlenecks

One key reason people move toward shared services is to avoid delivery bottlenecks. What if there is a large backlog of changes that need to be made in a single service? Let's imagine that we are rolling out the ability for a customer to see the genre of a track across our products, as well as adding a brand new type of stock: virtual musical ringtones for the mobile phone. The website team needs to make a change to surface the genre information, with the mobile app team working to allow users to browse, preview, and buy the ringtones. Both changes need to be made to the catalog service, but unfortunately half the team is out with the flu, and the other half is stuck diagnosing a production failure.

We have a couple of options that don't involve shared services to avoid this situation. The first is to just wait. The website and mobile application teams move on to something else. Depending on how important the feature is, or how long the delay is likely to be, this may be fine or it may be a major problem.

You could instead add people to the catalog team to help them move through their work faster. The more standardized the technology stack and programming idioms in use across your system, the easier it is for other people to make changes in your services. The flipside, of course, as we discussed earlier, is that standardization tends to reduce a team's ability to adopt the right solution for the job, and can lead to different sorts of inefficiencies. If the team is on the other side of the planet, this might be impossible, however.

Another option could be to split the catalog into a separate general music catalog and a ringtone catalog. If the change being made to support ringtones is fairly small, and the likelihood of this being an area in which we will develop heavily in the future is also quite low, this may well be premature. On the other hand, if there are 10 weeks of ringtone-related features stacked up, splitting out the service could make sense, with the mobile team taking ownership.

There is another model that could work well for us, though.

Internal Open Source

So what if we've tried our hardest, but we just can't find a way past having a few shared services? At this point, properly embracing the internal open source model can make a lot of sense.

With normal open source, a small group of people are considered core committers. They are the custodians of the code. If you want a change to an open source project, you either ask one of the committers to make the change for you, or else you make the change yourself and send them a pull request. The core committers are still in charge of the codebase; they are the owners.

Inside the organization, this pattern can work well too. Perhaps the people who worked on the service originally are no longer on a team together; perhaps they are now scattered across the organization. Well, if they still have commit rights, you can find them and ask for their help, perhaps pairing up with them, or if you have the right tooling you can send them a pull request.

Role of the Custodians

We still want our services to be sensible. We want the code to be of decent quality, and the service itself to exhibit some sort of consistency in how it is put together. We also want to make sure that changes being made now don't make future planned changes much harder than they need to be. This means that we need to adopt the same patterns used in normal open source internally too, which means separating out a group of trusted committers (the core team), and untrusted committers (people from outside the team submitting changes).

The core team needs to have some way of vetting and approving the changes. It needs to make sure the changes are idiomatically consistent—that is, that they follow the general coding guidelines of the rest of the codebase. The people doing the vetting are therefore going to have to spend time working with the submitters to make sure the change is of sufficient quality.

Good gatekeepers put a lot of work into this, communicating clearly with the submitters and encouraging good behavior. Bad gatekeepers can use this as an excuse to exert power over others or have religious wars about arbitrary technical decisions. Having seen both sets of behavior, I can tell you one thing is clear: either way it takes time. When considering allowing untrusted committers to submit changes to your codebase, you have to decide if the overhead of being a gatekeeper is worth the trouble: could the core team be doing better things with the time it spends vetting patches?

Maturity

The less stable or mature a service is, the harder it will be to allow people outside the core team to submit patches. Before the key spine of a service is in place, the team may not know what *good* looks like, and therefore may struggle to know what a good submission looks like. During this stage, the service itself is undergoing a high degree of change.

Most open source projects tend to not take submissions from a wider group of untrusted committers until the core of the first version is done. Following a similar model for your own organizations makes sense. If a service is pretty mature, and is rarely changed—for example, our cart service—then perhaps that is the time to open it up for other contributions.

Tooling

To best support an internal open source model, you'll need some tooling in place. The use of a distributed version control tool with the ability for people to submit pull requests (or something similar) is important. Depending on the size of the organization, you may also need tooling to allow for a discussion and evolution of patch requests; this may or may not mean a full-blown code review system, but the ability to comment inline on patches is very useful. Finally, you'll need to make it very easy for a committer to build and deploy your software, and make it available for others. Typically this involves having well-defined build and deployment pipelines and centralized artifact repositories.

Bounded Contexts and Team Structures

As mentioned before, we look to draw our service boundaries around bounded contexts. It therefore follows that we would like our teams aligned along bounded contexts too. This has multiple benefits. First, a team will find it easier to grasp domain concepts within a bounded context, as they are interrelated. Second, services within a bounded context are more likely to be services that talk to each other, making system design and release coordination easier. Finally, in terms of how the delivery team interacts with the business stakeholders, it becomes easier for the team to create good relationships with the one or two experts in that area.

The Orphaned Service?

So what about services that are no longer being actively maintained? As we move toward finer-grained architectures, the services themselves become smaller. One of the goals of smaller services, as we have discussed, is the fact that they are simpler. Simpler services with less functionality may not need to change for a while. Consider the humble cart service, which provides some fairly modest capabilities: Add to Cart, Remove from Cart, and so on. It is quite conceivable that this service may not have to change for months after first being written, even if active development is still going on. What happens here? Who owns this service?

If your team structures are aligned along the bounded contexts of your organization, then even services that are not changed frequently still have a de facto owner. Imagine a team that is aligned with the consumer web sales context. It might handle the website, cart, and recommendation services. Even if the cart service hasn't been changed in months, it would naturally fall to this team to make the change. One of the benefits of microservices, of course, is that if the team needs to change the service to add a new feature and not find it to its liking, rewriting it shouldn't take too long at all.

That said, if you've adopted a truly polyglot approach, making use of multiple technology stacks, then the challenges of making changes to an orphaned service could be compounded if your team doesn't know the tech stack any longer.

Case Study: RealEstate.com.au

REA's core business is real estate. But this encompasses multiple different facets, each of which operates as a single line of business (LOB). For example, one line of business deals with residential property in Australia, another commercial, while another might relate to one of REA's overseas businesses. These lines of business have IT delivery teams (or *squads*) associated with them; some may have only a single squad, while the biggest has four. So for residential property, there are multiple teams involved with creating the website and listing services to allow people to browse property. People rotate between these teams every now and then, but tend to stay within that line of business for extended periods, ensuring that the team members can build up a strong awareness of that part of the domain. This in turn helps the communication between the various business stakeholders and the team delivering features for them.

Each squad inside a line of business is expected to own the entire lifecycle of the services it creates, including building, testing and releasing, supporting, and even decommissioning. A core delivery services team provides advice and guidance to these teams, as well as tooling to help it get the job done. A strong culture of automation is key, and REA makes heavy use of AWS as a key part of enabling the teams to be more autonomous. Figure 10-1 illustrates how this all works.

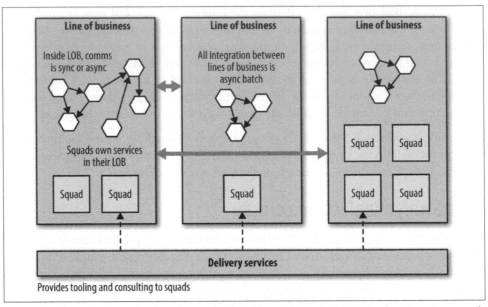

Figure 10-1. An overview of Realestate.com.au's organizational and team structure, and alignment with architecture

It isn't just the delivery organization that is aligned to how the business operates. It extends to the architecture too. One example of this is integration methods. Within an LOB, all services are free to talk to each other in any way they see fit, as decided by the squads who act as their custodians. But between LOBs, all communication is mandated to be asynchronous batch, one of the few cast-iron rules of the very small architecture team. This coarse-grained communication matches the coarse-grained communication that exists between the different parts of the business too. By insisting on it being batch, each LOB has a lot of freedom in how it acts and manages itself. It could afford to take its services down whenever it wanted, knowing that as long as it can satisfy the batch integration with other parts of the business and its own business stakeholders, no one would care.

This structure has allowed for significant autonomy of not only the teams but also the different parts of the business. From a handful of services a few years ago, REA now has hundreds, with more services than people, and is growing at a rapid pace. The ability to deliver change has helped the company achieve significant success in the local market to the point where it is expanding overseas. And, most heartening of all, from talking to the people there I get the impression that both the architecture and organizational structure as they stand now are just the latest iteration rather than the destination. I daresay in another five years REA will look very different again.

Those organizations that are adaptive enough to change not only their system architecture but also their organizational structure can yield huge benefits in terms of improved autonomy of teams and faster time to market for new features and functionality. REA is just one of a number of organizations that are realizing that system architecture doesn't exist in a vacuum.

Conway's Law in Reverse

So far, we've spoken about how the organization impacts the system design. But what about the reverse? Namely, can a system design change the organization? While I haven't been able to find the same quality of evidence to support the idea that Conway's law works in reverse, I've seen it anecdotally.

Probably the best example was a client I worked with many years ago. Back in the days when the Web was fairly nascent, and the Internet was seen as something that arrived on an AOL floppy disk through the door, this company was a large print firm that had a small, modest website. It had a website because it was the thing to do, but in the grand scheme of things it was fairly unimportant to how the business operated. When the original system was created, a fairly arbitrary technical decision was made as to how the system would work.

The content for this system was sourced in multiple ways, but most of it came from third parties who were placing ads for viewing by the general public. There was an input system that allowed content to be created by the paying third parties, a central system that took that data and enriched it in various ways, and an output system that created the final website that the general public could browse.

Whether the original design decisions were right at the time is a conversation for historians, but many years on the company had changed quite a bit and I and many of my colleagues were starting to wonder if the system design was fit for the company's present state. Its physical print business had diminished significantly, and the revenues and therefore business operations of the organization were now dominated by its online presence.

What we saw at that time was an organization tightly aligned to this three-part system. Three channels or divisions in the IT side of the business aligned with each of the input, core, and output parts of the business. Within those channels, there were separate delivery teams. What I didn't realize at the time was that these organizational structures didn't predate the system design, but actually grew up around it. As the print side of the business diminished, and the digital side of the business grew, the system design inadvertently lay the path for how the organization grew.

In the end we realized that whatever the shortcomings of the system design were, we would have to make changes to the organizational structure to make a shift. Many years later, that process remains a work in progress!

People

No matter how it looks at first, it's always a people problem.
—Gerry Weinberg,
The Second Law of Consulting

We have to accept that in a microservice environment, it is harder for a developer to just think about writing code in his own little world. He has to be more aware of the implications of things like calls across network boundaries, or the implications of failure. We've also talked about the ability of microservices to make it easier to try out new technologies, from data stores to languages. But if you're moving from a world where you have a monolithic system, where the majority of your developers have just had to use one language and remain completely oblivious to the operational concerns, then throwing them into the world of microservices may be a rude awakening for them.

Likewise, pushing power into development teams to increase autonomy can be fraught. People who have in the past thrown work over the wall to someone else are accustomed to having someone else to blame, and may not feel comfortable being fully accountable for their work. You may even find contractual barriers to having your developers carry support pagers for the systems they support!

Although this book has mostly been about technology, people are not just a side issue to be considered; they are the people who built what you have now, and will build what happens next. Coming up with a vision for how things should be done without considering how your current staff will feel about this or without considering what capabilities they have is likely to lead to a bad place.

Each organization has its own set of dynamics around this topic. Understand your staff's appetite to change. Don't push them too fast! Maybe you still have a separate team handle frontline support or deployment for a short period of time, giving your developers time to adjust to other new practices. You may, however, have to accept that you need different sorts of people in your organization to make all this work. Whatever your approach, understand that you need to be clear in articulating the responsibilities of your people in a microservices world, and also be clear why those responsibilities are important to you. This can help you see what your skill gaps might be, and think about how to close them. For many people, this will be a pretty scary journey. Just remember that without people on board, any change you might want to make could be doomed from the start.

Summary

Conway's law highlights the perils of trying to enforce a system design that doesn't match the organization. This leads us to trying to align service ownership to colocated teams, which themselves are aligned around the same bounded contexts of the organization. When the two are not in alignment, we get tension points as outlined throughout this chapter. By recognizing the link between the two, we'll make sure the system we are trying to build makes sense for the organization we're building it for.

Some of what we covered here touched on the challenges of working with organizations at scale. However, there are other technical considerations that we need to worry about when our systems start to grow beyond a few discrete services. We'll address those next.

CHAPTER 11

Microservices at Scale

When you're dealing with nice, small, book-sized examples, everything seems simple. But the real world is a more complex space. What happens when our microservice architectures grow from simpler, more humble beginnings to something more complex? What happens when we have to handle failure of multiple separate services or manage hundreds of services? What are some of the coping patterns when you have more microservices than people? Let's find out.

Failure Is Everywhere

We understand that things can go wrong. Hard disks can fail. Our software can crash. And as anyone who has read the fallacies of distributed computing (*http://bit.ly/ 1En0t51*) can tell you, we know that the network is unreliable. We can do our best to try to limit the causes of failure, but at a certain scale, failure becomes inevitable. Hard drives, for example, are more reliable now than ever before, but they'll break eventually. The more hard drives you have, the higher the likelihood of failure for an individual unit; failure becomes a statistical certainty at scale.

Even for those of us not thinking at extreme scale, if we can embrace the possibility of failure we will be better off. For example, if we can handle the failure of a service gracefully, then it follows that we can also do in-place upgrades of a service, as a planned outage is much easier to deal with than an unplanned one.

We can also spend a bit less of our time trying to stop the inevitable, and a bit more of our time dealing with it gracefully. I'm amazed at how many organizations put processes and controls in place to try to stop failure from occurring, but put little to no thought into actually making it easier to recover from failure in the first place.

Baking in the assumption that everything can and will fail leads you to think differently about how you solve problems.

I saw one example of this thinking while spending some time on the Google campus many years ago. In the reception area of one of the buildings in Mountain View was an old rack of machines, there as a sort of exhibit. I noticed a couple of things. First, these servers weren't in server enclosures, they were just bare motherboards slotted into the rack. The main thing I noticed, though, was that the hard drives were attached by velcro. I asked one of the Googlers why that was. "Oh," he said, "the hard drives fail so much we don't want them screwed in. We just rip them out, throw them in the bin, and velcro in a new one."

So let me repeat: at scale, even if you buy the best kit, the most expensive hardware, you cannot avoid the fact that things can and will fail. Therefore, you need to assume failure can happen. If you build this thinking into everything you do, and plan for failure, you can make different trade-offs. If you know your system can handle the fact that a server can and will fail, why bother spending much on it at all? Why not use a bare motherboard with cheaper components (and some velcro) like Google did, rather than worrying too much about the resiliency of a single node?

How Much Is Too Much?

We touched on the topic of cross-functional requirements in Chapter 7. Understanding cross-functional requirements is all about considering aspects like durability of data, availability of services, throughput, and acceptable latency of services. Many of the techniques covered in this chapter and elsewhere talk about approaches to implement these requirements, but only you know exactly what the requirements themselves might be.

Having an autoscaling system capable of reacting to increased load or failure of individual nodes might be fantastic, but could be overkill for a reporting system that only needs to run twice a month, where being down for a day or two isn't that big of a deal. Likewise, figuring out how to do blue/green deployments to eliminate downtime of a service might make sense for your online ecommerce system, but for your corporate intranet knowledge base it's probably a step too far.

Knowing how much failure you can tolerate, or how fast your system needs to be, is driven by the users of your system. That in turn will help you understand which techniques will make the most sense for you. That said, your users won't always be able to articulate what the exact requirements are. So you need to ask questions to help extract the right information, and help them understand the relative costs of providing different levels of service.

As I mentioned previously, these cross-functional requirements can vary from service to service, but I would suggest defining some general cross-functionals and then overriding them for particular use cases. When it comes to considering if and how to scale out your system to better handle load or failure, start by trying to understand the following requirements:

Response time/latency
How long should various operations take? It can be useful here to measure this with different numbers of users to understand how increasing load will impact the response time. Given the nature of networks, you'll always have outliers, so setting targets for a given percentile of the responses monitored can be useful. The target should also include the number of concurrent connections/users you will expect your software to handle. So you might say, "We expect the website to have a 90th-percentile response time of 2 seconds when handling 200 concurrent connections per second."

Availability
Can you expect a service to be down? Is this considered a 24/7 service? Some people like to look at periods of acceptable downtime when measuring availability, but how useful is this to someone calling your service? I should either be able to rely on your service responding or not. Measuring periods of downtime is really more useful from a historical reporting angle.

Durability of data
How much data loss is acceptable? How long should data be kept for? This is highly likely to change on a case-by-case basis. For example, you might choose to keep user session logs for a year or less to save space, but your financial transaction records might need to be kept for many years.

Once you have these requirements in place, you'll want a way to systematically measure them on an ongoing basis. You may decide to make use of performance tests, for example, to ensure your system meets acceptable performance targets, but you'll want to make sure you are monitoring these stats in production as well!

Degrading Functionality

An essential part of building a resilient system, especially when your functionality is spread over a number of different microservices that may be up or down, is the ability to safely degrade functionality. Let's imagine a standard web page on our ecommerce site. To pull together the various parts of that website, we might need several microservices to play a part. One microservice might display the details about the album being offered for sale. Another might show the price and stock level. And we'll probably be showing shopping cart contents too, which may be yet another microservice. Now if one of those services is down, and that results in the whole web page being unavailable, then we have arguably made a system that is less resilient than one that requires only one service to be available.

What we need to do is understand the impact of each outage, and work out how to properly degrade functionality. If the shopping cart service is unavailable, we're probably in a lot of trouble, but we could still show the web page with the listing. Perhaps we just hide the shopping cart or replace it with an icon saying "Be Back Soon!"

With a single, monolithic application, we don't have many decisions to make. System health is binary. But with a microservice architecture, we need to consider a much more nuanced situation. The right thing to do in any situation is often not a technical decision. We might know what is technically possible when the shopping cart is down, but unless we understand the business context we won't understand what action we should be taking. For example, perhaps we close the entire site, still allow people to browse the catalog of items, or replace the part of the UI containing the cart control with a phone number for placing an order. But for every customer-facing interface that uses multiple microservices, or every microservice that depends on multiple downstream collaborators, you need to ask yourself, "What happens if this is down?" and know what to do.

By thinking about the criticality of each of our capabilities in terms of our cross-functional requirements, we'll be much better positioned to know what we can do. Now let's consider some things we can do from a technical point of view to make sure that when failure occurs we can handle it gracefully.

Architectural Safety Measures

There are a few patterns, which collectively I refer to as *architectural safety measures*, that we can make use of to ensure that if something does go wrong, it doesn't cause nasty ripple-out effects. These are points it is essential you understand, and should strongly consider standardizing in your system to ensure that one bad citizen doesn't bring the whole world crashing down around your ears. In a moment, we'll take a look at a few key safety measures you should consider, but before we do, I'd like to share a brief story to outline the sort of thing that can go wrong.

I was a technical lead on a project where we were building an online classified ads website. The website itself handled fairly high volumes, and generated a good deal of income for the business. Our core application handled some display of classified ads itself, and also proxied calls to other services that provided different types of products, as shown in Figure 11-1. This is actually an example of a *strangler application*, where a new system intercepts calls made to legacy applications and gradually replaces them altogether. As part of this project, we were partway through retiring the older applications. We had just moved over the highest volume and biggest earning product, but much of the rest of the ads were still being served by a number of older applications. In terms of both the number of searches and the money made by these applications, there was a very long tail.

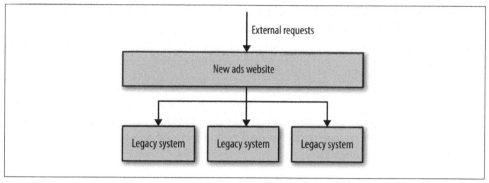

Figure 11-1. A classified ads website strangling older legacy applications

Our system had been live for a while and was behaving very well, handling a not insignificant load. At that time we must have been handling around 6,000–7,000 requests per second during peak, and although most of that was very heavily cached by reverse proxies sitting in front of our application servers, the searches for products (the most important aspect of the site) were mostly uncached and required a full server round-trip.

One morning, just before we hit our daily lunchtime peak, the system started behaving slowly, then gradually started failing. We had some level of monitoring on our new core application, enough to tell us that each of our application nodes was hitting a 100% CPU spike, well above the normal levels even at peak. In a short period of time, the entire site went down.

We managed to track down the culprit and bring the site back up. It turned out one of the downstream ad systems, one of the oldest and least actively maintained, had started responding very slowly. Responding very slowly is one of the worst failure modes you can experience. If a system is just not there, you find out pretty quickly. When it's just *slow*, you end up waiting around for a while before giving up. But whatever the cause of the failure, we had created a system that was vulnerable to a cascading failure. A downstream service, over which we had little control, was able to take down our whole system.

While one team looked at the problems with the downstream system, the rest of us started looking at what had gone wrong in our application. We found a few problems. We were using an HTTP connection pool to handle our downstream connections. The threads in the pool itself had timeouts configured for how long they would wait when making the downstream HTTP call, which is good. The problem was that the workers were all taking a while to time out due to the slow downstream system. While they were waiting, more requests went to the pool asking for worker threads. With no workers available, these requests themselves hung. It turned out the connection pool library we were using did have a timeout for waiting for workers, but this was *disabled by default*! This led to a huge build-up of blocked threads. Our application normally had 40 concurrent connections at any given time. In the space of five minutes, this situation caused us to peak at around 800 connections, bringing the system down.

What was worse was that the downstream service we were talking to represented functionality that less than 5% of our customer base used, and generated even less revenue than that. When you get down to it, we discovered the hard way that systems that just act slow are *much* harder to deal with than systems that just fail fast. In a distributed system, latency kills.

Even if we'd had the timeouts on the pool set correctly, we were also sharing a single HTTP connection pool for all outbound requests. This meant that one slow service could exhaust the number of available workers all by itself, even if everything else was healthy. Lastly, it was clear that the downstream service in question wasn't healthy, but we kept sending traffic its way. In our situation, this meant we were actually making a bad situation worse, as the downstream service had no chance to recover. We ended up implementing three fixes to avoid this happening again: getting our *timeouts* right, implementing *bulkheads* to separate out different connection pools, and implementing a *circuit breaker* to avoid sending calls to an unhealthy system in the first place.

The Antifragile Organization

In his book *Antifragile* (Random House), Nassim Taleb talks about things that actually benefit from failure and disorder. Ariel Tseitlin used this concept to coin the concept of the antifragile organization (*http://bit.ly/1e9i40t*) in regards to how Netflix operates.

The scale at which Netflix operates is well known, as is the fact that Netflix is based entirely on the AWS infrastructure. These two factors mean that it has to embrace failure well. Netflix goes beyond that by actually *inciting* failure to ensure that its systems are tolerant of it.

Some organizations would be happy with *game days*, where failure is simulated by systems being switched off and having the various teams react. During my time at Google, this was a fairly common occurrence for various systems, and I certainly think that many organizations could benefit from having these sorts of exercises regularly. Google goes beyond simple tests to mimic server failure, and as part of its annual DiRT (Disaster Recovery Test) exercises (*http://bit.ly/15CnW3a*) it has simulated large-scale disasters such as earthquakes. Netflix also takes a more aggressive approach, by writing programs that cause failure and running them in production on a daily basis.

The most famous of these programs is the Chaos Monkey, which during certain hours of the day will turn off random machines. Knowing that this can and will happen in production means that the developers who create the systems really have to be prepared for it. The Chaos Monkey is just one part of Netflix's Simian Army of failure bots. The Chaos Gorilla is used to take out an entire availability center (the AWS equivalent of a data center), whereas the Latency Monkey simulates slow network connectivity between machines. Netflix has made these tools available under an open source license (*http://bit.ly/1fsqzaH*). For many, the ultimate test of whether your system really is robust might be unleashing your very own Simian Army on your production infrastructure.

Embracing and inciting failure through software, and building systems that can handle it, is only part of what Netflix does. It also understands the importance of learning from the failure when it occurs, and adopting a blameless culture when mistakes do happen. Developers are further empowered to be part of this learning and evolving process, as each developer is also responsible for managing his or her production services.

By causing failure to happen, and building for it, Netflix has ensured that the systems it has scale better, and better support the needs of its customers.

Not everyone needs to go to the sorts of extremes that Google or Netflix do, but it is important to understand the mindset shift that is required with distributed systems. Things will fail. The fact that your system is now spread across multiple machines (which can and will fail) across a network (which will be unreliable) can actually make your system more vulnerable, not less. So regardless of whether you're trying to provide a service at the scale of Google or Netflix, preparing yourself for the sorts of failure that happen with more distributed architectures is pretty important. So what do we need to do to handle failure in our systems?

Timeouts

Timeouts are something it is easy to overlook, but in a downstream system they are important to get right. How long can I wait before I can consider a downstream system to actually be down?

Wait too long to decide that a call has failed, and you can slow the whole system down. Time out too quickly, and you'll consider a call that might have worked as failed. Have no timeouts at all, and a downstream system being down could hang your whole system.

Put timeouts on all out-of-process calls, and pick a default timeout for everything. Log when timeouts occur, look at what happens, and change them accordingly.

Circuit Breakers

In your own home, circuit breakers exist to protect your electrical devices from spikes in the power. If a spike occurs, the circuit breaker gets blown, protecting your expensive home appliances. You can also manually disable a circuit breaker to cut the power to part of your home, allowing you to work safely on the electrics. Michael Nygard's book *Release It!* (Pragmatic Programmers) shows how the same idea can work wonders as a protection mechanism for our software.

Consider the story I shared just a moment ago. The downstream legacy ad application was responding very slowly, before eventually returning an error. Even if we'd got the timeouts right, we'd be waiting a long time before we got the error. And then we'd try it again the next time a request came in, and wait. It's bad enough that the downstream service is malfunctioning, but it's making us go slow too.

With a circuit breaker, after a certain number of requests to the downstream resource have failed, the circuit breaker is blown. All further requests fail fast while the circuit breaker is in its blown state. After a certain period of time, the client sends a few requests through to see if the downstream service has recovered, and if it gets enough healthy responses it resets the circuit breaker. You can see an overview of this process in Figure 11-2.

How you implement a circuit breaker depends on what a *failed* request means, but when I've implemented them for HTTP connections I've taken failure to mean either a timeout or a 5XX HTTP return code. In this way, when a downstream resource is down, or timing out, or returning errors, after a certain threshold is reached we automatically stop sending traffic and start failing fast. And we can automatically start again when things are healthy.

Getting the settings right can be a little tricky. You don't want to blow the circuit breaker too readily, nor do you want to take too long to blow it. Likewise, you really want to make sure that the downstream service is healthy again before sending traffic. As with timeouts, I'd pick some sensible defaults and stick with them everywhere, then change them for specific cases.

While the circuit breaker is blown, you have some options. One is to queue up the requests and retry them later on. For some use cases, this might be appropriate, especially if you're carrying out some work as part of an asynchronous job. If this call is being made as part of a synchronous call chain, however, it is probably better to fail fast. This could mean propagating an error up the call chain, or a more subtle degrading of functionality.

If we have this mechanism in place (as with the circuit breakers in our home), we could use them manually to make it safer to do our work. For example, if we wanted to take a microservice down as part of routine maintenance, we could manually blow all the circuit breakers of the dependent systems so they fail fast while the microservice is offline. Once it's back, we can reset the circuit breakers and everything should go back to normal.

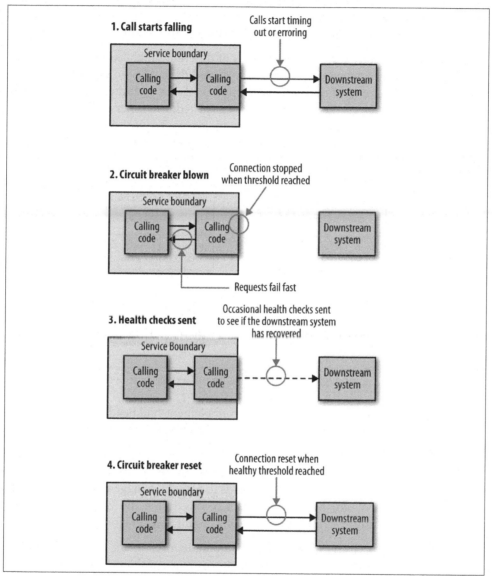

Figure 11-2. An overview of circuit breakers

Bulkheads

In another pattern from *Release It!*, Nygard introduces the concept of a *bulkhead* as a way to isolate yourself from failure. In shipping, a bulkhead is a part of the ship that can be sealed off to protect the rest of the ship. So if the ship springs a leak, you can close the bulkhead doors. You lose part of the ship, but the rest of it remains intact.

In software architecture terms, there are lots of different bulkheads we can consider. Returning to my own experience, we actually missed the chance to implement a bulkhead. We should have used different connection pools for each downstream connection. That way, if one connection pool gets exhausted, the other connections aren't impacted, as we see in Figure 11-3. This would ensure that if a downstream service started behaving slowly in the future, only that one connection pool would be impacted, allowing other calls to proceed as normal.

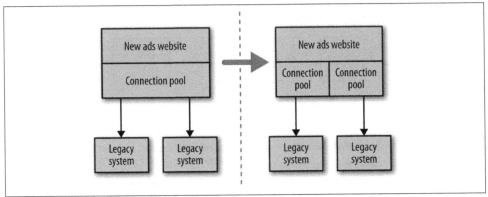

Figure 11-3. Using a connection pool per downstream service to provide bulkheads

Separation of concerns can also be a way to implement bulkheads. By teasing apart functionality into separate microservices, we reduce the chance of an outage in one area affecting another.

Look at all the aspects of your system that can go wrong, both inside your microservices and between them. Do you have bulkheads in place? I'd suggest starting with separate connection pools for each downstream connection at the very least. You may want to go further, however, and consider using circuit breakers too.

We can think of our circuit breakers as an automatic mechanism to seal a bulkhead, to not only protect the consumer from the downstream problem, but also to potentially protect the downstream service from more calls that may be having an adverse impact. Given the perils of cascading failure, I'd recommend mandating circuit breakers for all your synchronous downstream calls. You don't have to write your own, either. Netflix's Hystrix library (*http://bit.ly/1wxQtwW*) is a JVM circuit breaker abstraction that comes with some powerful monitoring, but other implementations exist for different technology stacks, such as Polly for .NET (*http://bit.ly/1CIDFuT*), or the circuit_breaker mixin for Ruby (*http://bit.ly/1CIDFLp*).

In many ways, bulkheads are the most important of these three patterns. Timeouts and circuit breakers help you free up resources when they are becoming constrained, but bulkheads can ensure they don't become constrained in the first place. Hystrix allows you, for example, to implement bulkheads that actually reject requests in certain conditions to ensure that resources don't become even more saturated; this is known as *load shedding*. Sometimes rejecting a request is the best way to stop an important system from becoming overwhelmed and being a bottleneck for multiple upstream services.

Isolation

The more one service depends on another being up, the more the health of one impacts the ability of the other to do its job. If we can use integration techniques that allow a downstream server to be offline, upstream services are less likely to be affected by outages, planned or unplanned.

There is another benefit to increasing isolation between services. When services are isolated from each other, much less coordination is needed between service owners. The less coordination needed between teams, the more autonomy those teams have, as they are able to operate and evolve their services more freely.

Idempotency

In *idempotent* operations, the outcome doesn't change after the first application, even if the operation is subsequently applied multiple times. If operations are idempotent, we can repeat the call multiple times without adverse impact. This is very useful when we want to replay messages that we aren't sure have been processed, a common way of recovering from error.

Let's consider a simple call to add some points as a result of one of our customers placing an order. We might make a call with the sort of payload shown in Example 11-1.

Example 11-1. Crediting points to an account

```
<credit>
  <amount>100</amount>
  <forAccount>1234</account>
</credit>
```

If this call is received multiple times, we would add 100 points multiple times. As it stands, therefore, this call is not idempotent. With a bit more information, though, we allow the points bank to make this call idempotent, as shown in Example 11-2.

Example 11-2. Adding more information to the points credit to make it idempotent

```
<credit>
  <amount>100</amount>
  <forAccount>1234</account>
  <reason>
    <forPurchase>4567</forPurchase>
  </reason>
</credit>
```

Now we know that this credit relates to a specific order, 4567. Assuming that we could receive only one credit for a given order, we could apply this credit again without increasing the overall number of points.

This mechanism works just as well with event-based collaboration, and can be especially useful if you have multiple instances of the same type of service subscribing to events. Even if we store which events have been processed, with some forms of asynchronous message delivery there may be small windows where two workers can see the same message. By processing the events in an idempotent manner, we ensure this won't cause us any issues.

Some people get quite caught up with this concept, and assume it means that subsequent calls with the same parameters can't have *any* impact, which then leaves us in an interesting position. We really would still like to record the fact that a call was received in our logs, for example. We want to record the response time of the call and collect this data for monitoring. The key point here is that it is the underlying business operation that we are considering idempotent, not the entire state of the system.

Some of the HTTP verbs, such as GET and PUT, are defined in the HTTP specification to be idempotent, but for that to be the case, they rely on your service handling these calls in an idempotent manner. If you start making these verbs nonidempotent, but callers think they can safely execute them repeatedly, you may get yourself into a mess. Remember, just because you're using HTTP as an underlying protocol doesn't mean you get everything for free!

Scaling

We scale our systems in general for one of two reasons. First, to help deal with failure: if we're worried that something will fail, then having more of it will help, right? Second, we scale for performance, either in terms of handling more load, reducing latency, or both. Let's look at some common scaling techniques we can use and think about how they apply to microservice architectures.

Go Bigger

Some operations can just benefit from more grunt. Getting a bigger box with faster CPU and better I/O can often improve latency and throughput, allowing you to process more work in less time. However, this form of scaling, often called *vertical scaling*, can be expensive—sometimes one big server can cost more than two smaller servers with the same combined raw power, especially when you start getting to really big machines. Sometimes our software itself cannot do much with the extra resources available to it. Larger machines often just give us more CPU cores, but not enough of our software is written to take advantage of them. The other problem is that this form of scaling may not do much to improve our server's resiliency if we only have one of them! Nonetheless, this can be a good quick win, especially if you're using a virtualization provider that lets you resize machines easily.

Splitting Workloads

As outlined in Chapter 6, having a single microservice per host is certainly preferable to a multiservice-per-host model. Initially, however, many people decide to coexist multiple microservices on one box to keep costs down or to simplify host management (although that is an arguable reason). As the microservices are independent processes that communicate over the network, it should be an easy task to then move them onto their own hosts to improve throughput and scaling. This can also increase the resiliency of the system, as a single host outage will impact a reduced number of microservices.

Of course, we could also use the need for increased scale to split an existing microservice into parts to better handle the load. As a simplistic example, let's imagine that our accounts service provides the ability to create and manage individual customers' financial accounts, but also exposes an API for running queries to generate reports. This query capability places a significant load on the system. The query capacity is considered noncritical, as it isn't needed to keep orders flowing in during the day. The ability to manage the financial records for our customers *is* critical, though, and we can't afford for it to be down. By splitting these two capabilities into separate services, we reduce the load on the critical accounts service, and introduce a new accounts reporting service that is designed not only with querying in mind (perhaps using some of the techniques we outlined in Chapter 4), but also as a noncritical system doesn't need to be deployed in as resilient a way as the core accounts service.

Spreading Your Risk

One way to scale for resilience is to ensure that you don't put all your eggs in one basket. A simplistic example of this is making sure that you don't have multiple services on one host, where an outage would impact multiple services. But let's consider what *host* means. In most situations nowadays, a *host* is actually a virtual concept. So what if I have all of my services on different hosts, but all those hosts are actually virtual hosts, running on the same physical box? If that box goes down, I could lose multiple services. Some virtualization platforms enable you to ensure that your hosts are distributed across multiple different physical boxes to reduce this chance.

For internal virtualization platforms, it is a common practice to have the virtual machine's root partition mapped to a single SAN (storage area network). If that SAN goes down, it can take down all connected VMs. SANs are big, expensive, and designed not to fail. That said, I have had big expensive SANs fail on me at least twice in the last 10 years, and each time the results were fairly serious.

Another common form of separation to reduce failure is to ensure that not all your services are running in a single rack in the data center, or that your services are distributed across more than one data center. If you're using an underlying service provider, it is important to know if a service-level agreement (SLA) is offered and plan accordingly. If you need to ensure your services are down for no more than four hours every quarter, but your hosting provider can only guarantee a downtime of eight hours per quarter, you have to either change the SLA, or come up with an alternative solution.

AWS, for example, is split into regions, which you can think of as distinct clouds. Each region is in turn split into two or more availability zones (AZs). AZs are AWS's equivalent of a data center. It is essential to have services distributed across multiple availability zones, as AWS does not offer any guarantees about the availability of a single node, or even an entire availability zone. For its compute service, it offers only a 99.95% uptime over a given monthly period of the region as a whole, so you'll want to distribute your workloads across multiple availability zones inside a single region. For some people, this isn't good enough, and instead they run their services across multiple regions too.

It should be noted, of course, that because providers give you an SLA *guarantee*, they will tend to limit their liability! If them missing their targets costs you customers and a large amount of money, you might find yourself searching through contracts to see if you can claw anything back from them. Therefore, I would strongly suggest you understand the impact of a supplier failing in its obligations to you, and work out if you need to have a plan B (or C) in your pocket. More than one client I've worked with has had a disaster recovery hosting platform with a different supplier, for example, to ensure they weren't too vulnerable to the mistakes of one company.

Load Balancing

When you need your service to be resilient, you want to avoid single points of failure. For a typical microservice that exposes a synchronous HTTP endpoint, the easiest way to achieve this is to have multiple hosts running your microservice instance, sitting behind a load balancer, as shown in Figure 11-4. To consumers of the microservice, you don't know if you are talking to one microservice instance or a hundred.

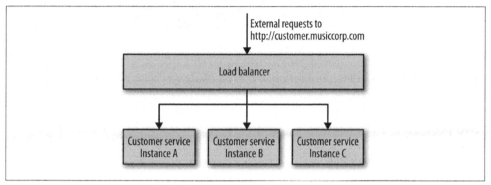

Figure 11-4. An example of a load balancing approach to scale the number of customer service instances

Load balancers come in all shapes and sizes, from big and expensive hardware appliances to software based load balancers like mod_proxy. They all share some key capabilities. They distribute calls sent to them to one or more instances based on some algorithm, remove instances when they are no longer healthy, and hopefully add them back in when they are.

Some load balancers provide useful features. A common one is *SSL termination*, where inbound HTTPS connections to the load balancer are transformed to HTTP connections once they hit the instance itself. Historically, the overhead of managing SSL was significant enough that having a load balancer handle this process for you was fairly useful. Nowadays, this is as much about simplifying the set-up of the individual hosts running the instance. The point of using HTTPS, though, is to ensure that the requests aren't vulnerable to a man-in-the-middle attack, as we discussed in Chapter 9, so if we use SSL termination, we are potentially exposing ourselves somewhat. One mitigation is to have all the instances of the microservice inside a single VLAN, as we see in Figure 11-5. A VLAN is a virtual local area network, that is isolated in such a way that requests from outside it can come only via a router, and in this case our router is also our SSL-terminating load balancer. The only communication to the microservice from outside the VLAN comes over HTTPS, but internally everything is HTTP.

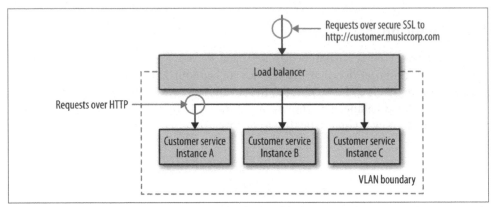

Figure 11-5. Using HTTPS termination at the load balancer with a VLAN for improved security

AWS provides HTTPS-terminating load balancers in the form of ELBs (elastic load balancers) and you can use its security groups or virtual private clouds (VPCs) to implement the VLAN. Otherwise, software like mod_proxy can play a similar role as a software load balancer. Many organizations have hardware load balancers, which can be difficult to automate. In such circumstances I have found myself advocating for software load balancers sitting *behind* the hardware load balancers to allow teams the freedom to reconfigure these as required. You do want to watch for the fact that all too often the hardware load balancers themselves are single points of failure! Whatever approach you take, when considering the configuration of a load balancer, treat it as you treat the configuration of your service: make sure it is stored in version control and can be applied automatically.

Load balancers allow us to add more instances of our microservice in a way that is transparent to any service consumers. This gives us an increased ability to handle load, and also reduce the impact of a single host failing. However, many, if not most, of your microservices will have some sort of persistent data store, probably a database sitting on a different machine. If we have multiple microservice instances on different machines, but only a single host running the database instance, our database is still a single source of failure. We'll talk about patterns to handle this shortly.

Worker-Based Systems

Load balancing isn't the only way to have multiple instances of your service share load and reduce fragility. Depending on the nature of the operations, a worker-based system could be just as effective. Here, a collection of instances all work on some shared backlog of work. This could be a number of Hadoop processes, or perhaps a number of listeners to a shared queue of work. These types of operations are well suited to batch work or asynchronous jobs. Think of tasks like image thumbnail processing, sending email, or generating reports.

The model also works well for *peaky* load, where you can spin up additional instances on demand to match the load coming in. As long as the work queue itself is resilient, this model can be used to scale both for improved throughput of work, but also for improved resiliency—the impact of a worker failing (or not being there) is easy to deal with. Work will take longer, but nothing gets lost.

I've seen this work well in organizations where there is lots of unused compute capacity at certain times of day. For example, overnight you might not need as many machines to run your ecommerce system, so you can temporarily use them to run workers for a reporting job instead.

With worker-based systems, although the workers themselves don't need to be that reliable, the system that contains the work to be done does. You could handle this by running a persistent message broker, for example, or perhaps a system like Zookeeper. The benefit here is that if we use existing software for this purpose, someone has done much of the hard work for us. However, we still need to know how to set up and maintain these systems in a resilient fashion.

Starting Again

The architecture that gets you started may not be the architecture that keeps you going when your system has to handle very different volumes of load. As Jeff Dean said in his presentation "Challenges in Building Large-Scale Information Retrieval Systems" (WSDM 2009 conference), you should "design for ~10× growth, but plan to rewrite before ~100×." At certain points, you need to do something pretty radical to support the next level of growth.

Recall the story of Gilt, which we touched on in Chapter 6. A simple monolithic Rails application did well for Gilt for two years. Its business became increasingly successful, which meant more customers and more load. At a certain tipping point, the company had to redesign the application to handle the load it was seeing.

A redesign may mean splitting apart an existing monolith, as it did for Gilt. Or it might mean picking new data stores that can handle the load better, which we'll look at in a moment. It could also mean adopting new techniques, such as moving from synchronous request/response to event-based systems, adopting new deployment platforms, changing whole technology stacks, or everything in between.

There is a danger that people will see the need to rearchitect when certain scaling thresholds are reached as a reason to build for massive scale from the beginning. This can be disastrous. At the start of a new project, we often don't know exactly what we want to build, nor do we know if it will be successful. We need to be able to rapidly experiment, and understand what capabilities we need to build. If we tried building for massive scale up front, we'd end up front-loading a huge amount of work to prepare for load that may never come, while diverting effort away from more important activities, like understanding if anyone will want to actually use our product. Eric Ries tells the story of spending six months building a product that no one ever downloaded. He reflected that he could have put up a link on a web page that 404'd when people clicked on it to see if there was any demand, spent six months on the beach instead, and learned just as much!

The need to change our systems to deal with scale isn't a sign of failure. It is a sign of success.

Scaling Databases

Scaling stateless microservices is fairly straightforward. But what if we are storing data in a database? We'll need to know how to scale that too. Different types of databases provide different forms of scaling, and understanding what form suits your use case best will ensure you select the right database technology from the beginning.

Availability of Service Versus Durability of Data

Straight off, it is important to separate the concept of availability of the service from the durability of the data itself. You need to understand that these are two different things, and as such they will have different solutions.

For example, I could store a copy of all data written to my database in a resilient filesystem. If the database goes down, my data isn't lost, as I have a copy, but the database itself isn't available, which may make my microservice unavailable too. A more common model would be using a standby. All data written to the primary database gets copied to the standby replica database. If the primary goes down, my data is safe, but without a mechanism to either bring it back up or promote the replica to the primary, we don't have an available database, even though our data is safe.

Scaling for Reads

Many services are read-mostly. Think of a catalog service that stores information for the items we have for sale. We add records for new items on a fairly irregular basis, and it wouldn't at all be surprising if we get more than 100 reads of our catalog's data for every write. Happily, scaling for reads is much easier than scaling for writes. Caching of data can play a large part here, and we'll discuss that in more depth shortly. Another model is to make use of *read replicas*.

In a relational database management system (RDBMS) like MySQL or Postgres, data can be copied from a primary node to one or more replicas. This is often done to ensure that a copy of our data is kept safe, but we can also use it to distribute our reads. A service could direct all writes to the single primary node, but distribute reads to one or more read replicas, as we see in Figure 11-6. The replication from the primary database to the replicas happens at some point after the write. This means that with this technique reads may sometimes see *stale* data until the replication has completed. Eventually the reads will see the consistent data. Such a setup is called *eventually consistent*, and if you can handle the temporary inconsistency it is a fairly easy and common way to help scale systems. We'll look into this in more depth shortly when we look at the CAP theorem.

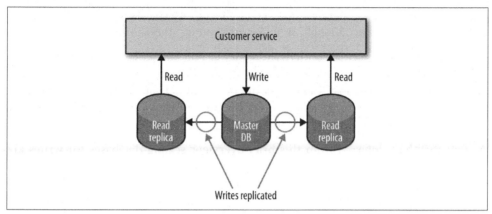

Figure 11-6. Using read replicas to scale reads

Years ago, using read replicas to scale was all the rage, although nowadays I would suggest you look to caching first, as it can deliver much more significant improvements in performance, often with less work.

Scaling for Writes

Reads are comparatively easy to scale. What about writes? One approach is to use *sharding*. With sharding, you have multiple database nodes. You take a piece of data to be written, apply some hashing function to the key of the data, and based on the result of the function learn where to send the data. To pick a very simplistic (and actually bad) example, imagine that customer records A–M go to one database instance, and N–Z another. You can manage this yourself in your application, but some databases, like Mongo, handle much of it for you.

The complexity with sharding for writes comes from handling queries. Looking up an individual record is easy, as I can just apply the hashing function to find which instance the data should be on, and then retrieve it from the correct shard. But what about queries that span the data in multiple nodes—for example, finding all the customers who are over 18? If you want to query all shards, you either need to query each individual shard and join in memory, or have an alternative read store where both data sets are available. Often querying across shards is handled by an asynchronous mechanism, using cached results. Mongo uses map/reduce jobs, for example, to perform these queries.

One of the questions that emerges with sharded systems is, what happens if I want to add an extra database node? In the past, this would often require significant downtime—especially for large clusters—as you might have to take the entire database down and rebalance the data. More recently, more systems support adding extra shards to a live system, where the rebalancing of data happens in the background; Cassandra, for example, handles this very well. Adding shards to an existing cluster isn't for the faint of heart, though, so make sure you test this thoroughly.

Sharding for writes may scale for write volume, but may not improve resiliency. If customer records A–M always go to Instance X, and Instance X is unavailable, access to records A–M can be lost. Cassandra offers additional capabilities here, where we can ensure that data is replicated to multiple nodes in a *ring* (Cassandra's term for a collection of Cassandra nodes).

As you may have inferred from this brief overview, scaling databases for writes are where things get very tricky, and where the capabilities of the various databases really start to become differentiated. I often see people changing database technology when they start hitting limits on how easily they can scale their existing write volume. If this happens to you, buying a bigger box is often the quickest way to solve the problem, but in the background you might want to look at systems like Cassandra, Mongo, or Riak to see if their alternative scaling models might offer you a better long-term solution.

Shared Database Infrastructure

Some types of databases, such as the traditional RDBMS, separate the concept of the database itself and the schema. This means one running database could host multiple, independent schemas, one for each microservice. This can be very useful in terms of reducing the number of machines we need to run our system, but we are introducing a significant single point of failure. If this database infrastructure goes down, it can impact multiple microservices at once, potentially resulting in a catastrophic outage. If you are running this sort of setup, make sure you consider the risks. And be very sure that the database itself is as resilient as it can be.

CQRS

The Command-Query Responsibility Segregation (CQRS) pattern refers to an alternate model for storing and querying information. With normal databases, we use one system for performing modifications to data and querying the data. With CQRS, part of the system deals with commands, which capture requests to modify state, while another part of the system deals with queries.

Commands come in requesting changes in state. These commands are validated, and if they work, they will be applied to the model. Commands should contain information about their intent. They can be processed synchronously or asynchronously, allowing for different models to handle scaling; we could, for example, just queue up inbound requests and process them later.

The key takeaway here is that the internal models used to handle commands and queries are themselves completely separate. For example, I might choose to handle and process commands as events, perhaps just storing the list of commands in a data store (a process known as *event sourcing*). My query model could query an event store and create projections from stored events to assemble the state of domain objects, or could just pick up a feed from the command part of the system to update a different type of store. In many ways, we get the same benefits of read replicas that we discussed earlier, without the requirement that the backing store for the replicas be the same as the data store used to handle data modifications.

This form of separation allows for different types of scaling. The command and query parts of our system could live in different services, or on different hardware, and could make use of radically different types of data store. This can unlock a large number of ways to handle scale. You could even support different types of read format by having multiple implementations of the query piece, perhaps supporting a graph-based representation of your data, or a key/value-based form of your data.

Be warned, however: this sort of pattern is quite a shift away from a model where a single data store handles all our CRUD operations. I've seen more than one experienced development team struggle to get this pattern right!

Caching

Caching is a commonly used performance optimization whereby the previous result of some operation is stored, so that subsequent requests can use this stored value rather than spending time and resources recalculating the value. More often than not, caching is about eliminating needless round-trips to databases or other services to serve results faster. Used well, it can yield huge performance benefits. The reason that HTTP scales so well in handling large numbers of requests is that the concept of caching is built in.

Even with a simple monolithic web application, there are quite a few choices as to where and how to cache. With a microservice architecture, where each service is its own source of data and behavior, we have many more choices to make about where and how to cache. With a distributed system, we typically think of caching either on the client side or on the server side. But which is best?

Client-Side, Proxy, and Server-Side Caching

In client-side caching, the client stores the cached result. The client gets to decide when (and if) it goes and retrieves a fresh copy. Ideally, the downstream service will provide hints to help the client understand what to do with the response, so it knows when and if to make a new request. With proxy caching, a proxy is placed between the client and the server. A great example of this is using a reverse proxy or content delivery network (CDN). With server-side caching, the server handles caching responsibility, perhaps making use of a system like Redis or Memcache, or even a simple in-memory cache.

Which one makes the most sense depends on what you are trying to optimize. Client-side caching can help reduce network calls drastically, and can be one of the fastest ways of reducing load on a downstream service. In this case, the client is in charge of the caching behavior, and if you want to make changes to how caching is done, rolling out changes to a number of consumers could be difficult. Invalidation of stale data can also be trickier, although we'll discuss some coping mechanisms for this in a moment.

With proxy caching, everything is opaque to both the client and server. This is often a very simple way to add caching to an existing system. If the proxy is designed to cache generic traffic, it can also cache more than one service; a common example is a reverse proxy like Squid or Varnish, which can cache any HTTP traffic. Having a proxy between the client and server does introduce additional network hops, although in my experience it is very rare that this causes problems, as the performance optimizations resulting from the caching itself outweigh any additional network costs.

With server-side caching, everything is opaque to the clients; they don't need to worry about anything. With a cache near or inside a service boundary, it can be easier to reason about things like invalidation of data, or track and optimize cache hits. In a situation where you have multiple types of clients, a server-side cache could be the fastest way to improve performance.

For every public-facing website I've worked on, we've ended up doing a mix of all three approaches. But for more than one distributed system, I've gotten away with no caching at all. But it all comes down to knowing what load you need to handle, how fresh your data needs to be, and what your system can do right now. Knowing that you have a number of different tools at your disposal is just the beginning.

Caching in HTTP

HTTP provides some really useful controls to help us cache either on the client side or server side, which are worth understanding even if you aren't using HTTP itself.

First, with HTTP, we can use `cache-control` directives in our responses to clients. These tell clients if they should cache the resource at all, and if so how long they should cache it for in seconds. We also have the option of setting an `Expires` header, where instead of saying how long a piece of content can be cached for, we specify a time and date at which a resource should be considered stale and fetched again. The nature of the resources you are sharing determines which one is most likely to fit. Standard static website content like CSS or images often fit well with a simple `cache-control` time to live (TTL). On the other hand, if you know in advance when a new version of a resource will be updated, setting an `Expires` header will make more sense. All of this is very useful in stopping a client from even needing to make a request to the server in the first place.

Aside from `cache-control` and `Expires`, we have another option in our arsenal of HTTP goodies: Entity Tags, or ETags. An ETag is used to determine if the value of a resource has changed. If I update a customer record, the URI to the resource is the same, but the value is different, so I would expect the ETag to change. This becomes powerful when we're using what is called a *conditional GET*. When making a GET request, we can specify additional headers, telling the service to send us the resource only if some criteria are met.

For example, let's imagine we fetch a customer record, and its ETag comes back as o5t6fkd2sa. Later on, perhaps because a `cache-control` directive has told us the resource should be considered stale, we want to make sure we get the latest version. When issuing the subsequent GET request, we can pass in a `If-None-Match: o5t6fkd2sa`. This tells the server that we want the resource at the specified URI, unless it already matches this ETag value. If we already have the up-to-date version, the service sends us a `304 Not Modified` response, telling us we have the latest version. If there is a newer version available, we get a `200 OK` with the changed resource, and a new ETag for the resource.

The fact that these controls are built into such a widely used specification means we get to take advantage of a lot of preexisting software that handles the caching for us. Reverse proxies like Squid or Varnish can sit transparently on the network between client and server, storing and expiring cached content as required. These systems are geared toward serving huge numbers of concurrent requests very fast, and are a standard way of scaling public-facing websites. CDNs like AWS's CloudFront or Akamai can ensure that requests are routed to caches near the calling client, making sure that traffic doesn't go halfway round the world when it doesn't need to. And more prosaically, HTTP client libraries and client caches can handle a lot of this work for us.

ETags, `Expires`, and `cache-control` can overlap a bit, and if you aren't careful you can end up giving conflicting information if you decide to use all of them! For a more in-depth discussion of the various merits, take a look at the book *REST In Practice* (*http://bit.ly/rest-practice*) (O'Reilly) or read section 13 of the HTTP 1.1 specification (*http://bit.ly/1JOSoVh*), which describes how both clients and servers are supposed to implement these various controls.

Whether you decide to use HTTP as an interservice protocol, caching at the client and reducing the need for round-trips to the client is well worth it. If you decide to pick a different protocol, understand when and how you can provide hints to the client to help it understand how long it can cache for.

Caching for Writes

Although you'll find yourself using caching for reads more often, there are some use cases where caching for writes make sense. For example, if you make use of a write-behind cache, you can write to a local cache, and at some later point the data will be flushed to a downstream source, probably the canonical source of data. This can be useful when you have bursts of writes, or when there is a good chance that the same data will be written multiple times. When used to buffer and potentially batch writes, write-behind caches can be a useful further performance optimization.

With a write-behind cache, if the buffered writes are suitably persistent, even if the downstream service is unavailable we could queue up the writes and send them through when it is available again.

Caching for Resilience

Caching can be used to implement resiliency in case of failure. With client-side caching, if the downstream service is unavailable, the client could decide to simply use cached but potentially stale data. We could also use something like a reverse proxy to serve up stale data. For some systems, being available even with stale data is better than not returning a result at all, but that is a judgment call you'll have to make. Obviously, if we don't have the requested data in the cache, then we can't do much to help, but there are ways to mitigate this.

A technique I saw used at the *Guardian*, and subsequently elsewhere, was to crawl the existing *live* site periodically to generate a static version of the website that could be served in the event of an outage. Although this crawled version wasn't as fresh as the cached content served from the live system, in a pinch it could ensure that a version of the site would get displayed.

Hiding the Origin

With a normal cache, if a request results in a cache miss, the request goes on to the origin to fetch the fresh data with the caller blocking, waiting on the result. In the normal course of things, this is to be expected. But if we suffer a massive cache miss, perhaps because an entire machine (or group of machines) that provide our cache fail, a large number of requests will hit the origin.

For those services that serve up highly cachable data, it is common for the origin itself to be scaled to handle only a fraction of the total traffic, as most requests get served out of memory by the caches that sit in front of the origin. If we suddenly get a thundering herd due to an entire cache region vanishing, our origin could be pummelled out of existence.

One way to protect the origin in such a situation is never to allow requests to go to the origin in the first place. Instead, the origin itself populates the cache asynchronously when needed, as shown in Figure 11-7. If a cache miss is caused, this triggers an event that the origin can pick up on, alerting it that it needs to repopulate the cache. So if an entire shard has vanished, we can rebuild the cache in the background. We could decide to block the original request waiting for the region to be repopulated, but this could cause contention on the cache itself, leading to further problems. It's more likely if we are prioritizing keeping the system stable that we would fail the original request, but it would fail fast.

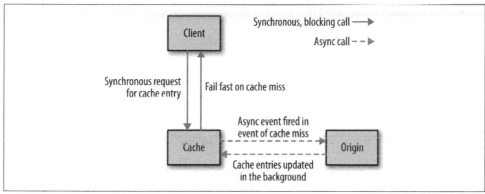

Figure 11-7. Hiding the origin from the client and populating the cache asynchronously

This sort of approach may not make sense for some situations, but it can be a way to ensure the system remains up when parts of it fail. By failing requests fast, and ensuring we don't take up resources or increase latency, we avoid a failure in our cache from cascading downstream and give ourselves a chance to recover.

Keep It Simple

Be careful about caching in too many places! The more caches between you and the source of fresh data, the more stale the data can be, and the harder it can be to determine the freshness of the data that a client eventually sees. This can be especially problematic with a microservice architecture where you have multiple services involved in a call chain. Again, the more caching you have, the harder it will be to assess the freshness of any piece of data. So if you think a cache is a good idea, keep it simple, stick to one, and think carefully before adding more!

Cache Poisoning: A Cautionary Tale

With caching we often think that if we get it wrong the worst thing that can happen is we serve stale data for a bit. But what happens if you end up serving stale data forever? Earlier I mentioned the project I worked on where we were using a strangler application to help intercept calls to multiple legacy systems with a view of incrementally retiring them. Our application operated effectively as a proxy. Traffic to our application was routed through to the legacy application. On the way back, we did a few housekeeping things; for example, we made sure that the results from the legacy application had proper HTTP cache headers applied.

One day, shortly after a normal routine release, something odd started happening. A bug had been introduced whereby a small subset of pages were falling through a logic condition in our cache header insertion code, resulting in us not changing the header at all. Unfortunately, this downstream application had also been changed sometime previously to include an `Expires: Never` HTTP header. This hadn't had any effect earlier, as we were overriding this header. Now we weren't.

Our application made heavy use of Squid to cache HTTP traffic, and we noticed the problem quite quickly as we were seeing more requests bypassing Squid itself to hit our application servers. We fixed the cache header code and pushed out a release, and also manually cleared the relevant region of the Squid cache. However, that wasn't enough.

As I mentioned earlier, you can cache in multiple places. When it comes to serving up content to users of a public-facing web application, you could have multiple caches between you and your customer. Not only might you be fronting your website with something like a CDN, but some ISPs make use of caching. Can you control those caches? And even if you could, there is one cache that you have little control over: the cache in a user's browser.

Those pages with `Expires: Never` stuck in the caches of many of our users, and would never be invalidated until the cache became full or the user cleaned them out manually. Clearly we couldn't make either thing happen; our only option was to change the URLs of these pages so they were refetched.

Caching can be very powerful indeed, but you need to understand the full path of data that is cached from source to destination to really appreciate its complexities and what can go wrong.

Autoscaling

If you are lucky enough to have fully automatable provisioning of virtual hosts, and can fully automate the deployment of your microservice instances, then you have the building blocks to allow you to automatically scale your microservices.

For example, you could also have the scaling triggered by well-known trends. You might know that your system's peak load is between 9 a.m. and 5 p.m., so you bring up additional instances at 8:45 a.m., and turn them off at 5:15 p.m.. If you're using something like AWS (which has very good support for autoscaling built in), turning off instances you don't need any longer will help save money. You'll need data to understand how your load changes over time, from day to day, week to week. Some businesses have obvious seasonal cycles too, so you may need data going back a fair way to make proper judgment calls.

On the other hand, you could be reactive, bringing up additional instances when you see an increase in load or an instance failure, and remove instances when you no longer needed them. Knowing how fast you can scale up once you spot an upward trend is key. If you know you'll only get a couple of minutes' notice about an increase in load, but scaling up will take you at least 10 minutes, you know you'll need to keep extra capacity around to bridge this gap. Having a good suite of load tests is almost essential here. You can use them to test your autoscaling rules. If you don't have tests that can reproduce different loads that will trigger scaling, then you're only going to find out in production if you got the rules wrong. And the consequences of failure aren't great!

A news site is a great example of a type of business where you may want a mix of predictive and reactive scaling. On the last news site I worked on, we saw very clear daily trends, with views climbing from the morning to lunchtime and then starting to decline. This pattern was repeated day in, day out, with traffic less pronounced at the weekend. That gave you a fairly clear trend that could drive proactive scaling up (and down) of resources. On the other hand, a big news story would cause an unexpected spike, requiring more capacity at often short notice.

I actually see autoscaling used much more for handling failure of instances than for reacting to load conditions. AWS lets you specify rules like "There should be at least 5 instances in this group," so if one goes down a new one is automatically launched. I've seen this approach lead to a fun game of whack-a-mole when someone forgets to turn off the rule and then tries to take down the instances for maintenance, only to see them keep spinning up!

Both reactive and predictive scaling are very useful, and can help you be much more cost effective if you're using a platform that allows you to pay only for the computing resources you use. But they also require careful observation of the data available to you. I'd suggest using autoscaling for failure conditions first while you collect the data. Once you want to start scaling for load, make sure you are very cautious about scaling down too quickly. In most situations, having more computing power at your hands than you need is much better than not having enough!

CAP Theorem

We'd like to have it all, but unfortunately we know we can't. And when it comes to distributed systems like those we build using microservice architectures, we even have a mathematical proof that tells us we can't. You may well have heard about the CAP theorem, especially in discussions about the merits of various different types of data stores. At its heart it tells us that in a distributed system, we have three things we can trade off against each other: *consistency*, *availability*, and *partition tolerance*. Specifically, the theorem tells us that we get to keep two in a failure mode.

Consistency is the system characteristic by which I will get the same answer if I go to multiple nodes. Availability means that every request receives a response. Partition tolerance is the system's ability to handle the fact that communication between its parts is sometimes impossible.

Since Eric Brewer published his original conjecture, the idea has gained a mathematical proof. I'm not going to dive into the math of the proof itself, as not only is this not that sort of book, but I can also guarantee that I would get it wrong. Instead, let's use some worked examples that will help us understand that under it all, the CAP theorem is a distillation of a very logical set of reasoning.

We've already talked about some simple database scaling techniques. Let's use one of these to probe the ideas behind the CAP theorem. Let's imagine that our inventory service is deployed across two separate data centers, as shown in Figure 11-8. Backing our service instance in each data center is a database, and these two databases talk to each other to try to synchronize data between them. Reads and writes are done via the local database node, and replication is used to synchronize the data between the nodes.

Now let's think about what happens when something fails. Imagine that something as simple as the network link between the two data centers stops working. The synchronization at this point fails. Writes made to the primary database in DC1 will not propagate to DC2, and vice versa. Most databases that support these setups also support some sort of queuing technique to ensure that we can recover from this afterward, but what happens in the meantime?

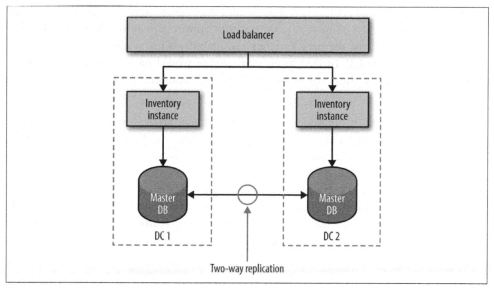

Figure 11-8. Using multiprimary replication to share data between two database nodes

Sacrificing Consistency

Let's assume that we don't shut the inventory service down entirely. If I make a change now to the data in DC1, the database in DC2 doesn't see it. This means any requests made to our inventory node in DC2 see potentially stale data. In other words, our system is still *available* in that both nodes are able to serve requests, and we have kept the system running despite the *partition*, but we have lost *consistency*. This is often called a *AP* system. We don't get to keep all three.

During this partition, if we keep accepting writes then we accept the fact that at some point in the future they have to be resynchronized. The longer the partition lasts, the more difficult this resynchronization can become.

The reality is that even if we don't have a network failure between our database nodes, replication of data is not instantaneous. As touched on earlier, systems that are happy to cede consistency to keep partition tolerance and availability are said to be *eventually consistent*; that is, we expect at some point in the future that all nodes will see the updated data, but it won't happen at once so we have to live with the possibility that users see old data.

Sacrificing Availability

What happens if we need to keep consistency and want to drop something else instead? Well, to keep consistency, each database node needs to know the copy of the data it has is the same as the other database node. Now in the partition, if the database nodes can't talk to each other, they cannot coordinate to ensure consistency. We are unable to guarantee consistency, so our only option is to refuse to respond to the request. In other words, we have sacrificed availability. Our system is consistent and partition tolerant, or CP. In this mode our service would have to work out how to degrade functionality until the partition is healed and the database nodes can be resynchronized.

Consistency across multiple nodes is really hard. There are few things (perhaps nothing) harder in distributed systems. Think about it for a moment. Imagine I want to read a record from the local database node. How do I know it is up to date? I have to go and ask the other node. But I also have to ask that database node to not allow it to be updated while the read completes; in other words, I need to initiate a transactional read across multiple database nodes to ensure consistency. But in general people don't do transactional reads, do they? Because transactional reads are slow. They require locks. A read can block an entire system up. All consistent systems require some level of locking to do their job.

As we've already discussed, distributed systems have to expect failure. Consider our transactional read across a set of consistent nodes. I ask a remote node to lock a given record while the read is initiated. I complete the read, and ask the remote node to release its lock, but now I can't talk to it. What happens now? Locks are really hard to get right even in a single process system, and are significantly more difficult to implement well in a distributed system.

Remember when we talked about distributed transactions in Chapter 5? The core reason they are challenging is because of this problem with ensuring consistency across multiple nodes.

Getting multinode consistency right is so hard that I would strongly, *strongly* suggest that if you need it, don't try to invent it yourself. Instead, pick a data store or lock service that offers these characteristics. Consul, for example, which we'll discuss shortly, implements a strongly consistent key/value store designed to share configuration between multiple nodes. Along with "Friends don't let friends write their own crypto" should go "Friends don't let friends write their own distributed consistent data store." If you think you need to write your own CP data store, read all the papers on the subject first, then get a PhD, and then look forward to spending a few years getting it wrong. Meanwhile, I'll be using something off the shelf that does it for me, or more likely trying *really hard* to build eventually consistent AP systems instead.

Sacrificing Partition Tolerance?

We get to pick two, right? So we've got our eventually consistent AP system. We have our consistent, but hard to build and scale, CP system. Why not a CA system? Well, how can we sacrifice partition tolerance? If our system has no partition tolerance, it can't run over a network. In other words, it needs to be a single process operating locally. CA systems don't exist in distributed systems.

AP or CP?

Which is right, AP or CP? Well, the reality is *it depends*. As the people building the system, we know the trade-off exists. We know that AP systems scale more easily and are simpler to build, and we know that a CP system will require more work due to the challenges in supporting distributed consistency. But we may not understand the business impact of this trade-off. For our inventory system, if a record is out of date by five minutes, is that OK? If the answer is yes, an AP system might be the answer. But what about the balance held for a customer in a bank? Can that be out of date? Without knowing the context in which the operation is being used, we can't know the right thing to do. Knowing about the CAP theorem just helps you understand that this trade-off exists and what questions to ask.

It's Not All or Nothing

Our system as a whole doesn't need to be either AP or CP. Our catalog could be AP, as we don't mind too much about a stale record. But we might decide that our inventory service needs to be CP, as we don't want to sell a customer something we don't have and then have to apologize later.

But individual services don't even need to be CP or AP.

Let's think about our points balance service, where we store records of how many loyalty points our customers have built up. We could decide that we don't care if the balance we show for a customer is stale, but that when it comes to updating a balance we need it to be consistent to ensure that customers don't use more points than they have available. Is this microservice CP, or AP, or is it both? Really, what we have done is push the trade-offs around the CAP theorem down to individual service capabilities.

Another complexity is that neither consistency nor availability is all or nothing. Many systems allow us a far more nuanced trade-off. For example, with Cassandra I can make different trade-offs for individual calls. So if I need strict consistency, I can perform a read that blocks until all replicas have responded confirming the value is consistent, or until a specific quorum of replicas have responded, or even just a single node. Obviously, if I block waiting for all replicas to report back and one of them is unavailable, I'll be blocking for a long time. But if I am satisfied with just a simple quorum of nodes reporting back, I can accept some lack of consistency to be less vulnerable to a single replica being unavailable.

You'll often see posts about people *beating* the CAP theorem. They haven't. What they have done is create a system where some capabilities are CP, and some are AP. The mathematical proof behind the CAP theorem holds. Despite many attempts at school, I've learned that you don't beat math.

And the Real World

Much of what we've talked about is the electronic world—bits and bytes stored in memory. We talk about consistency in an almost child-like fashion; we imagine that within the scope of the system we have created, we can stop the world and have it all make sense. And yet so much of what we build is just a reflection of the real world, and we don't get to control that, do we?

Let's revisit our inventory system. This maps to real-world, physical items. We keep a count in our system of how many albums we have. At the start of the day we had 100 copies of *Give Blood* by The Brakes. We sold one. Now we have 99 copies. Easy, right? By what happens if when the order was being sent out, someone knocks a copy of the album onto the floor and it gets stepped on and broken? What happens now? Our systems say 99, but there are 98 copies on the shelf.

What if we made our inventory system AP instead, and occasionally had to contact a user later on and tell him that one of his items is actually out of stock? Would that be the worst thing in the world? It would certainly be much easier to build, scale, and ensure it is correct.

We have to recognize that no matter how consistent our systems might be in and of themselves, they cannot know everything that happens, especially when we're keeping records of the real world. This is one of the main reasons why AP systems end up being the right call in many situations. Aside from the complexity of building CP systems, they can't fix all our problems anyway.

Service Discovery

Once you have more than a few microservices lying around, your attention inevitably turns to knowing where on earth everything is. Perhaps you want to know what is running in a given environment so you know what you should be monitoring. Maybe it's as simple as knowing where your accounts service is so that those microservices that use it know where to find it. Or perhaps you just want to make it easy for developers in your organization to know what APIs are available so they don't reinvent the wheel. Broadly speaking, all of these use cases fall under the banner of *service discovery*. And as always with microservices, we have quite a few different options at our disposal for dealing with it.

All of the solutions we'll look at handle things in two parts. First, they provide some mechanism for an instance to register itself and say, "I'm here!" Second, they provide a way to find the service once it's registered. Service discovery gets more complicated, though, when we are considering an environment where we are constantly destroying and deploying new instances of services. Ideally, we'd want whatever solution we pick to cope with this.

Let's look at some of the most common solutions to service delivery and consider our options.

DNS

It's nice to start simple. DNS lets us associate a name with the IP address of one or more machines. We could decide, for example, that our accounts service is always found at *accounts.musiccorp.com*. We would then have that entry point to the IP address of the host running that service, or perhaps have it resolve to a load balancer that is distributing load across a number of instances. This means we'd have to handle updating these entries as part of deploying our service.

When dealing with instances of a service in different environments, I have seen a convention-based domain template work well. For example, we might have a template defined as *<servicename>-<environment>.musiccorp.com*, giving us entries like *accounts-uat.musiccorp.com* or *accounts-dev.musiccorp.com*.

A more advanced way of handling different environments is to have different domain name servers for different environments. So I could assume that *accounts.musiccorp.com* is where I always find the accounts service, but it could resolve to different hosts depending on where I do the lookup. If you already have your environments sitting in different network segments and are comfortable with managing your own DNS servers and entries, this could be quite a neat solution, but it is a lot of work if you aren't getting other benefits from this setup.

DNS has a host of advantages, the main one being it is such a well-understood and well-used standard that almost any technology stack will support it. Unfortunately, while a number of services exist for managing DNS inside an organization, few of them seem designed for an environment where we are dealing with highly disposable hosts, making updating DNS entries somewhat painful. Amazon's Route53 service does a pretty good job of this, but I haven't seen a self-hosted option that is as good yet, although (as we'll discuss shortly) Consul may help us here. Aside from the problems in updating DNS entries, the DNS specification itself can cause us some issues.

DNS entries for domain names have a *time to live* (TTL). This is how long a client can consider the entry fresh. When we want to change the host to which the domain name refers, we update that entry, but we have to assume that clients will be holding on to the old IP for *at least* as long as the TTL states. DNS entries can get cached in multiple places (even the JVM will cache DNS entries unless you tell it not to), and the more places they are cached in, the more stale the entry can be.

One way to work around this problem is to have the domain name entry for your service point to a load balancer, which in turn points to the instances of your service, as shown in Figure 11-9. When you deploy a new instance, you can take the old one out of the load-balancer entry and add the new one. Some people use DNS round-robining, where the DNS entries themselves refer to a group of machines. This technique is extremely problematic, as the client is hidden from the underlying host, and therefore cannot easily stop routing traffic to one of the hosts should it become sick.

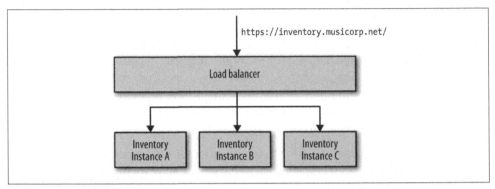

Figure 11-9. Using DNS to resolve to a load balancer to avoid stale DNS entries

As mentioned, DNS is well understood and widely supported. But it does have one or two downsides. I would suggest investigating whether it is a good fit for you before picking something more complex. For a situation where you have only single nodes, having DNS refer directly to hosts is probably fine. But for those situations where you need more than one instance of a host, have DNS entries resolve to load balancers that can handle putting individual hosts into and out of service as appropriate.

Dynamic Service Registries

The downsides of DNS as a way of finding nodes in a highly dynamic environment have led to a number of alternative systems, most of which involve the service registering itself with some central registry, which in turn offers the ability to look up these services later on. Often, these systems do more than just providing service registration and discovery, which may or may not be a good thing. This is a crowded field, so we'll just look at a few options to give you a sense of what is available.

Zookeeper

Zookeeper (*http://zookeeper.apache.org/*) was originally developed as part of the Hadoop project. It is used for an almost bewildering array of use cases, including configuration management, synchronizing data between services, leader election, message queues, and (usefully for us) as a naming service.

Like many similar types of systems, Zookeeper relies on running a number of nodes in a cluster to provide various guarantees. This means you should expect to be running at least three Zookeeper nodes. Most of the smarts in Zookeeper are around ensuring that data is replicated safely between these nodes, and that things remain consistent when nodes fail.

At its heart, Zookeeper provides a hierarchical namespace for storing information. Clients can insert new nodes in this hierarchy, change them, or query them. Furthermore, they can add watches to nodes to be told when they change. This means we could store the information about where our services are located in this structure, and as a client be told when they change. Zookeeper is often used as a general configuration store, so you could also store service-specific configuration in it, allowing you to do tasks like dynamically changing log levels or turning off features of a running system. Personally, I tend to shy away from the use of systems like Zookeeper as a configuration source, as I think it can make it harder to reason about the behavior of a given service.

Zookeeper itself is fairly generic in what it offers, which is why it is used for so many use cases. You can think of it just as a replicated tree of information that you can be alerted about when it changes. This means that you'll typically build things on top of it to suit your particular use case. Luckily, client libraries exist for most languages out there.

In the grand scheme of things, Zookeeper could be considered *old* by now, and doesn't provide us that much functionality out of the box to help with service discovery compared to some of the newer alternatives. That said, it is certainly tried and tested, and widely used. The underlying algorithms Zookeeper implements are quite hard to get right. I know one database vendor, for example, that was using Zookeeper just for leader election in order to ensure that a primary node got properly promoted during failure conditions. The client felt that Zookeeper was too heavyweight and spent a long time ironing out bugs in its own implementation of the PAXOS algorithm to replace what Zookeeper did. People often say you shouldn't write your own cryptography libraries. I'd extend that by saying you shouldn't write your own distributed coordination systems either. There is a lot to be said for using existing stuff that just works.

Consul

Like Zookeeper, Consul (*http://www.consul.io/*) supports both configuration management and service discovery. But it goes further than Zookeeper in providing more support for these key use cases. For example, it exposes an HTTP interface for service discovery, and one of Consul's killer features is that it actually provides a DNS server out of the box; specifically, it can serve SRV records, which give you both an IP and port for a given name. This means if part of your system uses DNS already and can support SRV records, you can just drop in Consul and start using it without any changes to your existing system.

Consul also builds in other capabilities that you might find useful, such as the ability to perform health checks on nodes. This means that Consul could well overlap the capabilities provided by other dedicated monitoring tools, although you would more likely use Consul as a source of this information and then pull it into a more comprehensive dashboard or alerting system. Consul's highly fault-tolerant design and focus on handling systems that make heavy use of ephemeral nodes does make me wonder, though, if it may end up replacing systems like Nagios and Sensu for some use cases.

Consul uses a RESTful HTTP interface for everything from registering a service, querying the key/value store, or inserting health checks. This makes integration with different technology stacks very straightforward. One of the other things I really like about Consul is that the team behind it has split out the underlying cluster management piece. Serf, which Consul sits on top of, handles detection of nodes in a cluster, failure management, and alerting. Consul then adds service discovery and configuration management. This separation of concerns appeals to me, which should be no surprise to you given the themes that run through this book!

Consul is very new, and given the complexity of the algorithms it uses, this would normally make me hesitant in recommending it for such an important job. That said, Hashicorp, the team behind it, certainly has a great track record in creating very useful open source technology (in the form of both Packer and Vagrant), the project is being actively developed, and I've spoken to a few people who are happily using it in production. Given that, I think it is well worth a look.

Eureka

Netflix's open source Eureka system (*http://bit.ly/15Co2I7*) bucks the trend of systems like Consul and Zookeeper in that it doesn't also try to be a general-purpose configuration store. It is actually very targeted in its use case.

Eureka also provides basic load-balancing capabilities in that it can support basic round-robin lookup of service instances. It provides a REST-based endpoint so you can write your own clients, or you can use its own Java client. The Java client provides additional capabilities, such as health checking of instances. Obviously if you bypass Eureka's own client and go directly to the REST endpoint, you're on your own there.

By having the clients deal with service discovery directly, we avoid the need for a separate process. However, you do require that every client implement service discovery. Netflix, which standardizes on the JVM, achieves this by having all clients use Eureka. If you're in a more polyglot environment, this may be more of a challenge.

Rolling Your Own

One approach I have used myself and seen done elsewhere is to roll your own system. On one project we were making heavy use of AWS, which offers the ability to add tags to instances. When launching service instances, I would apply tags to help define what the instance was and what it was used for. These allowed for some rich metadata to be associated with a given host, for example:

- service = accounts
- environment = production
- version = 154

I could then use the AWS APIs to query all the instances associated with a given AWS account to find machines I cared about. Here, AWS itself is handling the storing of the metadata associated with each instance, and providing us with the ability to query it. I then built command-line tools for interacting with these instances, and making dashboards for status monitoring becomes fairly easy, especially if you adopt the idea of having each service instance exposing health check details.

The last time I did this we didn't go as far as having services use the AWS APIs to find their service dependencies, but there is no reason why you couldn't. Obviously, if you want upstream services to be alerted when the location of a downstream service changes, you're on your own.

Don't Forget the Humans!

The systems we've looked at so far make it easy for a service instance to register itself and look up other services it needs to talk to. But as humans we sometimes want this information too. Whatever system you pick, make sure you have tools available that let you build reports and dashboards on top of these registries to create displays for humans, not just for computers.

Documenting Services

By decomposing our systems into finer-grained microservices, we're hoping to expose lots of seams in the form of APIs that people can use to do many, hopefully wonderful, things. If you get your discovery right, we know where things are. But how do we know what those things do, or how to use them? One option is obviously to have documentation about the APIs. Of course, documentation can often be out of date. Ideally, we'd ensure that our documentation is always up to date with the microservice API, and make it easy to see this documentation when we know where a service endpoint is. Two different pieces of technology, Swagger and HAL, try to make this a reality, and both are worth looking at.

Swagger

Swagger lets you describe your API in order to generate a very nice web UI that allows you to view the documentation and interact with the API via a web browser. The ability to execute requests is very nice: you can define POST templates, for example, making it clear what sort of content the server expects.

To do all of this, Swagger needs the service to expose a sidecar file matching the Swagger format. Swagger has a number of libraries for different languages that does this for you. For example, for Java you can annotate methods that match your API calls, and the file gets generated for you.

I like the end-user experience that Swagger gives you, but it does little for the incremental exploration concept at the heart of hypermedia. Still, it's a pretty nice way to expose documentation about your services.

HAL and the HAL Browser

By itself, the Hypertext Application Language (HAL) (*http://bit.ly/hal-spec*) is a standard that describes standards for hypermedia controls that we expose. As we covered in Chapter 4, hypermedia controls are the means by which we allow clients to progressively explore our APIs to use our service's capabilities in a less coupled fashion than other integration techniques. If you decide to adopt HAL's hypermedia standard, then not only can you make use of a wide number of client libraries for consuming the API (at the time of writing, the HAL wiki listed 50 supporting libraries for a number of different languages), but you can also make use of the HAL browser, which gives you a way to explore the API via a web browser.

Like Swagger, this UI can be used not only to act as living documentation, but also to execute calls against the service itself. Executing calls isn't quite as slick, though. Whereas with Swagger you can define templates to do things like issue a POST request, with HAL you're more on your own. The flipside to this is that the inherent power of hypermedia controls lets you much more effectively explore the API exposed by the service, as you can follow links around very easily. It turns out that web browsers are pretty good at that sort of thing!

Unlike with Swagger, all the information needed to drive this documentation and sandbox is embedded in the hypermedia controls. This is a double-edged sword. If you are already using hypermedia controls, it takes little effort to expose a HAL browser and have clients explore your API. However, if you aren't using hypermedia, you either can't use HAL or have to retrofit your API to use hypermedia, which is likely to be an exercise that breaks existing consumers.

The fact that HAL also describes a hypermedia standard with some supporting client libraries is an added bonus, and I suspect is a big reason why I've seen more uptake of HAL as a way of documenting APIs than Swagger for those people already using hypermedia controls. If you're using hypermedia, my recommendation is to go with HAL over Swagger. But if you're not using hypermedia and can't justify the switch, I'd definitely suggest giving Swagger a go.

The Self-Describing System

During the early evolution of SOA, standards like Universal Description, Discovery, and Integration (UDDI) emerged to help people make sense of what services were running. These approaches were fairly heavyweight, which led to alternative techniques to try to make sense of our systems. Martin Fowler discussed the concept of the humane registry (*http://bit.ly/1CIDHTn*), where a much more lightweight approach is simply to have a place where humans can record information about the services in the organization in something as basic as a wiki.

Getting a picture of our system and how it is behaving is important, especially when we're at scale. We've covered a number of different techniques that will help us gain understanding directly from our system. By tracking the health of our downstream services together with correlation IDs to help us see call chains, we can get real data in terms of how our services interrelate. Using service discovery systems like Consul, we can see where our microservices are running. HAL lets us see what capabilities are being hosted on any given endpoint, while our health-check pages and monitoring systems let us know the health of both the overall system and individual services.

All of this information is available programatically. All of this data allows us to make our humane registry more powerful than a simple wiki page that will no doubt get out of date. Instead, we should use it to harness and display all the information our system will be emitting. By creating custom dashboards, we can pull together the vast array of information that is available to help us make sense of our ecosystem.

By all means, start with something as simple as a static web page or wiki that perhaps scrapes in a bit of data from the live system. But look to pull in more and more information over time. Making this information readily available is a key tool to managing the emerging complexity that will come from running these systems at scale.

Summary

As a design approach, microservices are still fairly young, so although we have some notable experiences to draw upon, I'm sure the next few years will yield more useful patterns in handling them at scale. Nonetheless, I hope this chapter has outlined some steps you can take on your journey to microservices at scale that will hold you in good stead.

In addition to what I have covered here, I recommend Michael Nygard's excellent book *Release It!*. In it he shares a collection of stories about system failure and some patterns to help deal with it well. The book is well worth a read (in fact, I would go so far as to say it should be considered essential reading for anyone building systems at scale).

We've covered quite a lot of ground, and we're nearing the end. In our next and final chapter, we will look to pull everything back together and summarize what we have learned in the book overall.

CHAPTER 12

Bringing It All Together

We've covered a fair amount in the previous chapters, from what microservices are to how to define their boundaries, and from integration technology to concerns about security and monitoring. And we even found time to work out how the role of the architect fits in. There is a lot to take in, as although microservices themselves may be small, the breadth and impact of their architecture are not. So here I'll try to summarize some of the key points covered throughout the book.

Principles of Microservices

We discussed the role that principles can play in Chapter 2. They are statements about how things should be done, and why we think they should be done that way. They help us frame the various decisions we have to make when building our systems. You should absolutely define your own principles, but I thought it worth spelling out what I see as being the key principles for microservice architectures, which you can see summarized in Figure 12-1. These are the principles that will help us create small autonomous services that work well together. We've already covered everything here at least once so far, so nothing should be new, but there is value in distilling it down to its core essence.

You can choose to adopt these principles wholesale, or perhaps tweak them to make sense in your own organization. But note the value that comes from using them in combination: the whole should be greater than the sum of the parts. So if you decide to drop one of them, make sure you understand what you'll be missing.

For each of these principles, I've tried to pull out some of the supporting practices that we have covered in the book. As the saying goes, there is more than one way to skin a cat: you might find your own practices to help deliver on these principles, but this should get you started.

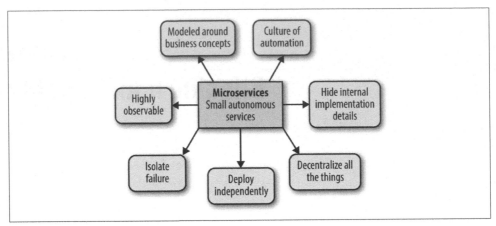

Figure 12-1. Principles of microservices

Model Around Business Concepts

Experience has shown us that interfaces structured around business-bounded contexts are more stable than those structured around technical concepts. By modeling the domain in which our system operates, not only do we attempt to form more stable interfaces, but we also ensure that we are better able to reflect changes in business processes easily. Use *bounded contexts* to define potential domain boundaries.

Adopt a Culture of Automation

Microservices add a lot of complexity, a key part of which comes from the sheer number of moving parts we have to deal with. Embracing a culture of automation is one key way to address this, and front-loading effort to create the tooling to support microservices can make a lot of sense. *Automated testing* is essential, as ensuring our services still work is a more complex process than with monolithic systems. Having a uniform command-line call to *deploy the same way everywhere* can help, and this can be a key part of adopting *continuous delivery* to give us fast feedback on the production quality of each check-in.

Consider using *environment definitions* to help you specify the differences from one environment to another, without sacrificing the ability to use a uniform deployment method. Think about creating *custom images* to speed up deployment, and embracing the creation of fully automated *immutable servers* to make it easier to reason about your systems.

Hide Internal Implementation Details

To maximize the ability of one service to evolve independently of any others, it is vital that we hide implementation details. Modeling *bounded contexts* can help, as this helps us focus on those models that should be shared, and those that should be hidden. Services should also *hide their databases* to avoid falling into one of the most common sorts of coupling that can appear in traditional service-oriented architectures, and use *data pumps* or *event data pumps* to consolidate data across multiple services for reporting purposes.

Where possible, pick *technology-agnostic APIs* to give you freedom to use different technology stacks. Consider using *REST*, which formalizes the separation of internal and external implementation details, although even if using remote procedure calls (RPCs), you can still embrace these ideas.

Decentralize All the Things

To maximize the autonomy that microservices make possible, we need to constantly be looking for the chance to delegate decision making and control to the teams that own the services themselves. This process starts with embracing *self service* wherever possible, allowing people to deploy software on demand, making development and testing as easy as possible, and avoiding the need for separate teams to perform these activities.

Ensuring that *teams own their services* is an important step on this journey, making teams responsible for the changes that are made, ideally even having them decide when to release those changes. Making use of *internal open source* ensures that people can make changes on services owned by other teams, although remember that this requires work to implement. *Align teams to the organization* to ensure that Conway's law works for you, and help your team become domain experts in the business-focused services they are creating. Where some overarching guidance is needed, try to embrace a *shared governance* model where people from each team collectively share responsibility for evolving the technical vision of the system.

This principle can apply to architecture too. Avoid approaches like enterprise service bus or orchestration systems, which can lead to centralization of business logic and dumb services. Instead, *prefer choreography over orchestration* and *dumb middleware, with smart endpoints* to ensure that you keep associated logic and data within service boundaries, helping keep things cohesive.

Independently Deployable

We should always strive to ensure that our microservices can and are deployed by themselves. Even when breaking changes are required, we should seek to *coexist versioned endpoints* to allow our consumers to change over time. This allows us to optimize for speed of release of new features, as well as increasing the autonomy of the teams owning these microservices by ensuring that they don't have to constantly orchestrate their deployments. When using RPC-based integration, *avoid tightly bound client/server stub generation* such as that promoted by Java RMI.

By adopting a *one-service-per-host* model, you reduce side effects that could cause deploying one service to impact another unrelated service. Consider using *blue/green* or *canary* release techniques to separate deployment from release, reducing the risk of a release going wrong. Use *consumer-driven contracts* to catch breaking changes before they happen.

Remember that it should be the norm, not the exception, that you can make a change to a single service and release it into production, without having to deploy any other services in lock-step. Your *consumers should decide when they update themselves*, and you need to accommodate this.

Isolate Failure

A microservice architecture can be more resilient than a monolithic system, but only if we understand and plan for failures in part of our system. If we don't account for the fact that a downstream call can and will fail, our systems might suffer catastrophic cascading failure, and we could find ourselves with a system that is much more fragile than before.

When using network calls, *don't treat remote calls like local calls*, as this will hide different sorts of failure mode. So make sure if you're using client libraries that the abstraction of the remote call doesn't go too far.

If we hold the tenets of *antifragility* in mind, and expect failure will occur anywhere and everywhere, we are on the right track. Make sure your *timeouts* are set appropriately. Understand when and how to use *bulkheads* and *circuit breakers* to limit the fallout of a failing component. Understand what the customer-facing impact will be if only one part of the system is misbehaving. Know what the implications of a network partition might be, and whether sacrificing *availability* or *consistency* in a given situation is the right call.

Highly Observable

We cannot rely on observing the behavior of a single service instance or the status of a single machine to see if the system is functioning correctly. Instead, we need a joined-up view of what is happening. Use *semantic monitoring* to see if your system is behaving correctly, by injecting *synthetic transactions* into your system to simulate real-user behavior. *Aggregate your logs*, and *aggregate your stats*, so that when you see a problem you can drill down to the source. And when it comes to reproducing nasty issues or just seeing how your system is interacting in production, use *correlation IDs* to allow you to trace calls through the system.

When Shouldn't You Use Microservices?

I get asked this question a lot. My first piece of advice would be that the less well you understand a domain, the harder it will be for you to find proper bounded contexts for your services. As we discussed previously, getting service boundaries wrong can result in having to make lots of changes in service-to-service collaboration—an expensive operation. So if you're coming to a monolithic system for which you don't understand the domain, spend some time learning what the system does first, and then look to identify clean module boundaries prior to splitting out services.

Greenfield development is also quite challenging. It isn't just that the domain is also likely to be new; it's that it is much easier to chunk up something you have than something you don't! So again, consider starting monolithic first and break things out when you're stable.

Many of the challenges you're going to face with microservices get worse with scale. If you mostly do things manually, you might be OK with 1 or 2 services, but 5 or 10? Sticking with old monitoring practices where you just look at stats like CPU and memory likewise might work OK for a few services, but the more service-to-service collaboration you do, the more painful this will become. You'll find yourself hitting these pain points as you add more services, and I hope the advice in this book will help you see some of these problems coming, and give you some concrete tips for how to deal with them. I spoke before about REA and Gilt taking a while to build the tooling and practices to manage microservices well, prior to being able to use them in any large quantity. These stories just reinforce to me the importance of starting gradually so you understand your organization's appetite and ability to change, which will help you properly adopt microservices.

Parting Words

Microservice architectures give you more options, and more decisions to make. Making decisions in this world is a far more common activity than in simpler, monolithic systems. You won't get all of these decisions right, I can guarantee that. So, knowing we are going to get some things wrong, what are our options? Well, I would suggest finding ways to make each decision small in scope; that way, if you get it wrong, you only impact a small part of your system. Learn to embrace the concept of evolutionary architecture, where your system bends and flexes and changes over time as you learn new things. Think not of big-bang rewrites, but instead of a series of changes made to your system over time to keep it supple.

Hopefully by now I've shared with you enough information and experiences to help you decide if microservices are for you. If they are, I hope you think of this as a journey, not a destination. Go incrementally. Break your system apart piece by piece, learning as you go. And get used to it: in many ways, the discipline to continually change and evolve our systems is a far more important lesson to learn than any other I have shared with you through this book. Change is inevitable. Embrace it.

Index

technology-facing tests, 132
templates, 22
test doubles, 137
Test Pyramid, 132, 144
test snow cone, 136
test-driven design (TDD), 134
testing
  canary releasing, 149
  considerations for, 135
  consumer-driven tests, 144
  cross-functional, 151
  end-to-end tests, 138
  MTTR over MTBF, 150
  overview of, 153
  performance tests, 152
  post-production, 148
  scope of, 132
  selecting number of, 136
  semantic monitoring, 147
  separating deployment from release, 148
  service test implementation, 136
  types of tests, 131
third-party software, 73-78, 95
  building vs. buying, 73
  content management systems (CMS), 75
  Customer Relationship Management
    (CRM), 76
  customization of, 74
  integration issues, 74
  lack of control over, 74
  reporting databases, 95
  Strangler Application Pattern, 77
tight coupling, 30, 192
time to live (TTL), 237
timeouts, 211
transaction managers, 92
transactional boundaries, 89-93
transactions
  compensating, 91
  distributed, 92
Transport Layer Security (TLS), 175
two-phase commits, 92
type 2 virtualization, 123

U

UDDI (Universal Description, Discovery, and
  Integration), 242
unit tests
  Cohn's Test Pyramid, 132

  goals of, 134
  Marick's quadrant, 132
  scope of, 134
user interfaces, 67-73
  API composition, 68
  API gateways, 71
  API granularity, 67
  Cohn's Test Pyramid, 132
    (see also end-to-end tests)
  constraints, 68
  evolution of, 67
  fragment composition, 69
  hybrid approaches, 73

V

Vagrant, 124
versioning, 62-67
  catching breaking changes early, 63
  coexisting different endpoints, 64
  deferring breaking changes, 62
  multiple concurrent versions, 66
  semantic, 64
vertical scaling, 217
virtual private clouds (VPC), 183
virtualization
  hypervisors, 123
  traditional, 123
  type 2, 123
virtualization platforms
  Docker, 126
  Linux containers, 124
  on-demand, 1
  storage area networks in, 218
  Vagrant, 124
vision, 27

W

worker-based systems, 220
write-behind caches, 228

X

XML, 53

Z

Zed Attack Proxy (ZAP), 187
Zipkin, 163
Zookeeper, 238

About the Author

Sam Newman is a technologist at ThoughtWorks, where he currently splits his time between helping clients and working as an architect for ThoughtWorks' own internal systems. He has worked with a variety of companies in multiple domains around the world, often with one foot in the developer world, and another in the IT operations space. If you asked him what he does, he'd say, "I work with people to build better software systems." He has written articles, presented at conferences, and sporadically commits to open source projects.

Colophon

The animals on the cover of *Building Microservices* are honey bees (of the genus *Apis*). Of 20,000 known species of bees, only seven are considered honey bees. They are distinct because they produce and store honey, as well as building hives from wax. Beekeeping to collect honey has been a human pursuit for thousands of years.

Honey bees live in hives with thousands of individuals and have a very organized social structure. There are three castes: queen, drone, and worker. Each hive has one queen, who remains fertile for 3–5 years after her mating flight, and lays up to 2,000 eggs per day. Drones are male bees who mate with the queen (and die in the act because of their barbed sex organs). Worker bees are sterile females who fill many roles during their lifetime, such as nursemaid, construction worker, grocer, guard, undertaker, and forager. Foraging worker bees communicate with one another by "dancing" in particular patterns to share information about nearby resources.

All three castes of honey bee are similar in appearance, with wings, six legs, and a body segmented into a head, thorax, and abdomen. They have short fuzzy hairs in a striped yellow and black pattern. Their diet is made up exclusively of honey, which is created by a process of partially digesting and regurgitating sugar-rich flower nectar.

Bees are crucial to agriculture, as they pollinate crops and other flowering plants while they collect pollen and nectar. On average, each hive of bees gathers 66 pounds of pollen a year. In recent years, the decline of many bee species has been cause for concern and is known as "colony collapse disorder." It is still unclear what is causing this die-off: some theories include parasites, insecticide use, or disease, but no effective preventative measures have been found to date.

Many of the animals on O'Reilly covers are endangered; all of them are important to the world. To learn more about how you can help, go to *animals.oreilly.com*.

The cover image is from Johnson's *Natural History*. The cover fonts are URW Typewriter and Guardian Sans. The text font is Adobe Minion Pro; the heading font is Adobe Myriad Condensed; and the code font is Dalton Maag's Ubuntu Mono.

Get even more for your money.

Join the O'Reilly Community, and register the O'Reilly books you own. It's free, and you'll get:

- $4.99 ebook upgrade offer
- 40% upgrade offer on O'Reilly print books
- Membership discounts on books and events
- Free lifetime updates to ebooks and videos
- Multiple ebook formats, DRM FREE
- Participation in the O'Reilly community
- Newsletters
- Account management
- 100% Satisfaction Guarantee

Signing up is easy:

1. Go to: oreilly.com/go/register
2. Create an O'Reilly login.
3. Provide your address.
4. Register your books.

Note: English-language books only

To order books online:
oreilly.com/store

For questions about products or an order:
orders@oreilly.com

To sign up to get topic-specific email announcements and/or news about upcoming books, conferences, special offers, and new technologies:
elists@oreilly.com

For technical questions about book content:
booktech@oreilly.com

To submit new book proposals to our editors:
proposals@oreilly.com

O'Reilly books are available in multiple DRM-free ebook formats. For more information:
oreilly.com/ebooks

Lightning Source UK Ltd.
Milton Keynes UK
UKOW04f1004190417

299385UK00002B/2/P